The Future of Islam in the Middle East

The Future of Islam in the Middle East

Fundamentalism in Egypt, Algeria, and Saudi Arabia

MAHMUD A. FAKSH

Westport, Connecticut
London

Library of Congress Cataloging-in-Publication Data

Faksh, Mahmud A.
    The Future of Islam in the Middle East : fundamentalism in Egypt,
Algeria, and Saudi Arabia / Mahmud A. Faksh.
      p. cm.
    Includes bibliographical references (p.   ) and index.
    ISBN 0–275–95128–6 (alk. paper)
    1. Islamic fundamentalism—Arab countries—History—20th century.
I. Title.
    BP63.A65F35   1997
    297'.0956'09049—dc20   96–9564

British Library Cataloguing in Publication Data is available.

Library of Congress Catalog Card Number: 96–9564
ISBN: 0–275–95128–6

First published in 1997

Praeger Publishers, 88 Post Road West, Westport, CT 06881
An imprint of Greenwood Publishing Group, Inc.

Printed in the United States of America

The paper used in this book complies with the
Permanent Paper Standard issued by the National
Information Standards Organization (Z39.48–1984).

10 9 8 7 6 5 4 3 2

For Orouba, Arij, and Noor,
the treasures of my life

WITHDRAWN

Contents

Acknowledgments

I would like to extend my appreciation to my longtime dear friend and counsel, Betty G. Seaver, for her instructive comments throughout the different stages of the manuscript. I am likewise grateful to Marion C. Salinger of Duke University, an admirable woman of letters and grace, for her observations on the manuscript. My thanks are also due to Lynn Ann Rollins of the Office of Sponsored Programs at the University of Southern Maine for her kind professional service in putting the manuscript in the proper format.

Introduction

The post–Gulf War period has been rife with speculation about an imminent fundamentalist Islamic explosion in the Middle East. One has heard, and still hears, that the coming avalanche will sweep away the Arab status quo, already sundered by the Gulf "Arabquake," and will usher in an Islamic state system. It is true that Islamism, as a populist-cultural-religious force, has experienced an upsurge and has become increasingly assertive in the wake of the war, but its real fortunes as a political force have fallen far short of expectations, and it is now being thwarted on many fronts. Put simply, the revolution that was to envelop the Muslim heartland from North Africa to the Persian Gulf has not materialized. The Islamists have not fared well in the struggle against the powers that be: they are floundering. This study considers the likely future of Islamism in the context of the Islamic challenge in Egypt, Algeria, and Saudi Arabia.[1]

The current period of Islamic fundamentalism is not something altogether new; for the most part, it has simply taken on a new form and expression in response to conditions marked by rising tensions and frustrations. In the Islamic world, the belief has always been that the religion of Islam—its sources (the Qur'an and the *Sunna*, or prophetic traditions), its inherited ways, and its history—provides the principles that enable a virtuous and just society. Historically, Islam has gone through periods of expansion and vibrancy followed by periods of contraction and dormancy, punctuated by revivalist movements that rose and fell, each seeking to reinvigorate the faith and reestablish the "true" Islamic order in accord with its own vision. And the revivalist impulse in Islam lives on today.

Since the start of the nineteenth century, one can identify three periods of Islamic revival associated with the failure of various societies to deal with an accumulation of internal and external crises arising from sociopolitical and economic weakness and from foreign hegemony. These were revolts expressed in religious terms against the perceived deterioration and humiliation of the societies and their diminished place in the world—calls for a return to the roots of Islam. The first, in the nineteenth century, was championed by such movements as the Wahhabis in Arabia, the Mahdis in Sudan, the Sanusis in North Africa (Libya), and Islamic reform in Egypt.[2] The second period climaxed in the 1940s with the ascendancy of two major fundamentalist movements: al-Ikhwan al-Muslimoun (the Muslim Brotherhood) in Egypt and Jama'at-i-Islami (the Muslim Society) in the Indian subcontinent.

The third, and longest, period of Islamic revival began in the aftermath of the 1967 Arab defeat by Israel and continued throughout the 1970s amid social and economic dislocations, class disparities, and authoritarian state structures. Islamism became a formidable force in the 1980s after the Iranian Islamic revolution of 1978–1979, sweeping across the region from the Maghreb to the Gulf. Vast stretches of Muslim lands have since come under its sweep. This is Islam as a political force—that is, "political Islam"—challenging established regimes, shaking Arab political life to its foundations, and calling for a revival of the early Islamic ethos of governance. It seeks states and societies under Islamic regimes. Power is the objective; Islam, as a religio-political ideology, is the vehicle. Power is the bedrock of political Islam. To the Muslim activists, religion is the manifestation of faith and power, and "faith itself gets 'incarnated' in the state."[3] Thus, an Islamic state is the sine qua non in the struggle against the existing secular state.

The Islamic tide climaxed in the immediate post–Gulf War period as more and more countries seemed about to be swept under. Some Islamists even declared its "inevitable" triumph. Hasan al-Turabi, one of the leading Islamist theoreticians and head of the military-backed ruling National Islamic Front in Sudan since 1989, described the war as "a blessing in disguise" because it increased the popularity of the Islamic movements among the masses and undermined many governments, which "must go popular or perish." With a Marxist-like historical determinism, he went on: "There is a course of history that makes the establishment of Islamic states almost inevitable."[4] The growing challenge posed by Muslim militants throughout the Middle East is obvious. Countries such as Egypt, Algeria, Tunisia, and Jordan, as well as Israel and the Palestinian National Authority, among others, have been caught up in an escalating cycle of fundamentalist violence. Even traditional-conservative Saudi Arabia could not escape.

Why has today's fundamentalism grown so assertive and militant? The mass appeal of Islamism has its roots in worldly frustrations and denials, and those frustrations and denials have been given a religious idiom. In Egypt, Algeria, Saudi Arabia, and elsewhere, Islamism is basically an indigenous response to prevalent socioeconomic and political problems. Demographic imbalances (the growth in population, rural-urban migration, and concomitant "ruralization" of cities), social dislocation (the breakdown of traditional structures and ethos), mass impoverishment, "Leviathan" states, and cultural and spiritual disturbances (the loss of identity and moral decay) have all animated the fundamentalist appeal. Indeed, the phenomenon of Islamism is more a reflection of the magnitude of the crisis—especially among the multitudinous masses of the destitute, unemployed, and underprivileged—than a manifestation of a desire for a theocracy. In other words, Islamism is a product of the failed modernization policies of the past fifty years, which have eventuated in unmet expectations and consequent militancy.[5] In this milieu, Islam, promising salvation and fulfillment, is the lodestar, particularly so in a culture that fuses the religious and public spheres and at a time when secular ideologies are discredited. Not surprisingly, then, Islamic fundamentalism is a movement on the march.

The fundamentalist appeal notwithstanding, this study focuses on the limits of Islamic fundamentalism as a system of thought and as a challenge to the established order. To counter the malaise in the Muslim body, the leading idealogues of Islamism have advanced various theoretical formulations of an "Islamic alternative." Despite the diversity within the Islamic movement, certain common ideological assumptions underlie the formulations and serve to bind the constituent groups. This study analyzes the strands of Muslim fundamentalist thought regarding society and state and identifies their inherent shortcomings in the context of regional and global conditions.

While the third period of the Islamic revival is still reverberating, Islamism's ability to challenge existing regimes is not infinite. Faced with a coalition of conservative and secular national states that are willing to use, and do use, assorted countermeasures, it is fast approaching exhaustion. Indeed, the perception of a possible triumphant Islamic fundamentalist movement has precipitated strategies of containment by national governments ranging from confrontation and repression to accommodation and co-optation. This study delineates the nature of the challenge and the responses to it that are likely to determine the fate of the current Islamic resurgence in Egypt, Algeria, and Saudi Arabia, countries in which the challenge is most crucial.

Islamic fundamentalism's challenge in Egypt and Algeria has been the most prominent and most militant. It has led to open confrontation and violence that have threatened social and political stability. Although both countries have utilized the strong arm of the state to quell the danger, Egypt's response was alloyed with co-optation and accommodation, thereby lessening the fault lines between state and society. The difference is reflective of each country's historical and contextual circumstances, which were determinative of the perceived level of threat and the nature of the response.

Egypt has a history of Islamic revivalism dating back to the second half of the nineteenth century—the Islamic call is deeply rooted. Concomitantly, Egyptian revivalism has been counterbalanced by the ascendant forces of liberalism and nationalism, which steered the country onto a modern path; modern liberalism has been woven into the cultural life of Egypt. However, the tradition of Islamic revivalism lives on in the mainstream fundamentalist

Muslim Brotherhood, whose existence has been "illegal" for much of its life-time, and in the militant fundamentalist groups that proliferated in the 1980s. In an ongoing struggle to contain the rising fundamentalism, the Egyptian state has employed a mix of heavy-handed repression of militants, adoption of religious themes and symbols, and—until recently—co-optation of main-stream Islamists.

Algeria's long colonial status meant that French cultural and educational influences were ascendant, bringing in their wake a European secular orienta-tion. The resultant culture, especially in the urban centers, had no counterbal-ancing Islamic reform movement. (The one exception was the founding of the Association of the Algerian Muslim Ulama in 1931 by Abdul Hamid Ben Badis, whose aim was to bring Islamic reform and revive the Arabic language after a century of French rule and settlement.) Secularism continued after indepen-dence in 1962 under the National Liberation Front (FLN), which promoted a nationalist-socialist agenda. The rise of the Islamic Salvation Front (FIS) dur-ing the countrywide civil disturbances in 1988 put it on a collision course with the secularist state structures and culture of the military-political estab-lishment. The religious-secular divide locked the fundamentalists and the state apparatus in the most violent confrontation since the war of independence.

Saudi Arabia has had no experience with Western colonialism or liberal secularism. The country has long been kept behind a veil of traditional Wahhabi Islam, the nexus of the Saudi state since its inception in 1932. Official Wahhabi fundamentalism is a given in Saudi Arabia. Despite its cloak of Islamicity, the kingdom has not been immune to the growth of Muslim extremism threaten-ing to undermine the Al-Saud rule. In addressing the danger, the state has utilized a combination of threats and intimidation, closer cooperation and consultation with the traditional orthodox *ulama* (religious leaders), and ac-commodation of modern professional groups and the business elite through limited measures creating openness (the establishment of the Majlis al-Shura, Consultative Council, for one) and sustained economic benefits.

In addition to the various strategies of containment, certain inherent limi-tations of Islamism could impede its march. The fundamentalists' radical agenda regarding state and society and regional issues does not square with the realities and changing circumstances in the Middle East, thereby dimin-ishing the prospects of fundamentalism. This study demonstrates that the ideo-logical formulations of Muslim fundamentalism are in complete contradis-tinction to modern regional and international contexts. In attempting to weave a future out of a distant idealized past *(salaf)* and to retreat behind a wall of Islamic cultural authenticity and identity, the fundamentalists seem frozen in time and oblivious to a changing, interactive world—a condition that could threaten to doom society to stagnation and regression. In today's interdepen-dent global environment, clinging to a glorious past in order to find a solution to perceived political and economic decline is highly dubious strategy.

Equally imporotant, the fundamentalists' claims of Islamic certainty and self-sufficiency—that Islam is a supreme, complete, and total way of life—have major implications for social and political freedom and equality. This self-righteous certainty—a one-size-fits-all answer—portends the denial of all other values and belief systems and the imposition of a stifling uniformity. Such a stance raises the question of the compatibility of Islamic doctrine and democracy. Would a fundamentalist Islamic state be democratic and respectful of individual rights? Would it tolerate diversity, pluralism, and opposing views? The answer is simply no. Shi'a fundamentalist Iran and Sunni fundamentalist Sudan are stark examples of intolerance and oppression. In fact, as this study shows, Muslim fundamentalist postulates are not conducive to the building of a liberal democracy. Rather, they have the potential of social and political absolutism. All the evidence clearly suggests that, despite their populist rhetoric and calls for mass empowerment and popular participation, today's fundamentalists are not the forerunners of democracy and freedom in the Middle East. They are not democrats; contrariwise, they are the new religious Bolsheviks in the unending cycle of Arab-Muslim authoritarianism.

Looking ahead, despite Hasan al-Turabi's assertion of the inevitability of the Islamic system, Islamism will be no more inevitably triumphant than communism. Will the dawn of a new millennium mark the eclipse of fundamentalism? It is evident that political Islam is now in retreat and in time will fade away. But the cultural and moral pull of Islamism will not give way soon. The language and motivation of Islam remain deeply entrenched in Middle Eastern societies.

NOTES

1. An assortment of labels has been given to the various manifestations of the Islamic revival in the Middle East today: Islamic fundamentalism, militant Islam, Islamic radicalism, and Islamism, among others. The two most common are Islamic fundamentalism and Islamism.

The terms *Islamic fundamentalism* and *Islamism* are used interchangeably hereafter in reference to Islamic movements or groups that use Islam as a political force to mobilize the public, gain control of governance, and reform society and state in accordance with their doctrinal religious agenda. They are not seeking to "modernize" Islam or to bring about its reformation in a theologoical sense. (In the Protestant religious sense, every Muslim is a "fundamentalist" because a central tenet of the faith is the cardinal belief that the Qur'an is the literal word of God transmitted through the Prophet Muhammad.) Rather, they appropriate Islam as an ideology for social and political action and lay claim to the right of fresh interpretation of its dogma on the basis of their particular understanding of the religious texts—the Qur'an and the *Sunna*, or prophetic traditions. Their objective is to "return" to some ancestral model (*salaf*), and hence they tend to glorify and idealize the past and vilify the present. As the self-appointed avant-garde of the society, these movements or groups engage in an activism that is often manifested in political militancy or political aggresiveness within and sometimes outside the existing national political structures.

2. The Mahdi movement was founded by Muhammad Ahmad (A.D. 1843–1885) and became a major force in the political life of Sudan. It was a religio-political movement that advocated revivalism, egalitarianism, and restoration of Islamic rule. Its leader proclaimed

himself *al-mahdi* (the messiah), led a relentless *jihad* (holy war) in the early 1880s against the Egyptian rulers of Sudan, and established a puritanical Islamic state. The Mahdi movement was destroyed in the late 1890s by Anglo-Egyptian forces, and the country became an Anglo-Egyptian condominium, with the British being the actual rulers. On the Mahdi movement, see P. M. Holt, *The Mahdist State in the Sudan, 1881–1898* (London: Oxford University Press, 1958).

The Sanusi movement was founded in the 1840s by Algerian-born Muhammad bin Ali al-Sanusi (1787–1859), who received his religious training in Fez (Morocco) and Mecca. It is basically a Sufi *tariqa* (mystical order) and a *salafi* (invoking ancestoral heritage) reform movement reasserting the faith of early Islam. It became firmly established in Cyrenaica (eastern province of Libya) and later spread into the interior of Libya and western Egypt. In 1911, it led the struggle against the Italian occupation of the country. Upon independence in 1951, Idris, head of the Sanusi order, was proclaimed king of the United Kingdom of Libya. He was overthrown on September 1, 1969, by the military junta led by Colonel Mu'ammar al-Qadhafi. See Hassan S. Haddad and Basheer K. Nijim, eds., *The Arab World: A Handbook* (Wilmette, Ill.: Medina Press, 1978) 102–3.

3. S. Parvez Manzoor, "The Future of Muslim Politics: Critique of the 'Fundamentalist' Theory of the Islamic State," *Futures* 23 (Apr. 1991): 294.

4. "Islam, Democracy, the State, and the West" (Summary of a lecture and roundtable discussion with Hasan al-Turabi, prepared by Louis J. Cantori and Arthur Lowrie), *Middle East Policy* 1. 3 (1992): 55.

5. On this theme, see Olivier Roy, *The Failure of Political Islam* (Cambridge: Harvard University Press, 1994).

The Future of Islam
in the Middle East

1

Islamic Fundamentalist Thought: An Analysis of Major Theoretical Formulations

More than two centuries ago the world of Islam first experienced Western political and military encroachments and the attendant pressures of modernity. The traditional Muslim culture and mode of life came increasingly under the disruptive influences of Western cultural penetration and hegemony and the threat of possible subsumption. The ongoing experience was tormenting and humiliating for a society and culture that not long before had felt superior to Europe and itself had incorporated others.[1] To deal with their predicament Muslims alternated—and to varying extents are still alternating—among three courses: (1) embracing modernity, advocated by Western-educated liberal modernists; (2) rejecting modernity and adhering steadfastly to Islam, advocated by Muslim fundamentalists; and (3) adapting Islam to modern national objectives, advocated by nationalist modernists.[2]

Western-educated liberal modernists were primarily a Eurocentered elite seeking to emulate the West and assimilate its ways. The expanding social and intellectual power of the Continent was for them both adversarial challenge and attractive force. In short, Europe was a model for progress, and the way to become like Europe was to liberate society from religion. Tradition was derided as a medieval holdover and modernity seen as inevitable. The former had to be displaced. Basically, liberal modernists found themselves largely isolated, viewed as blind followers and successive imitators of unbelievers. Their fortunes were confined mainly to modern Turkey under Mustafa Kemal Ataturk and, to a lesser extent, Iran under Reza Shah Pahlavi. Both countries Westernized and secularized their societies. Iran failed to uproot the Islamic tradition by not moving against the religious establishment as vigorously as Ataturk.[3] Ultimately, neither country succeeded as a viable developmental model. In fact, no Arab-Muslim state has openly followed the Turkish-Iranian example.

The nationalist modernists were more successful: they led the struggles for national independence and later promoted nation-building and development. They have continued to hold the reins in most Middle Eastern countries, pursuing policies of modernization and change. Unlike the Westernized liberal modernists, who denigrated Islam as an obstacle to social change and progress, the nationalist modernists sought to adapt Islam to national requirements, to mold it in the context of their modern schema of society. Their aim was to nationalize Islam, not to disown it. In other words, leaders such as Nasser and other like-minded nationalist modernists used Islam to serve state purposes, to fit their policies of development. Certainly this group did not seek to reform Islam, as was the case with nineteenth-century Muslim reformers, who called for Islamic renewal and a synthesis between Islam and modernity.[4] Rather, the supremacy of modernity over tradition was, for them, an evident article of faith.[5]

But the ascendancy of the nationalist modernists did not spell the withering away of Islam, as many secularists had assumed or hoped would happen. Establishing an Islamic order is a vision that has enthralled a good many Muslims over time and has resulted in a succession of revivalist calls. Indeed, many Islamic dynasties rose to power propelled by zealots of this vision.[6] The Islamic vision resonates with added intensity during social crises or after episodes of national disgrace inflicted by outside powers. The 1967 defeat by Israel, which signified the failure of nationalist-modernist regimes with secularist orientations; the subsequent socioeconomic and political participation crises; and increasing foreign political, cultural, and economic control have all brought increased strength to the fundamentalist message of retreat to an Islamic universe.

The fundamentalist call that has been sounding across the Muslim world for almost three decades, *al-Islam huwa al-hall* (Islam is the solution), promotes "the Return to Islam"[7] as an ideology for political action to remedy the malaise in the Muslim condition. This is political Islam: an activist, dynamic force inciting political involvement and direct action by Muslims to bring about the re-Islamization of their societies and the establishment of an Islamic order in accord with their fundamentalist rendering of religious doctrine. It seeks to realign politics with Islamic precepts and manifests itself in ways that are anti-Western, antisecularist, antimodernist, and anti–status quo. Equally important, it stands against formal religious bodies as part of the status quo, hence exhibiting a degree of antipathy to customary religious authorities. In its extreme form, it is even militant and violent. Surely the assertion of independence and activism in current Islamic fundamentalist thought is a source of worry and consternation for traditional religious leaders (the *ulama*) and government officials alike.

The fundamentalists today are not tradition-bound or passive in regard to interpretation of Islamic ideology. They assert the right of fresh interpretation and application of Islamic doctrine on the basis of the fundamental sources of that doctrine (the Qur'an and the *Sunna*, or prophetic traditions). They insist that nobody, including the *ulama* (religious scholars), has a monopoly over religio-legal interpretation and that all Muslims are entitled to *ijtihad* (individual interpretation of Islamic doctrine). According to Hasan al-Turabi, chief ideologue of the ruling National Islamic Front in Sudan, the right to exercise *ijtihad* is inherent in all Muslims and "should not be inhibited" by the claims of clerics to sole dominion.[8] Surely this is tantamount to a rebellion against the religious establishment, which has traditionally monopolized *ijtihad* as its exclusive prerogative. The *ulama* stand accused of lacking independence and of being generally subservient to the state. This helps explain the erosion in the credibility of "establishment Islam" and the anti-*ulama* sentiments among the young radical fundamentalists. In fact, many of today's fundamentalist leaders are more populist activists than religious scholars, preaching Islamic populism and participatory ethos, as against the formalism and exclusivism of the *ulama*, whom they accuse of reducing Islam to a mere ritual: prayers, fasting, and pilgrimage.

In the ongoing struggle over the role Islam ought to play in contemporary Muslim societies, the young fundamentalists are seeking to control the discourse of Islam, which has traditionally been the preserve of the established *ulama* class. Current Islamic discourse is best reflected in the various theoretical formulations advanced by Islamist groups striving to refashion society according to Islamic rules and traditional values. In fact, we have witnessed of late an exponential growth in Muslim fundamentalist thought that is directly proportional to the proliferation of "players" in the Islamic movement. The fundamentalist groups seek to transform the role of Islam in the polity by advocating an assertive and forceful political Islam. Their message—the reinstitution of an Islamic state and society according to their doctrinal vision of the world—is often phrased in a populist and revolutionary rhetoric.

What are the major theoretical constructs of modern Islamic fundamentalism? There is now consensus among students of Islam that fundamentalist Islam has diverse manifestations, elements or components, and contextual historical and societal conditions. It is a multifarious movement with no headquarters, no "Comintern" to serve as an overall command imposing a unified structure and coherent ideology. The programs, strategies, and tactics of Islamic groups vary among and within countries, as do their sometimes contending ideologies.

Their differences aside, the ultimate objective of all Islamists is the same: the restructuring of state-society relations in the image of Islam's early golden years. Hence, some common ideological themes run through fundamentalist discourse today, themes that are heavily influenced by the prominent Muslim thinkers and activists Abul Ala Maududi (1903–1979) of Pakistan, Sayyid Qutb (1906–1966) of Egypt, and Ayatollah Khomeini (1900–1989) of Iran. The thinking of these three men provides the theoretical paradigms that inspire contemporary Islamic fundamentalism. They, especially Qutb and

Khomeini, elaborated and popularized an Islamic worldview based on exclu-sivity and self-sufficiency that is increasingly assertive and combative.[9]

THEMES IN ISLAMIC FUNDAMENTALIST THOUGHT

Fusion of Religion and Politics

A common theme of fundamentalists is the necessity to end the separation of the public and religious spheres, to politicize Islam. They maintain that Islam has been dissociated from its role and mission in the polity since the inception of Islamic empires in A.D. 661. Indeed, many fundamentalists see the rise of the Omayyad dynasty (A.D. 661–750) as the beginning of secular-ized government.[10] In the eighth century, the Abbasids successfully revolted against the Omayyad state, accusing it of forsaking religion and morality for imperial rule and worldly temptations.[11] The Abbasid Caliphate (A.D. 750–1258) initially sought to remove the chasm that had separated religion from the Omayyad state by addressing the concerns of the disaffected religious leadership; eventually, however, the religious character of the state eroded, and the caliphate proceeded on an increasingly secularized political course. By the eleventh century, most Middle Eastern societies were "built around separate institutions of state and religion."[12] The Islamic state was far from being an inherently Islamic institution serving religious ends.

Over time, Islam was emptied of political meaning, and it came to have no significance in public life. With the rise of the nation-state system in the in-terwar period, the traditional religious institutions and roles (*ulama*; *Shari'a*, or Islamic law; *qadi*, or an Islamic judge in a *Shari'a* court; and *madrasa*, or religious parochial schools) were increasingly displaced by modern structures and functions. By the 1930s, "a duality of legal systems" was in place: Euro-pean codes and procedures regulating criminal, civil, and commercial mat-ters; and *Shari'a* holding sway over matters of personal status.[13] More and more people, especially among the educated elite, were living less and less within the bounds of *Shari'a*, so that it has virtually no presence in the na-tional political life of Middle Eastern states today. Most of these states have now opted for a national political life that relegates Islam to the private sphere.[14] Many of them have found it easier to evade *Shari'a* than to modify it. The widespread secularization of life is most evident in the growing numbers of those who consider Islam to be an inherited culture rather than a regulator of life. Islam, a religio-political order at its inception, therefore has been ossi-fied into a set of religious rituals and conventions presided over by the offi-cial clerics.

As a consequence of the disappearance of Islam from governance, funda-mentalists believe that the history of Muslim peoples, at least until now, has been marked by steady regression and decline. In the modern period, the pro-cess has culminated in the cultural and political hegemony of the West, the concomitant diffusion of national-secular orientations in almost all areas of life, and a "hideous schizophrenia" between religion and practical life.[15] Fundamentalists see Islam as more and more marginalized in the lives of Muslims, who are "Muslims in name only," leading in turn to the marginalization of the Islamic world.[16] Social, institutional, and cultural decay, fragmentation, and weakness have become so pervasive in the Muslim community that its viability is threatened. It is this bleak assessment that spurs the fundamentalists.

Fundamentalists seek to reinstate Islam as a religio-political order; it is looked upon as the panacea. According to Abul Ala Maududi, because Islam is both an ideology and a system of life comprising religious, legal, and moral aspects in accordance with God's commands, establishment of an Islamic order is prerequisite to the actualization of Muslim life. Only under an Islamic regime in which Qur'anic injunctions are implemented on personal and communal levels can a Muslim lead a truly Islamic life.[17] The state must therefore be an Islamic state because—unlike any other state—its scope of controls is coextensive with the totality of life: all spheres of human existence, temporal and spiritual, are under the purview of Islamic ideology.[18]

Sayyid Qutb characterizes Islam as such a "totalitarian, practical, and hegemonic" system; there is no separation between faith and life.[19] All human actions are considered to be acts of worship, and the Holy Qur'an and the *hadith* (sayings of the Prophet) are the foundation on which actions rest.[20] In consequence, rituals and practices (*ibadat*) are an integral part of the larger domain of human activities and politics (*mu'amalat*);[21] all human activities, including politics, are rooted in religion and are inseparable. The Islamic state is the nexus of the two realms. It is a state guided by a divine message as revealed in the Qur'an and the *Sunna* (traditions of the Prophet; his sayings [*hadith*] and deeds) and, as such, is the embodiment of "the Kingdom of God on the earth."[22]

As to Ayatollah Khomeini, his doctrine of the rule of the religious elite (*vilayat-i-faqih*) and his relentless political activism fomented the politicization of Shi'a Islam and brought the religious clergy to power in Iran.[23] The *mullahs* (Shi'a clerics) were turned into revolutionary soldiers, power grabbers, and practitioners of statecraft who rapidly disestablished the Shi'a clerical tradition of political apathy and withdrawal from official life. Thus, the victory of the clerics in Iran signaled the transformation of Shi'ism from a doctrine of political quietism, resignation, and even submissiveness into a doctrine of political activism and assertiveness.[24] In essence, Khomeini brought politics back to its home base, Islam, and operationalized the change by means of the direct rule of the men of religion—the clergy emerged as the new ruling class.[25]

The fusing of religion and politics is supported by early historical experience and intellectual tradition in the world of Islam, which posited a holistic, totalitarian view of life. At the inception of Islam, the Prophet Muhammad and his immediate caliphs, or successors, set out to construct a new order.[26]

This is at variance with the Christian concept that the earth is a "fallen realm"—indelibly tainted by the "original sin"—that cannot be put aright, the result of which is an inherent church-state dichotomy that leads to conflict and finally separation. The notion that church and state are distinct entities is as old as Christianity itself and is made manifest in the distinction between the things that are Caesar's and the things that are God's. It eventuated in the Western separation of church and state, which dates back to the beginnings of the modern European state system and the adoption of secularism some 300 years ago.

Almost the entire corpus of Islamic political thought springs from the common belief that the state is not in conflict with religion. Rather, "religion in Islam is essential for the state, and the state is essential for religion."[27] They are seen as correlative, not antagonistic, phenomena. Therefore, contrary to Western thinking, which bases the state on the social contract theory, Islamic tradition has no equivalent secular theory of the state.[28] Simply put, the state is embedded in religion; its purpose is the fulfillment of divine imperatives. Thus, the formulation that Islam is *deen wa dunya* (a religion and a system of life) is basic to the faith of all Muslims. It is a formulation that the fundamentalists seek to operationalize and institutionalize.

Hakimiyya: Divine Sovereignty or Rule

For Muslim fundamentalists, the cardinal principle upon which the polity is based is *hakimiyya*, or divine sovereignty over all creation. Because the state is bound by religion, rule, or *hakimiyya*, belongs to God—in practice, this means the supremacy of *Shari'a*. Indeed, the idea of the absolute oneness of God and his exclusive sovereignty is the hallmark of a true Islamic polity. It is a polity ruled by God's laws, and all legitimate authority stems from him alone.[29] Submission is to the one God, and no one else. All other forms of human governance, as the source of authority and commands, are therefore tantamount to *shirk* (polytheism), a throwback to *jahiliyya* conditions (pre-Islamic paganism).[30] As Abul Ala Maududi put it, human control by one or more humans over other humans is a master-slave relationship, which negates God's express command.[31] Such a conception of the Islamic state might connote some form of theocracy, but not in the Christian sense of direct rule by a church or a priestly class, which has no equivalent in Islam (with the exception of Khomeini's Iran). Rather, it is a theocracy in the more general sense of a state under the rule of God.[32]

In accord with the notion of divine sovereignty, rulers are merely God's legitimate representatives (vicegerents) on earth. As such, they are the decision-makers and enforcers of *Shari'a*, but not the sovereign power in Islam.[33] All fundamentalists agree that the temporal ruler should be a very pious Muslim male who is also a knowledgeable leader, someone who heeds the will of God as made known in the Qur'an and the *Sunna*—the two fundamental sources of Islamic principles, values, and laws throughout the centuries. Although Maududi and Qutb do not confine the leadership position to the distinguished men of religion, Ayatollah Khomeini so decrees. According to the ayatollah, in the absence of duality of religious and political authority in Islam and because an Islamic government is obligated to fully implement *Shari'a,* only qualified jurist-theologians who combine a deep sense of justice and a thorough knowledge of the law are entitled to govern.

Thus, in challenging the shah's regime during his fifteen years in exile, Khomeini called upon the Shi'a religious leaders to assume a revolutionary role and take direct control of the state. This was in accord with his theory of *vilayat-i-faqih* (rule or authority of the leading jurist-theologian as a surrogate carrying out the authority of the "hidden" Imam), which he later incorporated as doctrine into the 1979 Constitution of the Islamic Republic of Iran.[34] The doctrine propounds the concept of the supreme Shi'a religious figure assuming the topmost leader-arbiter position ("the philosopher-king") of the Islamic state as the direct representative of the last Shi'a Imam during his occultation. Khomeini's theory established in Islam, for the first time, the direct rule of the clergy.[35]

To Maududi, leadership is a central issue in a Muslim community. It supersedes almost all other political issues because a society is a reflection of its leadership. Leaders provide general direction to, and set the value system of, the body politic.[36] The envisaged Islamic state, accordingly, is governed by a tightly knit group of certain dedicated believers, a sort of Muslim avant-garde, committed to realizing the Islamic transformation (*inqilab Islami*) of the society. The means to achieve the transformation would be steady and disciplined efforts to spread the Islamic message, heighten Islamic awareness and identification, and strengthen the foundation of the Islamic system. Maududi is inclined to believe that, once a comprehensive program of re-Islamization is put forth, the populace will willingly rally to the cause.[37] His preferred emphasis seems to be more on propagation and persuasion than on militant confrontation.

Likewise, Qutb believes that the leadership should have the support of the people. But the leadership would not be the compact group of Maududi's Islamic regime; Qutb's radical political activism would point toward an "anarchy of true believers," as Leonard Binder put it.[38] For Qutb, the principle of divine sovereignty is an affirmation of the equality of all humans and of individual human freedom—no person should be subjugated by another. This principle establishes the emancipation of the individual from the authority of others. Subjugation is exemplified by the slavery present in *jahiliyya* (pre-Islamic, or pagan) societies, which Islam came to destroy.[39] Qutb's main preoccupation is the waging of a relentless struggle against political orders that suppress individual freedom by claiming the people's obedience, which rightfully belongs to God, the supreme Sovereign.[40] In his schema, compared to Maududi's, one can detect a radical mixture of virtue and violence, the trademark of today's extremists.

Such a religion-based conception of rule and sovereignty in Islam entails the rejection of Western democracy, which is based on the sovereignty of the people, and popular sovereignty is regarded as constituting a rebellion against God. It is seen to be human-centered, not God-centered, and thus establishes the rule of human over human, an act of the profoundest arrogance in Islam. There is no sovereign human will in Islam. Human beings have free will and individual freedom only within the bounds of God's commands, as prescribed in the Qur'an and in the prophetic traditions. Maududi characterizes Islamic government as a "theodemocracy," which entitles Muslims, as vicegerents of God on earth, to a "limited popular sovereignty" under the paramountcy of God.[41] And Qutb argues that the principle of *shura* (consultation in public affairs), as stated in the Qur'an and practiced by the Prophet Muhammad and the early caliphs, does not equate with the Western notion of majority rule or sovereignty and its corollary of absolute freedom in legislation.[42] Another fundamentalist theorist, Syrian-born Said al-Hawwa, elaborated on this position by indicating that Islamic government differs from Western democracy in that it is a government of divine laws, not a government of man-made laws.[43]

In matters of legislation, then, fundamentalist theorists view the Islamic state as limited by the religious laws (*Shari'a*). Legislation should derive from established Islamic principles, or at least not contradict the spirit of *Shari'a*. Indeed, the application of *Shari'a*, as the legal system overseeing both the public and the private lives of the believers, is the stamp of an Islamic state, and the reconstitution of *Shari'a* is a common objective of Islamist groups.

Islamic Authenticity versus *Jahiliyya*

Another shared element in the Islamic discourse is the restoration and reassertion of Islamic authenticity in response to Western hegemony. Ever since its encounter with—and subsequent domination by—the West, Islam has been on the retreat. This is particularly so in the twentieth century, prompting one leading Islamist, Muhammad al-Bahi, to call it the century of eclipse.[44] The current onslaught of social modernization, or Westernization and secularism, along with the assimilative power and attraction of Western culture, is causing the erosion of authentic Islam. It poses a far greater danger than any past encroachments upon the old, cherished Islamic values and way of life. It is no wonder that Ayatollah Khomeini called the United States the "Great Satan." In Muslim thought, Satan is the source of evil and sin and also of temptation, infatuation, and lust, all of which should be condemned and eradicated. Western culture is, in the eyes of the fundamentalists, a paradigm of moral decay and of the consequent defilement of society. To Abul Ala Maududi and Sayyid Qutb and their Islamist cohort, it represents the new *jahiliyya*.[45]

Jahiliyya, which means pagan ignorance, is seen as descriptive of the conditions of pre-Islamic Arabia—godlessness, moral laxity, corruption, oppression—and is infused with moral and emotional themes: moral weakness in the absence of inner spiritual guidance, tyranny under unrestrained human will that rejects God's commands, and persecution and martyrdom of the righteous few by the forces of evil (the transgressors, *tughat*). All this is now manifest in modernity, which has come to stand for a "modern *jahiliyya*."

Qutb declares that humanity is now in a period of pagan ignorance similar to or surpassing the *jahiliyya* that was extinguished earlier by Islam. It permeates ideas and belief systems, custom and tradition, education and literature, and legal and governance structures. Everything about us is a product of our pagan ignorance.[46] This second *jahiliyya* is more pervasive and therefore more sinister in consequences and implications than was its pre-Islamic counterpart.[47] The intake of Western materialism, consumerism, and hedonism— "the white man's civilization"—is eating away at the moral and spiritual basis of Muslim society and augmenting cultural enslavement by the West.[48] In particular, the Western-dominated content of television and radio programs, cinema, and the arts and literature is vitiating Islamic culture and promoting immorality and decadence—a theme common to Muslim fundamentalists of all stripes.

But, for the fundamentalists, the most insidious aspect of the new *jahiliyya* is the internal dissemination of debilitating notions by Muslim reformers and rulers who are deemed to be secularists in Islamic disguise. They are more dangerous and destructive than the foreign infidels in leading the Muslim community astray. The reformists' attempts to reconcile Islam and modernity are dismissed as apologetic intellectual arguments made by a timid elite to a Western audience. Essentially, the Muslim reformists are viewed as cultural assimilationists who have been co-opted by the West and are its awed dupes in their willingness to compromise Islamic principles.[49]

To fundamentalists, the post-independence pseudo-Muslim rulers, desirous of mimicking the West, adopted nationalist-secularist policies that are inimical to Islam. They cite, as most evident, developments in Egypt under Nasser, Syria under the Ba'th, Iran under the shah, and Algeria under the National Liberation Front (FLN). In each of these national regimes, Islam was largely ignored and sometimes expressly repudiated. From the vantage point of the fundamentalists, Muslim laws and principles were discarded in favor of secular laws and values. Foreign ideologies of liberalism, socialism, and nationalism displaced Islamic ideas of community solidarity (*umma*) and social welfare.

The prevalent widespread "Westoxication"—intoxication with and subservience to the West—has greatly enhanced the diffusion of today's version of *jahiliyya* in Muslim societies, rendering their identities—in the eyes of the Muslim fundamentalists—increasingly marginal and subject to the West.[50] In the midst of this pervasive *jahiliyya*, Qutb warns, "We should not doubt for a moment what the inevitable result will be."[51] To him and his followers, the inevitable results of forsaking God and his commandments are social degradation, cultural bankruptcy, economic decline, and political authoritarianism. All this makes a return to roots, to Islamic authenticity, the earnest quest of all fundamentalists today.

Islamic Universalism (*Umma*) versus Nationalist Particularism (*Qawmiyya*)

Related to the theme of *jahiliyya* is the fundamentalists' opposition to nationalism. In fact, they posit that the contemporary *jahiliyya* is closely linked to the onset of nationalism and its twin, the secular nation-state, in the world of Islam, whose model is the European nation-state. Because the secular nation-state is also a product of nineteenth-century European colonialism, it is built around a national political identity, which contravenes the older, Muslim-based community identity.[52]

Since its inception, Islam has sought to abolish all the pagan connotations of nationalism, such as race, language, ethnicity, and tribe, and to establish a universal Muslim *umma* (community) based upon religious identification. The first Muslim commonwealth under Muhammad in Medina (A.D. 622–632) differed considerably from the tribal communities previously prevalent in Arabia in the sense that it was based not upon kinship, but upon faith and moral and spiritual principles. Membership in the political community and participation in public affairs were therefore defined by religion, not by ethnic, national, or tribal considerations. Today, under political Islam, religion is the primary source of political identity and loyalty. To Muslim fundamentalist thinkers of all kinds, the underlying strength of an Islamic order is its universality—the bond of religion is the heart of community solidarity. Contrariwise, nationalist particularism is the negation of Islamic universalism and breeds secularism and decline.

According to Sayyid Qutb, "A Muslim's nationality is his religion." He goes on to state that the Qur'an speaks of Muslims as members of a single *umma* regardless of ethnic, racial, and territorial affiliation.[53] He therefore rejects Arab nationalism as Western-inspired ideology and a form of modern *jahiliyya*. The Arabs, he maintains, could claim no place in the annals of world history were it not for Islam: Islam in its early days made them great; Islam instilled in them a new religious loyalty and a universal mission that did away with their tribal chauvinism and divisiveness; Islam enabled their transmission of a noble tradition and culture. Without Islam, they would have been inferior then, as is their situation today. Arabism in these times is no substitute for Islam, for the Arabs had no real existence as a nation before Islam. In fact, the current general regression of the Arabs in all areas of human endeavor renders them indolent and useless, with nothing to offer the world except their religion.[54] Qutb's activist opposition to Nasser's nationalist-secularist policies sent him to the gallows in 1966.

To Abul Ala Maududi, the message of Islam as revealed in the Qur'an is not nationality-based, nor is it the province of any specific national group. The Qur'an does not glorify the Aràbs or any other group of people based on nationalism. Rather, the Prophet of Islam struggled against the chauvinist identities of the various Arab tribes in order to establish a Muslim *umma*, wherein the only relevant bond is the religious bond, which supersedes all other affiliations.[55] The Islamic state therefore is not nationality-based; it is an ideological Qur'anic-based state that transcends race and nationality.[56]

Maududi believes that Islam and nationalism are antithetical and that there can be no accommodation between the two, contrary to what is espoused by many Muslim reformers. Such proposals of accommodation carry the seeds of the most dangerous Western import: secularism. To him, nationalism and its secular manifestations represent a flagrant denial of the sovereignty of God (*hakimiyya*) over the whole of the *umma*. In light of this Islamic principle, Maududi opposed the idea of a separate state of Pakistan, which was advanced by the Muslim League under Muhammad Ali Jinah during the independence movement in India in the 1940s. Muhammad Ali Jinah, with his modernist sentiments, set out to create a modern state of Pakistan as an expression of national self-determination for India's Muslims outside Hindu domination, not to found an ideological Islamic state. It was not meant to be an Islamic state subject to the rule of *Shari'a*, which, of course, further alienated Maududi.

Maududi rejected the league's "Islamic nationalism" theory as the basis of the proposed new state because "it does not differentiate between true Islamic universalism and limited territorial Islam."[57] To him, religion had no geographical bounds, and hence the territorial nation-state paradigm was not applicable. Further, nationalism would ultimately foster *jahiliyya* fanaticism and fratricide, a relapse to Arab tribal conditions. Instead of establishing a partitioned Muslim homeland, he urged his fellow Muslims to devote themselves to achieving the "Islamic transformation" (*inqilab Islami*) globally, unfettered by regionalism or nationalism. It would start with individual spiritual rejuvenation, education, and moral reform and work its way—under the leadership of a dedicated cadre of true Muslim believers—to the building of a world society based upon universal Islamic principles.[58]

As it turned out, following the partition of the Indian subcontinent, Maududi and his organization—the Jama'at-i-Islami (the Muslim Society)—moved to Pakistan, where they joined the *ulama* in pressing the newly created state to follow an Islamic course, domestically and internationally. In the next decades, Maududi continued to play a significant role in Pakistani politics, propagating his conception of an Islamic order under successive civilian and military regimes. Meanwhile, his organization failed to achieve any major electoral successes. Maududi died in 1979, the year that saw the Islamic revolution inaugurated in adjacent Iran. The Jama'at-i-Islami remains an influential political organization in Pakistan.[59]

Ayatollah Khomeini associates the return of *jahiliyya* with the advent of the Omayyad Empire in 661, whose rule was based upon Arab exclusiveness and elitism. He argues that the Omayyads promoted the Arabs over all other Muslim peoples, contravening the Islamic principles of universalism and egalitarianism. Arabism split *umma* unity and contributed to the degeneration of Islam and the onset of *jahiliyya*.[60] In this vein of Islamic universality, Khomeini presents himself not as an Iranian revolutionary leader, but as an Islamic revolutionary leader par excellence who could appeal to Muslims the world over to join the cause, a universal Islamic revolution.

It is obvious that Islamic fundamentalism is strongly opposed to modern nationalism for doctrinal-ideological and also practical reasons: it is antithetical to *umma* universality based upon Islamic identity; it spawns secularism, which threatens the Muslim way of life; and it inhibits *umma* unity and strength, rendering Islam a house divided.

Jihad

The answer of fundamentalists to the widespread diffusion of *jahilliyya* in Muslim societies is to reactivate the old Muslim duty of *jihad*: the duty to wage holy war against the internal and external enemies of Islam. This is a major theme in fundamentalist literature—one that is the most controversial and most threatening. It leads to a readiness to use force and violence and a willingness to challenge existing regimes. Indeed, the fundamentalist call, especially in its extreme expression, has reintroduced *jihad* as a form of political struggle and even rebellion and has given it a pivotal role in the strategy to combat the Muslim backslider. It is the revolutionary path of Islam that rejects the traditional notions of passivity and noninvolvement in public affairs.[61] Accordingly, direct action or force is now a principal preoccupation of radical Islamic fundamentalism.

The dynamic fundamentalist interpretation of *jihad* justifies its use for sociopolitical change in the name of Islam. Abul Ala Maududi declares that a committed group of Muslims armed with the power of faith and animated by the spirit of struggle is sure to bring about the desired transformation. Beliefs, then, have to be manifested in action through constant struggle—that is the essence of Islam.[62] There is no separation between doctrine and practice in Islam. True faith can be affirmed only by proper action in line with the teaching of the Qur'an and the *Sunna*.

Maududi elaborates his ideas on the Islamic obligation of *jihad* in *Al-Jihad fi Sabeel Allah* (Jihad in Islam). He defines *jihad* as a permanent revolutionary struggle to bring about the universal Islamic system. To that end, he envisages the founding of an "International Revolutionary Party" of committed Muslims—regardless of race, national origin, color, or social status—for the purpose of waging *jihad* against tyrannical and evil systems worldwide. Such warriors are members of *hizbullah* (the party of God), whose mission is to wipe out "oppression," "corruption," and "exploitation" wherever they exist, "using all means," and to establish "God's just order in the world." They seek to "shatter the myth of the divinity of demi-gods and fake deities and reinstate good in place of evil."[63] Maududi declares these actions are in line with the actions of the Prophets, who "without exception were Revolutionary Leaders, and the illustrious Prophet Muhammad . . . was the greatest Revolutionary Leader."[64]

Jihad has become in Maududi's thinking a legitimated struggle to wrest control of government from the wicked and transfer it to the believers. The struggle should be carried out in accordance with God's divine command to terminate human dominion over humans and establish the dominion of God. Such a conception of *jihad* does not differentiate between offensive and defensive *jihad*, a theoretical-legal formulation worked out by classical Muslim jurists. Nor does it see *jihad* in modernist apologetics' terms as merely a defensive means, and hence not in contravention of the norms of international law. Rather, Maududi views *jihad* as a total and continuous struggle in accord with God's injunction to establish God's universal sovereignty.

Sayyid Qutb was inspired by Maududi's advocacy of political struggle through direct action, especially the ideas Maududi espoused in his *Al-Jihad fi Sabeel Allah*. Like Maududi, Qutb declares *jihad* against tyrannicide a religious obligation incumbent upon the Muslim community. When the Muslim community is so debilitated by the godless *jahiliyya* culture, the obligation of *jihad* devolves upon the virtuous who have renounced that culture. The struggle is ingrained in the nature of Islam, which set out to "destroy the pagan kingdom of man and establish the kingdom of God on earth."[65] Thus, to Qutb, *jihad* in Islam is permanent, timeless, and borderless.

But Qutb's intellectual legacy to Islamic activism is his conceptualization of *jihad* as a struggle between dichotomous opposites—pre-Islamic *jahiliyya* society versus Islamic society—modeled after the historical antecedent of the Prophet's career in Mecca and in Medina (A.D. 610–632). In Medina, Muhammad founded the embryonic Islamic state based upon the injunctions of God as stipulated in the Qur'an. He pronounced *jihad* against the pagan Meccan tribes in order to be fighting for the way of God.[66] Thus, in early Islam, the world was viewed as comprising two separate, antagonistic entities: the believers of God, the purveyors of good; and the unbelievers, those in the party of Satan. In thus categorizing people, the lines in the struggle between belief and unbelief were clearly drawn, and the use of force in combatting *jahiliyya* was legitimized.

Qutb declares that today the "party of God"—the Muslim vanguard, the "self-appointed legions of divine guidance"[67]—is locked in mortal struggle with the "party of Satan" because of the scope and severity of current global *jahiliyya*.[68] Islamic government is nowhere to be found, Islamic law is not applied, and the sovereignty of God is not recognized. The entire world consequently becomes subject to *jihad* waged by the emergent Islamic vanguard—the only option left. The inevitability of *jihad* is dictated by the incompatibility of the two kinds of societies and by the requirement of the Islamic mission (*da'wa*) to liberate humankind from oppression and slavery.[69]

Most important, Qutb, an ideologue with an activist-revolutionary bent, utilizes the dichotomy—pre-Islamic *jahiliyya* society and Islamic society—to justify opposing the present "apostate" rulers and hence to sanction fighting against them. In so doing, he gives a new rendering of Islam and political power that radicalizes the way many contemporary Muslim activists think about their religion and politics. In his pioneering and most inspiring work, *Ma'alim fi al-Tariq*, (Signposts on the road),[70] he declares that, under present *jahiliyya* conditions, many leaders who say they are Muslims are in fact "unbelievers" and their governments are "un-Islamic." They are *jahiliyya* rulers, in the category of infidels. Therefore, it is the duty of believers to wage *jihad* to dislodge them. This stance confers the right to revolt, which is a departure from mainstream Sunni Islam. The official Sunni religious hierarchy has for the most part accepted and even legitimized those who wield the sword and usurp power, calling on Muslims to obey them or not to rebel against them.[71]

Further, Qutb's reasoning yields a new radical-activist interpretation of who is a Muslim by emphasizing deeds rather than the traditional view of self-identification and performance of rituals. The ideological definition of Islam gives radicals the power to challenge the Islamicity or legitimacy of anyone by *takfir*, branding that person as non-Muslim and therefore someone who must be killed.

Ayatollah Khomeini's conception of *jihad* is divinely sanctioned violence directed against internal and external enemies of Islam, and he takes his cue from the historical Shi'a theme of martyrdom. *Jihad* is exemplified in the self-sacrifice of the early Imams of Shi'a Islam, Hassan and Hussein, in the face of the Omayyads' "oppressive-tyrannical" rule. It is therefore waged simply to restore legitimate political authority to the rightful, designated religious leaders: these are the divinely inspired Imams and the supreme religious figures who are their representatives. All other forms of government that do not come under the rule of clerical custodians of the faith are by definition illegitimate and must be overthrown.[72] Hence, the dichotomy of opposites in Khomeini's scheme is not *jahiliyya* society versus Islamic society, as in Qutb's formulation; rather, it is legitimate divine authority versus illegitimate temporal power.

Khomeini called upon the Iranian religious leaders to guide the struggle against the tyrannical earthly power of the shah and to establish true Islamic government under the authority of the clergy, as proposed in his theory of *vilayat-i-faqih* (the authority of the leading jurist-theologian). He harnessed the independent power of the clergy in Shi'a Islam to act as a kind of opposition force on behalf of the people and mobilized them for political action against the state. Contrary to the Sunni religious leadership, which was largely co-opted by the state and cooperated with rulers, in Iran the Shi'a religious elite remained a powerful dissident social force, independent of and antago-

nistic to the state. He also appealed to the martyrdom theme in Shi'a historical experience by urging the Shi'a masses to follow the example of Hassan
and Hussein in the fight against injustice and oppression.[73] The message ener-
gized millions of Iranians who were ready to welcome martyrdom in the Islamic revolution against the shah. The Islamic tide ultimately swept away the
monarchy and ushered in the Islamic Republic of Iran in 1979.

CONCLUDING ASSESSMENT

It appears that these fundamentalist theoreticians have been instrumental
in transforming their religion from a generally passive belief system, even
under corrupt and repressive rulers, into an active revolutionary force, inciting *jihad* to establish the Islamic order. All of them advocate religion-based
solutions to the perceived problems of Muslim societies. They all look to a
bygone era for the model society and state. They set out not to create a new
society, but to revive an old one: the community of the Prophet and his early
successors (caliphs) in the seventh century, when Muslims were true to their
religion and therefore powerful and triumphant. Their ideology calls not for a
revolutionary change, but for a religio-political resurrection of what is gone.[74]
In fact, they do not look forward to a new era at all; rather, they want to
recreate the past. This explains why their key reference points and orienting
concepts regarding religion and politics, rule and legitimacy, state and society, and social and moral life are taken from the golden age of Islam. They
tend to disown much of Islamic history as a "deviation" from the ideal past, a
disgrace to Islam.

In their divinely ordained scheme, the state assumes a moral function that
encompasses the community and its social institutions. It is charged with maintaining the fabric of virtuous, civilized life according to *Shari'a*. All standards of conduct are implemented in accord with Qur'anic provisions. The
society is bound together by public virtue and righteousness. Morals and ethics are inseparable from law and politics; all are embedded in religion. The
Muslim state is in sharp contradistinction to the Western liberal state, whose
principal function is to protect individual life, liberty, and property. Also, unlike Western liberalism, the polity, the community, and collective values pre-
cede all aspects of individuality.

Further, all attempts at synthesizing Islam with so-called modernity—or
accommodating Islam to it—are rejected out of hand. Society and state have
to be recast in the image of true Islam, based upon a fundamentalist theoretical paradigm of total Islamic self-sufficiency—Islam as a complete system of
life. Indeed, all of these fundamentalist ideologues see Islam as holistic and
self-sufficient, obviating any possible symbiotic coexistence with any other
social and political system. The Muslim community (*umma*) is a "world" sufficient unto itself, embracing lives and laying claim to loyalties. Qur'anic

injunctions provide the moral and institutional foundation of the society.

All three fundamentalist theoreticians assert their belief in the Muslim community's exceptionalism and its universal role and mission as the best instrument (*khayru umma*) for the dissemination of virtue and the prohibition of vice.[75] Indeed, to these fundamentalists, the power of Islam stems from believer certainty that its message is the best for humankind and that Muslims are the best of God's peoples. Such a definition does not promote an "intercultural *éntente*" in a world fraught with animosities. Rather, the uncompromising conviction of preeminence makes a "clash of civilizations" inevitable. The Muslim fundamentalists, unable to transcend history, are its prisoners, committed to permanent struggle against "unbelievers" both inside and out.

Still, these religious ideologues are the most compelling voices of Muslim fundamentalism today, and their messages have resonated among younger generations of Muslim activists, who currently champion the cause of political Islam. We are now witnessing a growth in Muslim fundamentalist thought consequent to the proliferation of Islamist groups throughout the Middle East during the current wave of Islamic resurgence. Indeed, the roll call of leading Muslim ideologues and movements has grown exponentially, with diverse constructs and strategies, depending on contextual conditions. They include Muhammad Abdul Salam Farag of the Jihad Organization, Sheikh Omar Abdul Rahman of the Islamic Jama'a, Shukri Mustafa of al-Takfir wa al-Hijra (Apostasy and Flight), Salih Siriyya of the Islamic Liberation Party in Egypt; Muhammad Hussein Fadlallah of Hizbullah in Lebanon; Hasan al-Turabi of the National Islamic Front in Sudan; Rachid Al-Ghannouchi of the Islamic Tendency Movement (MTI), known in the late 1980s as al-Nahda (Renaissance) Party in Tunisia; Abbas Madani and Ali Belhaj of the Islamic Salvation Front (FIS) in Algeria; Sheikh Ahmad Yassin of Hamas in Gaza and the West Bank; Juhayman al-Utaibi, Safar al-Hawali, and Sheikh Salman Al-Auda of the neo-Wahhabi fundamentalists in Saudi Arabia; and Said al-Hawwa and Sheikh Muhammad al-Bayanuni of the Islamic Front in Syria—among others. Yet, despite this multiplicity and despite the particularist properties of each Islamist group, they share some denominators as they draw on the key assumptions of themes outlined above.

Virtually all Islamic fundamentalist groups seek to reestablish Islam as the foundation of a just political and social order to replace existing corrupt, un-Islamic systems. The creation of an Islamic state is required for the founding and subsequent preservation of an Islamic society and the Islamic way of life. Faith and state are intertwined in Islam. They all see Western democracy as alien to Islam, where governance is predicated on the rule of God. Therefore, all fundamentalists hold that God's law (*Shari'a*) is supreme and that no person or group can alter or nullify it to suit one's current whimsical inclinations. Further, they all believe that Islam provides a comprehensive moral and ethical code regulating individual and communal life at all levels. Based on this moral absolutism, the total application of *Shari'a* is an imperative for all fundamentalists. Additionally, they are united in opposition to those aspects of modernity, especially social modernization, that they find inimical to Islam, a belief system deemed superior to Western materialism. Finally, they all maintain that it is the duty of Muslims to reject the secular state and even resist it. The religious identity of the ruling elite is of significance in fundamentalist thinking. The political elite in an Islamic state should be Muslims not only in name, but also in practice. Thus, challenging the status quo is a given for activist Islamist groups; it is the way to establish a truly Islamic order.

NOTES

1. According to Eqbal Ahmed, with arrival of Western colonialism, "for the first time in its long and eventful history, Islamic civilization began to be defined in reference to another." Muslims "were reduced to serving another's history." See Eqbal Ahmed, "Islam and Politics," *The Islamic Impact*, ed. Yvonne Y. Haddad, Byron Haines, and Ellison Findly (Syracuse: Syracuse University Press, 1984), 20. The resulting trauma has evoked a strong longing for and identification with Islam's glorious past, which modern Muslim fundamentalists seek to recreate.

2. On this general theme, see Saad Eddin Ibrahim, "Egypt's Islamic Activism in the 1980s," *Third World Quarterly* 10 (Apr. 1988): 655–56; Albert Hourani, *Arabic Thought in the Liberal Age, 1798–1939* (London: Oxford University Press, 1962); Hourani, *A History of the Arab Peoples* (New York: Warner Books, 1991), pt. 4; Bernard Lewis, *The Middle East and the West* (New York: Harper & Row, 1964); Lewis, *Islam and the West* (Oxford: Oxford University Press, 1993); Lewis, "Islam and Liberal Democracy," *Atlantic* Feb. 1993: 89–98; Lewis, "The Roots of Muslim Rage," *Atlantic* Sept. 1990: 47–54; William Pfaff, "Islam and the West," *New Yorker* 28 Jan. 1991: 83–88.

3. Whereas in orthodox Sunni Islam the state historically has generally controlled the religious establishment by co-opting it into the administrative apparatus, in Shi'a Islam the clerics have always maintained their independence from the state and their autonomy. This is largely due to Shi'a traditional rejection of all temporal authority as illegitimate in the absence of the "hidden Imam," who went into occultation in the latter part of the ninth century. Shi'a clerics have been able in this way to preserve considerably their pivotal position and role as the guardians of the society.

4. These Muslim reformers include nineteenth- and early-twentieth-century figures such as Jamal Al-Din Al-Afghani, Muhammad Abdu, Sir Sayyid Ahmad Khan, Rashid Rida, Ali Abdul Raziq, and Ameer Ali. They sought to reconcile Western civilization with Islamic faith and culture. In the end, Islamic reformation produced a "fragile synthesis" that failed to take root. See Olivier Roy, "Le néofundamentalisme: des Frères musulmans au FIS algérien," *Esprit* Mar.–Apr. 1992: 78, 83.

5. This is the theme of Daniel Lerner's acclaimed study, *The Passing of Traditional Society: Modernizing the Middle East* (New York: Free Press, 1958).

6. The fourteenth-century Muslim thinker Ibn Khaldun illustrated the power of religious zeal in the rise and decline of dynasties throughout Islamic history in his classic study, *Al-Muqaddima* (Introduction to history) (Beirut: Dar al-Kitab al-Lubnani, 1983).

7. Not the return of Islam, for Islam is always there; it did not wither. Rather, it is the Muslims who departed from the "straight path." Now Muslims are going back to where

they belong, the Islamic way of life.

8. See "Islam, Democracy, the State, and the West" (Summary of a lecture and roundtable discussion with Hasan al-Turabi, prepared by Louis J. Cantori and Arthur Lowrie), *Middle East Policy* 1. 3 (1992): 60.

9. This is an approach radically different from that of nineteenth-century Muslim reformers, who were not as inspiring or as successful in reaching out to the masses. These reformers are now looked upon by Muslim fundamentalists as intellectual apologists who tried to defend Islam by giving it Western garb. The one exception to this wholesale rejection of early reformers was Jamal al-Din al-Afghani, who was viewed as a populist-Islamist with a revolutionary bent. See Said bin Said al-Alawi, "Qat' ma' Fikr 'Asr al-Nahda" (Split from the age of Renaissance thought), *al-Sharq al-Awsat* 9 Feb. 1995: 14. For a survey of Muslim revivalist thinkers, see Ali Rahnema, ed., *Pioneers of Islamic Revival* (London: Zed Books, 1995).

10. The Omayyads were a clan of the Meccan tribe of Quraysh who early on led the opposition to the Prophet Muhammad's mission before their embrace of Islam. Their rebellion against the fourth Caliph Ali (A.D. 656–661) brought the period of the Rightly Guided Caliphs (first four successors of the Prophet) to an end.

11. The Abbasids were another clan of the Arabian Quraysh tribe. It was during the eighth and the tenth centuries of their reign that Islamic civilization reached its apogee. The Abbasid caliphate was destroyed by the Monghul invasion in 1258.

12. Ira M. Lapidus, "The Golden Age: The Political Concepts of Islam," *Annals of the American Academy of Political and Social Science* no. 524 (Nov. 1992): 16.

13. The one exception to this secularization process was Saudi Arabia. See Hourani, *A History of the Arab Peoples*, 345–46.

14. On the theme of the separation of public and religious life, see Lapidus, "The Golden Age," 13–25.

15. Sayyid Qutb, *Al-Mustaqbal li-hatha al-Din* (Islam: The religion of the future) (n.p., n.d.), 34–35.

16. Abdul Qader Odeh, *Al-Islam wa Awda'una al-Qanuniyya* (Islam and our legal conditions) (Kuwait: Dar al-Qur'an, 1977), 51.

17. Abul Ala Maududi, *Al-Jihad fi Sabeel Allah* (Jihad in Islam) (Beirut: Dar Lubnan, 1969), 36. See his *Nazariyat al-Islam al-Siyasiyya* (Political theory of Islam) (Beirut: al-Risala,1979); *Nizam al-Hayat fi al-Islam* (System of life in Islam) (Damascus: Dal al-Qur'an, 1977).

18. Maududi, *Nazariyat al-Islam al-Siyasiyya*, 41–42; *Nizam al-Hayat fi al-Islam*.

19. Qutb, *Al-Mustaqbal li-hath al-Din*, 7.

20. Sayyid Qutb, *Al-'Adala al-Ijtima'iyya fi al-Islam* (Social justice in Islam) (Cairo: al-Nashr lil-Jami'iyyin, 1954).

21. Sayyid Qutb, *Fi Zilal al-Qur'an* (In the shadow of the Qur'an) (Beirut: Dar al-Shuruq, 1981), 932–33.

22. On the comprehensive nature of the Islamic system, see Qutb, *Al-Mustaqbal li-hatha al-Din*.

23. On the rule of the clerical elite, see Ayatollah Khomeini, *Al-Hukouma al-Islamiyya* (Islamic government), prepared and introduced by Dr. Hasan Hanafi (Cairo: n.p., 1979).

24. Fouad Ajami, *The Vanished Imam: Musa al-Sadr and the Shia of Lebanon* (Ithaca, N.Y.: Cornell University Press, 1986), 191.

25. This is in stark contrast to Maududi, Qutb, and other Sunni fundamentalist thinkers who rejected the notion of an Islamic state ruled solely by the clergy.

26. The fusion between Islam and politics goes back to the formative years of the Islamic state (A.D. 622–661) under the Prophet Muhammad and his early successors, the four Rightly Guided Caliphs. Surely Muhammad's example stands as a paradigm of nonseperation of religion and state. He started out as Prophet and went on to rule over a Muslim state with armies, revenues, and laws. See my "Basic Characteristics of an Islamic State System," *Journal of South Asian and Middle Eastern Studies* 5 (Winter 1981): 3–16; Muhammad Salim al-'Awwa, *Fi al-Nizam al-Siyasi li al-Dawla al-Islamiyya* (On the political system of the Islamic state) (Cairo: al-Maktab al-Masri, 1979).

27. Abdul Qader Odeh, *Al-Mal wa al-Hukm fi al-Islam* (Wealth and rule in Islam) (Cairo: al-Makhtar al-Masri, 1977), 86.

28. It was Ali Abdul Raziq who first tried to advocate a secular theory of the state in 1925, only one year after the caliphate was formally abolished by Mustafa Kemal Ataturk, the founder of modern Turkey. Abdul Raziq maintained that government and politics in the world of Islam have nothing to do with religion; they are secular matters with no religious foundation and therefore should be treated separately from religious or moral consider-ations. His assertions led to a stormy reaction by al-Azhar *ulama* (religious scholars) of Egypt, accusing him of secularism and of abandoning Islam. Abdul Raziq, *Al-Islam wa Usoul al-Hukm* (Islam and the principles of rule), ed. Muhammad 'Amara (Beirut: al-Mu'assasa al-Arabiyya, 1972). In the same vein, a contemporary Egyptian liberal thinker, former Superior Court Chief Justice Muhammad Said al-Ashmawi, rejects the notion that Islam is a religion and a state. See his *Al-Islam al-Siyasi* (Political Islam) (Cairo: Sina, 1989).

29. On this point, see Abul Ala Maududi, *Nazariyat al-Islam wa Hadieh fi al-Siyasa wa al-Qanun wa al-Dustur* (Islamic theory and guidance in politics, law, and constitution) (Beirut: al-Risala, 1969), 250–57.

30. Maududi, *Al-Jihad fi Sabeel Allah*, 22–23; Sayyid Qutb, *Al-Jihad fi Sabeel Allah* (Jihad in Islam) (Beirut: Dar Lubnan 1969), 107–8.

31. Maududi, *Nazariyat al-Islam al-Siyasiyya*, 14–20.

32. Bernard Lewis, *The Political Language of Islam* (Chicago: University of Chicago Press, 1991), 30. See also Maududi, *Nazariyat al-Islam al-Siyasiyya*, 28–32. In fact, the term *nomocracy* is more apt than *theocracy* because God's rule is established through his law, which is the source of government authority. For further elaboration on this point, see Majid Khadduri, "Nature of the Islamic State," *Islamic Culture* 21 (Oct. 1947): 327–31.

33. Maududi, *Nazariyat al-Islam wa Hadieh*, 259.

34. For the differing views on and interpretations of the Khomeini theory of some Iranian Shi'a theologians, see Said Amir Arjomand, *The Turban for the Crown: The Islamic Revo-lution in Iran* (New York: Oxford University Press, 1988), 155–60.

35. It represents a substantive readjustment and reinterpretation of the classic theory of *imamate*, or rule, in Shi'a Islam. For further discussion on this point, see Shahrough Akhavi, "The Clergy's Concept of Rule in Egypt and Iran," *Annals of the American Academy of Political and Social Science* no. 524 (Nov. 1992): 92–102. In arguing the case for rule by the upper echelons of the clerics, Khomeini invoked the *hadith* (saying of the Prophet) "The *ulama* are the heirs of the Prophet." The same *hadith* is employed by the Sunni religious leaders, but only to support the *ulama*'s role as the moral guide of the community. See Khomeini, *Al-Hukouma al-Islamiyya*.

36. Abul Ala Maududi, *Al-Usus al-Akhlaqiyya lil-Haraka al-Islamiyya* (The moral foun-dations of the Islamic movement) (Cairo: Dar al-Nashr, 1952).

37. Abul Ala Maududi, *Manhaj al-Inqilab al-Islami* (The course of the Islamic transfor-

mation) (Beirut: Mu'assasat al-Risala, 1975), 16–19.

38. Leonard Binder, *Islamic Liberalism: A Critique of Development Ideologies* (Chicago: University of Chicago Press, 1988), 177.

39. Qutb, *Al-Mustaqbal li-hatha al-Din*, 12.

40. Qutb, *Al-Jihad fi Sabeel Allah*, 102–4.

41. Maududi, *Nazariyat al-Islam al-Siyasiyya*, 31.

42. Sayyid Qutb, *Ma'alim fi al-Tariq* (Signposts on the road) (Beirut: Matba'at al-Risala, 1966).

43. Said al-Hawwa, *Jund Allah* (Soldiers of God) (Cairo: Maktabat Wahba, 1988). The same theme was echoed by *al-Muslimoun*, an Egyptian Islamic weekly: "The European idea that gives nations 'legal sovereignty' has no basis in our *Shari'a* because we cannot ascribe sovereignty to a human being . . . Islamic Shari'a represents the will of God, not the will of the state." See "Islam and the West: Everything the Other Is Not," *Economist* 1 Aug. 1992: 34.

44. Muhammad al-Bahi, *Mustaqbal al-Islam wa al-Qarn al-Khamis Ashar al-Hijri* (The future of Islam and the fifteenth Islamic century) (Cairo: Maktabat Wahba, 1978).

45. Maududi was the first Muslim thinker to articulate a structure of thought condemning modernity—exemplified in nationalism, secularism, and democracy—as alien and therefore incompatible with Islam. See his *Al-Islam wa al-Madaniyya al-Haditha* (Islam and modernity) (Cairo: Dar al-Ansar, 1978). This is in sharp contrast to earlier Muslim reformers, such as Jamal al-Din al-Afghani, Muhammad Abdu, and Sir Sayyid Ahmad Khan, who sought to accommodate Islam to modernity and show its compatibility with conditions of progress and strength in the modern world.

46. Qutb, *Ma'alim fi al-Tariq*, 23.

47. Qutb, *Fi Zilal al-Qur'an*, 510.

48. See Qutb, *Al-Mustaqbal li-hatha al-Din*, 24.

49. This is a common theme among virtually all contemporary Muslim fundamentalist thinkers. On this general theme, see Stephen Humphreys, "Islam and Political Values in Saudi Arabia, Egypt, and Syria," *Middle East Journal* 33 (Winter 1979): 1–19.

50. More specifically, "Westoxication" refers to the attraction to more "advanced" societies and their education, science, and culture. The Persian term *gharbzadegi* (intoxication with the West) was coined by a leading theoretician of the Iranian revolution, Ali Shari'ati, in describing the ills facing contemporary Iran. See Ervand Abrahamian, "Ali Shari'ati: Ideologue of the Iranian Revolution," *Merip Reports* Jan. 1982: 25–28; Fouad Ajami, "The Impossible Life of Moslem Liberalism: The Doctrines of Ali Shari'ati and Their Defeat," *New Republic* 2 June 1986: 26–32.

51. Qutb, *Al-Mustagbal li-hatha al-Din*, 137.

52. Lapidus, "The Golden Age," 21.

53. Qutb, *Ma'alim fi al-Tarig*, 179, 192.

54. Qutb, *Fi Zilal al-Qur'an*, 511–12. In lamenting the Arab condition today, Qutb seems to be in agreement with leftist thinkers such as Salah al-Din al-Bitar, one of the founding fathers of the Ba'th in Syria, who declared shortly before his assassination in Paris: "The Arabs have not created any original idea for the last two hundred years, devoting themselves entirely to copying others. The liberals transplanted Western European liberalism; the Marxists transferred ideas from Eastern Europe; the Nasserists and Ba'thists, being eclectic, borrowed here and there." Quoted in Emmanuel Sivan, *Radical Islam: Medieval Theology and Modern Politics* (New Haven, Conn.: Yale University Press, 1990), 157.

55. Abul Ala Maududi, *Bayna al-Da'wa al-Qawmiyya wa al-Rabita al-Islamiyya* (Be-

tween the nationalist call and the Islamic bond) (Cairo: Dar al-Ansar, 1967).

56. Maududi, *Manhaj al-Inqilab al-Islami*, 8–9.

57. Maududi, *Nazariyat al-Islam al-Siyasiyya*, 5.

58. Maududi, *Minhaj al-Inqilab al-Islami*, 16–19.

59. Sohail Hashmi, "Islamic Fundamentalism: Religious Assertiveness and Political Militancy," class lecture on Islamic civilization, University of Southern Maine, Portland, 21 Apr. 1992.

60. Ayatollah Khomeini, *Islam and Revolution*, translated and annotated by Hamid Algar (Berkeley, Calif.: Mizan Press, 1981), 332.

61. This activist interpretation of *jihad* as a political struggle that even sanctions rebellion runs contrary to much of mainstream Sunni Islamic jurisprudence, which emphasizes the doctrine of civil obedience. Indeed, modern activist fundamentalists reject the medieval Sunni Muslim jurists' theories that would legalize the duty of obedience to the powers that be regardless of the means that had been used in reaching the top. The Sunni rationale is that an unjust ruler is better for the preservation of the community than civil strife (*fitna*). The one notable to take exception to this line of reasoning was the fourteenth-century Damascene Muslim scholar Ahmad ibn Taymiyya (1263–1338). In his treatise *Al-Siyasa al-Shar'iyya* (Public policy in Islamic jurisprudence), he justifies rebellion against corrupt rulers who do not apply and enforce *Shari'a*. His doctrines are a main source of inspiration for modern fundamentalists. On this point, see Sivan, *Radical Islam*, 94–107.

62. Maududi, *Al-Usus al-Akhlaqiyyah lil-Haraka al-Islamiyya*, 20–52.

63. Maududi, *Al-Jihad fi Sabeel Allah*, 13–15, 19–32, 34.

64. Ibid., 28.

65. Qutb, *Al-Jihad fi Sabeel Allah*, 103–4, 129–30.

66. Qutb, *Ma'alim fi al-Tariq*, 75–109.

67. Salim Tamari, "Left in Limbo," *Middle East Report* Nov.-Dec. 1992: 16.

68. Qutb, *Fi Zilal al-Qur'an*, 1013–30.

69. Qutb, *Al-Jihad fi Sabeel Allah*, 109, 111, 128; *Ma'alim*, 80–102.

70. Qutb, *Ma'alim fi al-Tariq*. Written in the early 1960s, by 1988 the book had been reprinted more than thirty times in Egypt alone. See Saad Eddin Ibrahim, "Egypt's Islamic Activism in the 1980s," 654.

71. According to classical Muslim theorists, how a ruler obtained power is less important than how he uses it. However, all of them agreed that power should be used within the bounds of *Shari'a*. Thus, the model of political authority in Islam is based primarily on safeguarding and preserving the welfare of the Muslim community under the rule of *Shari'a*, as operationalized by the *ulama*.

72. Khomeini, *Islam and Revolution*; *Al-Hukouma al-Islamiyya*, 33–34, 56–73, 88–117. In Shi'a tradition, all governments not ruled by the House of Ali (fourth caliph and the Prophet's cousin and son-in-law) are by definition illegitimate. Therefore, in contrast to Sunni Islam, which did not develop a constitutional theory to delegitimize rulers, the right to revolt has always been theoretically justified in Shi'a Islam, especially against Sunni-dominated states.

73. According to Ali Shari'ati, the message of Hussein's martyrdom is that "all Shi'is, irrespective of time and space, had the sacred duty to oppose, resist and rebel against contemporary ills." Abrahamian, "Ali Shari'ati," 26.

74. On this theme, see Mary-Jane Deeb, "Militant Islam and the Politics of Redemption," *Annals of the American Academy of Political and Social Science* no. 524 (Nov. 1992): 52–65.

75. This assertion is predicated upon a Qur'anic verse that describes the Muslim community as "the best of peoples, evolved for mankind. Enjoining what is right and forbidding what is wrong." The Qur'an 3: 110.

2

The Appeal of
Islamic Fundamentalism

If the past few centuries were difficult and trying times for Muslims, marked by failures and defeats, the present is no less troubling. Today is no ordinary moment. Since the mid-1970s, the world of Islam has been in the throes of a widespread Islamic resurgence that has been increasing in militance and violence, and no near end seems in sight. The challenge is shaking the foundations of Arab politics, and tremors are reverberating throughout the Muslim heartland from the Maghreb to Western Asia. Its sources are many and wide-ranging, extending from the religious and emotive to the mundane. It is driven by a strong nostalgia for a glorious distant past and a deep yearning to resurrect Islamic power, but its immediate causes do not spring from religion.

The mass appeal of Islamism has its roots in secular circumstances, but they have been given a religious expression. Thus, the symbolism and idioms employed are religious, but the real concerns are social and economic and overridingly political—power and control. The movement is basically an ideology of protest against the deteriorating cultural and material conditions of Arab Muslim societies and the perceived hegemony of the West. In the world of Islam, where public and religious life are intertwined, sociopolitical discontent is often manifested in religious terms. Historically, Islam has always served as a vehicle for the expression of sociopolitical and economic dissent, particularly in times of crisis; and its idealistic and egalitarian character has provided the impetus for protest and even rebellion. Indeed, in the first Islamic century,[1] the appeal of Shi'a Islam among non-Arab minorities of Islam, especially the Persians, was partly a religious expression of their objection to the social and economic domination of the Arab elite, a subjugation clearly contrary to the universal egalitarianism of Islam.[2]

Today, in the fifteenth Muslim century, with mounting social and economic crises, and in the absence of a viable and secular orienting ideology of change,

Islam proffers its unique ideology of reform. The secular national ideologies and movements that rallied millions across the Arab world in the post-colonial era—Nasserism and Ba'thism and their corollaries of Arab socialism, Arab nationalism, and Arab unity—have all collapsed. The ideologies of nationalism, socialism, and national socialism bequeathed by nineteenth- and twentieth-century Europe have lost whatever transplanted vigor they once had and have even become discredited. They failed to deliver on their promises of national strength, social and economic development, and political freedom. Instead, they spawned authoritarian, repressive structures that stifled civil society, thwarted individual initiative, and nurtured bureaucratic inertia—resulting eventually in debilitation and accumulating losses. This was best illustrated in the 1967 war, when the Arabs lost confidence in themselves and their nationalist idols and icons, precipitating a movement in favor of a return to religious imperatives.[3] People found refuge in Islam as a faith and a way of life; a conversion from the modernist-secularist path. Secular nationalism devoid of Islam had turned Muslims against Muslims. Socialism had brought with it divisiveness and regression. Both undermined the Islamic foundation of the community and produced decline.

The ensuing disarray in the Arab world was most evident in the often confused and contradictory reactions to the Kuwait crisis of 1990–1991. In the Gulf War, the Arabs watched from the sidelines as foreign powers went about the business of reordering the Arab house. The events testified to their national incapacities to act in concert and to their paralyzing reliance on the West to solve their problems, even after fifty years of being on their own. In the end, the near-destruction of Iraq put to rest once and for all Arab pretensions to national strength, independence, and solidarity. It cast the regimes in a revealing light as impotent, servile, and fratricidal. Hence, the moral verdict rendered was against the Arab order that favored an Islamic alternative.

In the absence of coherent responses and with the continued imposition of Western will, little wonder that slogans such as "Islam is the solution," "an Islamic state and society are the answer," and "Islam is our life"—glib and general though they may be—rang true in the minds of many who believed themselves adrift in lives gone awry. For too long, Arabs had been deluded, intoxicated, and paralyzed by foreign doctrinal imports—Marxism, liberalism, and secular nationalism—confusing them with progress. What their leaders had been doing was just mimicking the West, "Bolshevizing" or "liberalizing" Islam, trying to look "modern."[4] In the process, they divested themselves of their Muslim culture and turned into hollow imitators, in thrall to their models.

Ultimately, the failure of modernization policies underscored the bankruptcy of the alien schemes and turned Muslims inward in search of indigenous ways of life and governance. This, of course, in the context of these societies, could only mean Islamization. If the secular Western ideologies had all been unavailing, Islam—the region's own ideology—would be the best instrument for success. As Abdul Sallam Yassin, a Moroccan fundamentalist-activist leader, succinctly put it: Both "West and East have failed. The future is Islam."[5] It is clear that in this ideological-political arena, which is currently devoid of optimism, Islam holds out the prospect of salvation and diminished despair. The hope thus engendered has acquired political meaning, and some are taking direct action to work out the Islamic principles.

Equally important in the drawing power of Islamic fundamentalism is that, despite all the modern ideologies that have been tried and found wanting, Islam remains the source of cultural authenticity and national identity for most Arab Muslims. Without question, the pervasiveness of the Islamic cultural fiber in the life of Arabs makes it an integral part of their national-self definition. Muhammad Hasanein Heikal, the leading veteran Egyptian journalist, probably spoke for multitudes when he said, "Only Islam makes sense, is authentic" to them.[6]

Little wonder that imported ideologies never penetrated the deeper instincts of the Muslim masses. These external thought systems remained alien to the cultural context and were intrusive. Popular culture in much of the Arab world remains deeply imbedded in the Islamic religion. Hence, one of the major strengths of the Islamic movement is its appeal to Islam, an integral part of the individual and national psyches. More than anything else, Islam motivates the people of the Middle East. It is their faith and culture; it is their life and mentality. In the words of Ishaq al-Farhan, a fundamentalist leader of Jordan's Jabhat al-'Amal al-Islami (the Islamic Action Front, or IAF), "When [Islamic activists] preach through mosques or educational and social institutions, they are only responding to the pulse of the people."[7] Islamism is not a counterculture; it is a reaffirmation of an existing old culture that remains central to all Muslims.

The hold of Islam on the masses gives the Islamic movement a natural advantage over all other ideologies. It enables the movement to capture the people's imagination, to inspire them, and to mobilize them for political action. To that end, the mosque and its affiliate bodies (Qur'anic schools, religious study groups, and charitable foundations) and the independent networks of Islamic educational, social welfare, and medical services furnish the organizational support in the battle for the people's hearts and minds. Islamic groups have built and utilized these institutions as an alternative to inadequate or inefficient government services to enhance their position with the masses.

Indeed, the proliferation of independent local mosques with independent preachers has provided effective platforms of dissent outside government control. Ibrahim Nugud, a former communist leader in Sudan, bitterly comments: "To organize a communist group, we had to find safe houses. To organize an Islamic political group, you can meet openly five times a day [for prayers], in the mosque."[8] Many of the Islamic movements do have as their foundation neighborhood mosques or Islamic study circles. Not surprisingly, there is now an ongoing struggle between the government and Islamic groups in Egypt,

Algeria, Tunisia, Jordan, and the Palestinian territories, among others, for the control of mosques and their preachers.[9]

The issue of culture and identity, which figures prominently in the fundamentalist appeal today, is closely linked to the notion of Western hegemony, its nemesis. Surely the religious basis of Arab culture sets it apart from other cultures, especially those of the secular West. In this context, the preservation of Islamic cultural authenticity (*al-turath*) and identification against an aggressive, expansionist modern Western civilization, which threatens to bring the entire globe—including Islam—into its orbit, gives the fundamentalists a reason for being and for struggling. The cultural ascendancy of the West represents a "cultural-ideological invasion," or a new imperialism, which only Islam can combat.[10] In the face of this onslaught, the fundamentalists stand fast against "cultural surrender" and "identity betrayal."

The fundamentalist leaders are not traditionalists who are ignorant of the world. Rather, in contrast to the traditional conservative men of religion whom they oppose, they are men of today, products of modern education.[11] They are sophisticated enough to realize that modernity is an imperiling force, the greatest challenge to a cherished way of life. The new cultural imperialism of the West is as big a danger as any physical threat. It implants materialism, moral decadence, and societal weakness—the seeds of Muslim degeneration.

The issue of culture and identity is related to another important issue: independence. Should the Arabs follow the lead of outsiders and should foreign cultural penetration go unchecked, the result would be an even greater dependence on others, mainly Westerners. On the other hand, to be independent is to assert idiosyncratic values in charting the Arab course, which could mean only Islam. This reasoning makes of Islam a wellspring of cultural nationalism that is both assertive and defiant. It is somewhat reminiscent of Nasser's nationalist theme, *Irfa' ra'sak ya akhi* (Raise your head, stand tall, be counted, my Arab brother)—inspiring the masses against their oppressors, but with an Islamic twist. Such a response is typical of a culture that was once vibrant and stood tall, but now finds itself besieged by the very forces it disdained. A resurgent Islam gives promise of "turning the clock back."

In a way, today's Islamic fundamentalism is a continuation of the postcolonial, anti-Western nationalist struggle, but now couched in the language of radical Islam and in a new form. It is "the reincarnation of the nationalist movement with . . . an Islamic face."[12] In many respects, the Islamists espouse the nationalists' agenda—independence, national strength, social justice, and authenticity—but express it with a religious cast. No wonder, then, that the Islamic activists have championed the struggle for "decolonization at the cultural level"[13]—part and parcel of anti-Western Third Worldism—and advocated a revival of a pristine Islamic identity and culture.[14] Actually, the movement has a worldview and an understanding of the global political system similar to those of other Third World nationalist ideologies and movements.[15] An essential element of Islamic fundamentalism today is its assertion that it is crowning the struggle against colonialism by eradicating its most pervasive vestige: Western cultural hegemony, the chief source of their countries' failings.

Islam, then, has taken on the character of a quasi–national liberation doctrine. This is clearly evident to Hasan al-Turabi: "Today if you want to assert indigenous values, originality and independence against the West, then Islam is the only doctrine."[16] This puts the Westernized elites, who are looked upon as transplanted Westerners, in the enemy camp. The Muslim Arabs who abandoned their identity and slavishly emulated Western ways are deemed to be a "fifth column" in Islam's midst. In fact, the Islamic discourse has become so pervasive that even Arab nationalists have invoked Islamist themes such as *jihad* (holy war), *iman* (faith), and *ghadba lillah* (a rage for God) in the struggle against the Western powers.[17] But the use of religious idioms by nationalists should not be surprising; there has always been a strain of religious fervor in the many strands of political discourse in the Middle East.[18]

Above all, Islamic fundamentalism is more a response to economic conditions than a desire to build a theocracy. The fact that it has flourished since the 1980s is an indication of the parallel socioeconomic crises in many countries of the Middle East, crises that exemplify for their victims the failure of modernization. One such component of modernization, education, turned out not to be the key to opportunities in the context of limited economies. The spread of education only swelled the ranks of unemployed and underemployed graduates in economies that offered few openings outside the bloated public sector.[19] The waves of educated young people flooding into a saturated job market every year face a bleak present and an even bleaker future.

Another component of modernization, urbanization, was fueled by spiraling population growth and rural migration. Rampant urban decay has been the result. By 1990, more than half the population of a dozen (out of twenty) Arab countries lived in cities—each of which was burdened, if not overwhelmed, by a ballooning populace pressing against a limited, exhausted infrastructure in steady decline.[20] The deterioration and suffocation of urban life were inevitable.

In many cases, Cairo for one, city blended seamlessly with countryside as villages were overrun and absorbed. Further, the pull of the city for deprived millions in the countryside created "ruralized" enclaves within city confines, changing the nature of cohesion and collectivity in many ways.[21] One way was to transfuse village religious tradition and conservative ethos into the new setting. Cities of the Middle East now are megacenters with few of their former positive cosmopolitan characteristics. But most distressing—and dangerous—are the immense and inexorably growing pools of angry surplus labor: desperate people trying to extract an existence from nothingness. The masses of the migrant poor were kept "out," permanently disenfranchised economically and politically. Their despondence, uprootedness, alienation, and traditional conservatism make for almost total susceptibility to the radical

Islamic appeal.[22] The fundamentalists translated their grievances, frustrations, and aspirations into language that is intelligible to them: the language of Islam.

A third component of modernization, economic growth, especially during the oil boom of the 1970s, had induced structural imbalances and economic disequilibrium: a burgeoning public sector and increasing disparities in wealth. Most of the growth has been in the service sector of the economy, especially government services, and consumer-related industries. This has worked to the detriment of agricultural and industrial expansion, which has lagged behind in most Arab countries.[23] Alarmingly, the 2 percent average annual growth in agricultural production in Arab countries during the 1980s was below the average rate of population increase of more than 3 percent.[24] Equally consequential, the political and social structures in most of these countries, along with the expanding population, are not conducive to a more equitable distribution of income.[25] Rather, the gulf between the beneficiaries of growth, the few, and those who are left out, the many, has grown ever wider, making for a greater polarization of the societies.

In the end, the rising expectations that accompanied the onset of modernization have been crushed by harsh socioeconomic realities. The ever more disillusioned young form what Rachid Al-Ghannouchi, leader of Tunisia's Islamic Tendency Movement (later the banned al-Nahda Party, or Renaissance), called a "lost generation."[26] Caught between an uncertain future and the lure of the past, they constitute a chief recruitment pool for the Islamic movements. The swelling legions of malcontents among the young educated members of the middle and lower-middle classes have joined forces with the impoverished masses. Joblessness, general government inefficiency and ineptitude, and worsening economic conditions have reached crisis proportions in countries such as Egypt, Algeria, Tunisia, and Jordan, where unemployment among young university graduates is mounting. Even presumably economically secure Saudi Arabia finds itself in similar straits.

For Egypt, the egalitarian-socialist society promised in the 1952 revolution never materialized. Nasser's dreams of fundamental change went unfulfilled, and the 1967 defeat doomed the experiment in social and economic engineering. Egypt's seemingly intractable problems of overpopulation, limited resources, and unemployment did not abate. The existential fact: "In 1840, Egypt's population was 5 million; the cultivated land was 5 million acres. Today, the population is 60 million, the cultivated land a little more than 5 million."[27]

Sadat's policies of economic liberalization and openness (*infitah*) and Mubarak's free-market and privatization measures, coupled with a scaling down of government social services and subsidies, have compounded the hardships of Egypt's growing army of poor and unemployed and exacerbated a disparity between rich and poor that is reminiscent of monarchic days.[28] The tilt toward the West—away from the Nasserist socialist order—for political and economic support has not eased the plight of Egypt's "underclass." Not only did the vaunted economic growth not lead to the hoped-for higher standard of living, but also the nouveau riche expanded the pyramid of privilege: it now included the new elite of entrepreneurs and commissioned agents representing the interests of multinational corporations. Meanwhile, concomitant consumerism engendered demands and needs—and rising expectations—that could not be met by the limited economy. This left the bulk of Egyptians feeling like "undesirables" in the new "consumer society."[29] The poor remained disenfranchised in the free-market arena.

It appears that, in timeless Egypt, the more things changed, the more they stayed the same. The failed revolution and the subsequent harder times generated widespread frustration and anger, particularly among the young, educated cohort with time on its hands.[30] With progressively shrinking resources and heightened inflated expectations by increasing numbers, including the multitudes of *fellahin* (peasants) as urban Egypt spilled over into rural Egypt, a breakdown seems to be inevitable. The land of the once-mighty pharaohs does not stand alone at the Arab brink.

Algeria is a stark case of a revolution that has fallen short of the revolutionaries' expectations. For almost thirty years since independence in 1962, and until a brief adoption of multipartism in 1989, the single-party rule of the revolutionary war leaders—the National Liberation Front (FLN)—had led the country straight into the abyss. The highly centralized socialist state under Houari Boumedienne (1965–1978) nurtured an authoritarian triumvirate structure of military, bureaucratic, and party elites (the state's nomenclature) atop an expanding populace with dwindling opportunities and growing economic pains. The consequences were increasing sociopolitical segmentation and a greater income differential. The much-touted industrialization yielded not economic improvement or a higher standard of living, but rather economic dislocations, a dependency on food imports, and hyperinflationary pressures—all severely detrimental to the Algerian welfare state system.[31] Even so, the ruling elites retained their state-endowed privileges, comforts, and indulgences, seen as the "*nomenclature's* honey."[32]

President Chadli Benjedid's (1979–1992) economic reforms in the early 1980s aggravated the country's economic woes, making a bad situation worse. The drop in oil prices in the mid-1980s, which resulted in a loss of nearly 40 percent of the country's revenues, further exacerbated economic pains, especially given the fact that oil exports constitute more than 90 percent of Algeria's foreign earnings.[33] The teetering welfare-state system gave way to a "culture of corruption," and greater hardships, disparities, and alienation ensued.[34] The gulf between the ruling establishment and the bulk of the Algerian population grew ever wider.[35] Rising unemployment, deepening and widening poverty, and mounting foreign debt have become symbols of the system's monumental failure.[36]

The FLN's gross mismanagement of a statist economy, its increasingly corrupt and inefficient rule, and the vast enrichment of a favored political class have finally caught up with the party, generating an explosion of grievances against a so-called politico-financial mafia controlling the country and milking its resources. The economic riots of October 1988, which spurred the initial openings toward reform and democratization, were a turning point in Algeria's history, but history failed to turn. The democratic experiment was aborted shortly thereafter by a military-political establishment fearful of a fundamentalist takeover. Algeria was plunged into its most violent political upheaval since its revolution more than three decades ago.

It was among the multitudinous destitute, unemployed, and underprivileged of the Arab world—of which Egypt and Algeria stand as examples—that the fundamentalists set up camp and propagated their message. Many of the desperation-driven heeded the call, turning a deaf ear to their governments' trumpeting of the "Islamic threat." Impoverishment and faith converged to stimulate and sustain an Islamic resurgence promising spiritual and material salvation. In conditions of adversity and gloom, Muslims share in the common human drive to seek a way out. To a large extent, the fundamentalists' popularity derives from the presence of poverty, which is also at the base of the surge in Islamic violence. Economic deprivation and disparities have been particularly marked in countries where Islamic violence is most prevalent such as Egypt and Algeria. Both the Islamic Salvation Front (FIS) in Algeria and the Islamic groups in Egypt draw their support largely from among the urban poor, especially the unemployed young, who are plumbing the depths of despair.

The Islamic activists took up the cause of the poor and those with no "connections," articulating their demands. They called for honest and responsible government, social justice, and a more equitable distribution of income; set up a network of social services and welfare programs in the areas of health, education, housing, and employment; and pressed for empowerment of the people against closed elitist arrangements that dispossess most, if not all, of the poor. The lure of Islamism will persist so long as there exist these visible reasons for disquietude. And chances are that the fundamentalists will press on with the injection of their moral vision into the world's business, for it is implicit in their conception of Islam as a just, moral order that they carry on the struggle.

The Arabs are no better off in the 1990s than before. The Gulf War did nothing about the disparities between rich and poor Arab countries whose elimination the Islamists had sought, nor between the rich and poor within.[37] Rather, it accentuated the divisions and heightened resentment and mistrust between the haves and the have-nots, a schism that originated in the sudden oil wealth following upon the October 1973 war. Also, the Gulf War made plain to Islamists that the West is ready and willing to protect the rich Arabs against the poor and to punish foes in order to safeguard its interests.[38] In Muslim eyes, the demonstration of Western power underscored the Arab world's asymmetrical dependency relationship with the West. The price for protection for the rich Arab rulers is subservience; they are beholden.

Obviously, the new Arab wealth did not translate into an independent power resource. The thinking in the 1970s that the oil-rich states would be dealing with the West from a position of strength had dissipated, in the manner of a desert mirage. Contrariwise, the oil income furthered dependency and weakness. The industrialized nations are the Arab oil nations' best customers, their best places in which to invest their petrodollars, and their principal source of capital goods and technology. Their growing dependence became all the more glaring in the 1980s, during the height of the Islamic fundamentalist movement in the train of the Ayatollah Khomeini revolution, when more Arab countries than ever sought close alignment with the United States—a move that accelerated after the Gulf War. Further, contingents of foreign personnel serving in economic and security fields are daily reminders of the increasing reliance of those countries on outsiders. But to fundamentalists, the most dangerous outcomes of these phenomena are the loosening of moral bearings and the rupture of normative order, eventuating in ever more weakness.

The Gulf War inevitably compounded the economic problems of the Arab countries, imposing financial losses put by one estimate at $438 billion, an amount "more than three times [the Arab countries'] foreign debt, or enough to provide decent shelter for every Arab."[39] This blow was accompanied by heightened balance-of-payment problems because of the drop-off in expatriate remittances. Budgets were being written in red ink. Also, the war entailed the cessation of economic transactions with Iraq pursuant to the UN-directed international sanctions and embargo. It is estimated that the international embargo against Iraq has cost Jordan alone some $9 billion.[40] Above all, the war precipitated costly arms programs and security arrangements between the Arab Gulf countries and the West under the pretext of defense and stability. Since the war, Saudi Arabia has purchased U.S. weaponry in the amount of $30 billion,[41] an expenditure that comes on top of Saudi Arabia's hefty $65 billion share of the war's costs.[42]

All these financial burdens on the heels of an eight-year decline in real oil prices have drained treasuries and induced structural adjustments in countries as varied as Saudi Arabia and Egypt.[43] Since 1983, the Saudi kingdom has been running annual budget deficits of $4 to $18 billion, causing it to dip into its dollars reserve funds and borrow from international and domestic financial institutions.[44] Daunted, the government announced a 20 percent annual spending cut for 1994 and 1995,[45] a signal change from its customary open-handedness. Obviously, the treasury can no longer underwrite the Saudi welfare state, which has used its largesse to maintain autocratic royal family rule. This came at a time when per capita income had plunged from $17,000 in 1981 to $6,975 in 1993[46] and presumably was continuing its free fall. The repercussions of the shrinking economic pie were immediately felt in reduced government social programs and subsidies and decreasing job opportunities, thereby heightening the potential for sociopolitical instability.[47]

Today, many middle- and lower-middle-class young Saudis, caught in the throes of unemployment and underemployment, face an uncertain future and believe they are being denied their share of the country's wealth. In contrast to the boom years of the 1970s and early 1980s, their government can no longer guarantee jobs or provide free loans to start businesses to the thousands upon thousands of university graduates. Moreover, the saturated government bureaucracy is unable to absorb more degreeholders. In the private sector, less than 10 percent of the work force is of Saudi origin; the preference is for cheap and more efficient foreign labor.[48] Therefore, the kingdom is aswarm with hurting, unhappy young subjects whose plight appears all the more salient and acute in juxtaposition to the ostentatious lifestyles of the rulers, increasingly the object of resentment and attack. As elsewhere, the gap separating the thin top stratum of society from the very wide bottom stratum is expanding considerably.

These disparities have served to highlight the crisis of distribution and an attendant struggle for political authority, which played into the hands of the fundamentalists opposed to the royal family. The Islamists raised issues of equity and justice in open public discourse, and groups espousing the new Islamic rhetoric are growing more seductive and influential. The swelling ranks of disaffected and disadvantaged Saudis have provided recruits for radical Islamic groups that are openly challenging the corrupt status quo and the legitimacy of the Al-Saud rule.[49]

In addition to its adverse direct economic effects, the war added momentum and strength to the Islamic movement. For one thing, the defeat of Iraq by the Western-led coalition was deeply tormenting to all Arabs, albeit most had little sympathy for Saddam Hussein. It was a humbling of the Arab spirit akin to that inflicted in Palestine in 1948 and in the 1967 war with Israel, and it reverberated across the Muslim heartland from Morocco to Pakistan. Once again, the West had shown its muscle in the Middle East. The war, then, had the effect of invigorating the emergent Islamic political identity, which perceives the West as intent on weakening Muslims and Islam. Now the Islamists have come to the fore and staked out a role to reclaim Arab-Muslim independence and Islamic selfhood. This is in tune with the prevalent popular mood and greatly enhances the Islamists' zeal for mobilizing the masses against the status quo.

In effect, as Hasan al-Turabi maintained, the Gulf War popularized and radicalized the Islamic movements.[50] Thus, the United States and the Western allies trounced Arab radicalism in the war only to give a new stimulus to Islamic fundamentalism, which seeks to rid the region of foreign hegemony— a condition seen as a surrender to an imposed "pax-Americana." And the Arab rulers who signed on to the Western plans are now demonized as "enemies" of Islam, a constant theme in fundamentalist newspapers and literature.

The war additionally brought to light the vexing malaise in the Arab system of governance: oppressive regimes ruling over frail bodies politic. It laid out, for all the world to see, the impotence of the vanquished and the salvic strength of the victors. The Gulf monarchs stood revealed for what they are: handmaidens of the West. And Saddam Hussein stood revealed as no more than a secularist hoax, in the mold of Nasser and the Ba'th.[51] All were discredited before their peoples. As a consequence, the crisis of authority in most Arab countries is substantially more acute. One could say that the cry of one of the assassins of Sadat, "I killed Pharaoh"—in reference to idolatrous, tyrannical rulers—is symbolic of the crisis as it was felt then and is felt now by the young militant Islamic groups. It is such perceptions that have prompted ever more calls for wider popular participation as the only means to rejuvenate Arab societies.

Little wonder that the Islamist groups have espoused Islamic populism or populist politics as a dissenting voice against the ruling elites. Indeed, the appeal of Islamic fundamentalism is that it champions the cause of popular participation vis-à-vis the gross maldistribution of political power in many Arab countries. Since independence, these countries have been largely under the sway of various forms of authoritarianism: military-bureaucratic dictatorship, single-party state hegemony, or traditional monarchic autocracy. The pattern was interrupted only briefly by a few short-lived experimentations with representative democracy that soon succumbed to what is "normal."

Today there is no Arab state that fits under the rubric "democratic" in the Western sense. In no single case is government based on the consent of the governed, with constitutional rules and procedures guaranteeing participation and access to power by all groups. Arab systems are generally averse to the notion of open communication with and inclusion of their peoples in decision-making, which is essential to the democratic process. In fact, most Arab rulers despise free elections—a recipe for their downfall. The reality of current Arab-Muslim politics is best characterized as hegemonic, closed state structures superimposed on emasculated societies.

Modern Middle Eastern states have grown increasingly supreme in the lives of their people, overwhelming civil society and inhibiting freedoms. The political area is controlled by the dominant elites presiding over increasingly centralized state authority. They are intolerant of independent tendencies outside the realm of their fiefdoms and are bent on barring the citizenry from open political participation. They effectively keep the masses as spectators on the sidelines of the political field, watching the plays of the game from a distance. Indeed, this has been established practice from Morocco to Saudi Arabia: by and large, demands for political reform and popular involvement have either been suppressed or gone unheeded.

A few examples illustrate the point. In Egypt, the post-1952 political order is yet to become a fully open and competitive system. Political life remains circumscribed under the semiauthoritarian regime of President Hosni Mubarak.

In October 1993, Mubarak ran for a third six-year term virtually unopposed, reminiscent of predecessors Sadat and Nasser. The dominance of the government-controlled National Democratic Party is in line with the custom of single-party rule since the revolution. State-licensed opposition parties are ineffectual and divided. The Muslim Brotherhood, the most viable opposition group, has no legal status and is now facing a government campaign of containment. The People's Assembly is a pliant body, controlled by the ruling party, with little meaningful deliberative or opposition power.

In Saudi Arabia, the al-Saud family monopoly of power has been in place since the founding of the kingdom in 1932. The monarchy has kept a tight hold on the reins, shutting out possible aspirants and prohibiting challenges to its supremacy. All in all, the regime has reacted forcefully to independent opposition, stamping out any sign of dissent as potentially subversive and antiroyalist. The sixty-member Consultative Council (Majlis al-Shura), appointed in 1993, is an empty shell, devoid of any real parliamentary powers.

In Algeria, the dilapidated thirty-year-old single-party rule finally collapsed, only to give way to a military-controlled government that plunged the country into vicious disorder. The FLN socialist state neither acquired popular legitimacy nor achieved economic egalitarianism. It remained essentially an exclusivist power structure, run by a privileged military-bureaucratic elite superimposed upon a disgruntled populace. It inhibited popular participation and representation. The National Assembly was a dormant body, inconsequential to the country's political life. An attempt at democratization (1989–1992) was quickly squashed, and the country relapsed into its authoritarian ways.

Morocco is yet another example of a Middle Eastern monarchy engaged in the business of its own sustenance and survival. King Hassan, the second-longest-surviving Arab monarch—after the doyen, Hussein of Jordan—has since his ascent to the throne in the early 1960s kept all opposition groups in check and deftly thwarted all threats to his primacy. The principal opposition party, the Socialist Union of Popular Forces (USFP), has been circumscribed by the religious and royal powers of the monarchy and, in effect, has been precluded from accession to governance. Like many other Arab countries, party politics in Morocco remains shackled with various limitations and controls that render it inept.

In Syria and Iraq, homes of the two oldest and most fearful dictatorships in the Arab world, Hafiz al-Asad and Saddam Hussein, respectively, have presided over a party-state authoritarian structure spewing Ba'thi ideology, run and operated by an Alawi minoritarian group from the Latakia mountains, in the case of Syria, and by a Sunni minoritarian clique from the village of Tikrit, in the case of Iraq. In the process, each dictator has created his own communal, tribal- or family-based dynasty, ruthlessly repressing opposition.[52]

The suppression of rival political groups and ideologies in the Arab countries has ultimately worked to the advantage of the Islamic movement. In monopolizing legitimate political activity to the exclusion of the vast majority, the regimes created a vacuum that only the Islamists could fill. The mosque was the only free public space beyond the reach of the state that was left with some autonomy, and religion became the outlet for expressing resistance. "Politics has been driven into the mosque and the symbols of opposition have become avowedly religious."[53] The mobilization of Islam for political purposes catapulted the Islamists onto center stage as the sole leading political opposition. The absence of democracy, then, has patently fueled the Islamist movements. They are the product of "Leviathan" states that have bred political authoritarianism and economic decline—and a manifestation of the failure of Arab regimes to address participation and distribution in their societies.

Finally, the collapse of communist state structures in the former Soviet Union and Eastern Europe, which ruled with iron fists, and the spread of democratization worldwide are not lost on the Arab peoples generally and the Islamists in particular. These unfolding events resonated in the Arab world and called into question the authoritarian states therein, thus enhancing the cause of the fundamentalists as representatives of the "general will." Indeed, to many a fundamentalist, the demise of Soviet totalitarian communism is both a vindication of "eternal" Islamic ideology and a condemnation of leftist secular forces in the Arab world whose socialist model now stands invalidated.

Unlike the ephemeral secular ideologies, Islam is here to stay. Its power had been amply demonstrated in the routing of the USSR by the Afghan freedom fighters, the Mujahideen, which precipitated the decline of communism and accelerated the resurgence of radical Islamism.[54] Indeed, the holy war waged against the Soviet occupation of Afghanistan in the 1980s gave impetus to the militant Muslim revolutionaries, the "Arab Afghans": volunteers from half a dozen Arab countries, especially Egypt, Algeria, Saudi Arabia, and Tunisia, who fought alongside the Afghan Mujahideen. Bolstered by their participation in the victory over the Soviet Union, many of the Arab Afghans have brought their zeal to their home front, waging a religious war to destroy "infidel" governments. They inhabit the nightmares of those they seek to vanquish.

An equally momentous development that also enhanced the appeal of militant Islam in the 1980s was the Iranian Islamic revolution of 1978–1979. As the first popular Islamic movement to accede to state power, its willingness to defy the West, especially the United States and Israel, greatly boosted Islamic revolutionary fervor in the Middle East. The Khomeini legacy contributed to the mushrooming of Islamic fundamentalism as the leading political opposition force in the region and added energy and veracity to the actions of the militants. Yet, other than its emotive, vitalizing influence, Khomeinism had no standing as an exemplar for Arab Muslims. Traditional Sunni-Arab and Shi'a-Persian religious differences and national animosities militated against following Iran's lead, regardless of Islamic ideology. Iran, as the only Shi'a country in the Muslim world, does not serve as a model for the Sunni-dominated Arab states.

All of the above factors have stimulated the proliferation of Islamic fundamentalism in the Middle East. That Islamists have become assertive in Muslim countries as varied as Egypt, Algeria, Tunisia, Jordan, and Saudi Arabia, among others, shows how pervasive their activism has become in political life. This is clearly and particularly illustrated in Egypt, Algeria, and Saudi Arabia, where the challenge is most strident and most consequential for the region because of the centrality of these nations.

NOTES

1. The migration (*hijra*) in the summer of A.D. 622 of the Prophet and his few dozen followers from Mecca to Medina, where he founded the first Muslim commonwealth, marks the start of the Islamic calendar, *Anno Hijrae*.

2. No wonder that Ali Shari'ati, the leading theorist of the Islamic revolution in Iran, regarded Shi'ism as the ideology of protest in Islam. See Fouad Ajami, "The Impossible Life of Moslem Liberalism," *New Republic* 2 June 1986: 28.

3. The return to Islam became widely popular, especially among the disillusioned young, and expressed itself in many different forms. One form was the proliferation of religious literature across the Arab world. In Egypt, the best-seller of the 1970s was *My Itinerary from Doubt to Belief* by popular Egyptian writer Mustafa Mahmoud, who details his journey from belief in scientific positivism, materialism, and social engineering to belief in Islam. See Emmanuel Sivan, "Mubarak's Egypt," *Washington Quarterly* 5 (Winter 1982): 183.

4. It was the conservative Muslim thinker Salah al-Din al-Munajid who accused Nasser of Egypt and the Ba'th of Syria of pursuing "Godless socialism" and setting out on a course of the "Bolshevization of Islam." See his *A'midat al-Nakba* (The pillars of the disaster) (Beirut: Dar al-Kitab al-Jadid, 1967), 47, 49.

5. Quoted in Philip Revzin, "North Africa's Rulers Seeking to Stem Fundamentalism," *Wall Street Journal* 12 Aug. 1987: 12. Abdul Sallam Yassin, leader of the Islamic group al-Adl wa al-Ihsan (Justice and Charity), was jailed for three years beginning in 1975 for publishing 3,000 copies of an open letter calling on King Hassan of Morocco to implement *Shari'a*. He has been under house arrest since the beginning of the 1990s. See *al-Sharq al-Awsat* 16 Dec. 1995: 1. The theme was echoed in the motto of the Muslim Brotherhood demonstrators in Aleppo, Syria, while the author was a student there in the 1950s: *La-sharqiyya wa la-gharbiyya, hiya dawla Islamiyya* (Neither East nor West, ours is an Islamic state).

6. Quoted in Judith Miller, "The Islamic Wave," *New York Times Magazine* 31 May 1992: 25.

7. Quoted in Peter Ford, "Challenging Regimes, Koran in Hand," *Christian Science Monitor* 21 Apr. 1993: 11.

8. Quoted in Ford, "Challenging Regimes," 11.

9. See *al-Majalla* 15–21 Jan. 1995: 21–32.

10. On the theme of "cultural-ideological invasion," see Muhammad Jalal Kishk, *Al-Ghazw al-Fikri* (The cultural invasion) (Cairo: Dar al-Urubah, 1966); Kishk, *Al-Naksa wa al-Ghazw al-Fikri* (The setback and cultural invasion) (Beirut: Dar al-Kitab al-Arabi, 1969); Abdul Halim Iwis, *Thaqafat al-Muslim fi Wajh al-Tayyarat al-Mu'asira* (Muslim culture in the

face of modern trends) (Riyadh: Matabi' al-Firuzduq, 1979).

11. The Islamic movement is surprisingly strong among the educated. Many of the leaders and followers are university graduates, some even with doctoral degrees and active in professional fields and associations—physicians, engineers, and lawyers, among others. See Saad Eddin Ibrahim, "Egypt's Islamic Militants," *Merip Reports* Feb. 1982: 5–14; Ibrahim, "Egypt's Islamic Activism in the 1980s," *Third World Quarterly* 10 (Apr. 1988): 632–57; Nazih N. M. Ayubi, "The Politics of Militant Islamic Movements in the Middle East," *Journal of International Affairs* 36 (Fall/Winter 1982/83): 271–83; Hamied N. Ansari, "The Islamic Militants in Egyptian Politics," *International Journal of Middle East Studies* 16 (1984): 122–44; John P. Entelis and Lisa J. Arone, "Algeria in Turmoil: Islam, Democracy and the State," *Middle East Policy* 1. 2 (1992): 23–35; Azzedine Layachi and Abdel-Kader Haireche, "National Development and Political Protest: Islamists in the Maghreb Countries," *Arab Studies Quarterly* 14 (Spring/Summer 1992): 69–92; Leslie Cockburn and Andrew Cockburn, "Royal Mess," *New Yorker* 28 Nov. 1994: 54–72.

12. "Interview: Eric Rouleau Talks about the Peace Process and Political Islam," *Journal of Palestine Studies* 22 (Summer 1993): 55. Olivier Roy aptly describes today's Islamic assertiveness as "Islamo-nationalism." See Roy, *The Failure of Political Islam* (Cambridge: Harvard University Press, 1994), 130.

13. Caryle Murphy, "Wide Egyptian Unease Abets Muslim Radicals," *Washington Post* 11 Mar. 1993: A25.

14. The question of identity is not something new: it commenced with the inception of European colonialism in the nineteenth century. It became the rallying cry of Third World independence movements in the first half of the twentieth century. In the world of Islam, the historical encounter with the West prompted an Islamic self-definition opposite to the Western.

15. For an elaboration on this theme, see Shireen T. Hunter, "Islamic Fundamentalism: What It Really Is and Why It Frightens the West," *SAIS Review* 6 (Winter/Spring 1986): 189–200.

16. "Islam, Democracy, the State, and the West" (Summary of a lecture and roundtable discussion with Hasan al-Turabi, prepared by Louis J. Cantori and Arthur Lowrie), *Middle East Policy* 1. 3 (1992): 52. With confidence, al-Turabi called on Arab nationalists to "come home" to Islam; otherwise, "they have no future with the masses." He then went on to declare: "Besides, objectively, the future is ours [the Islamists']." See Miller, "The Islamic Wave," 40.

17. This was very evident during the Gulf War. See Ibrahim A. Karawan, "Arab Dilemmas in the 1990s: Breaking Taboos and Searching for Signposts," *Middle East Journal* 48 (Summer 1994): 433–54. But there remain deep ideological divisions between the Islamists and the Arabists. Add to this their differences over who would set the agenda and dominate the opposition.

18. For a thorough analysis, see Bernard Lewis, "The Return of Islam," *Commentary* 61 (Jan. 1979): 39–49.

19. On the dysfunctional socioeconomic consequences of the spread of education in Egypt, see my "Consequences of the Introduction and Spread of Modern Education: Education and National Integration in Egypt," *Modern Egypt: Studies in Politics and Society*, ed. Elie Kedourie and Sylvia G. Haim (London: Frank Cass, 1980), 42–55; and "The Chimera of Education for Development in Egypt: The Socio-Economic Roles of University Graduates," *Middle Eastern Studies* 13 (May 1977): 229–40.

20. See Arab Monetary Fund, *Al-Taqrir al-Iqtisadi al-Arabi al-Muwahhad* (Arab unified

economic report), Index 7/2 (1991): 169. (Cited hereafter as Arab Monetary Fund.) One stark example is the deteriorating infrastructure in Cairo, now a city of 15 million whose network of basic services is unchanged since its population numbered 4 million. See Edward Said, "The Phony Islamic Threat," *New York Times Magazine* 21 Nov. 1993: 65.

21. On the theme of "ruralization" of cities, see Albert Hourani, *A History of the Arab Peoples* (New York: Warner Books, 1991), 452.

22. Evidence of this can be found all across the Middle East, including modern secular Turkey. See Louise Lief, "An Old Oasis of Tolerance Runs Dry: Egypt's Women Face a New Islamic Backlash," *U.S. News and World Report* 29 Aug. 1994: 39, 41; Fouad Ajami, "The Battle for Egypt's Soul," *U.S. News and World Report* 27 June 1994: 42–44; "Taking Up Space in Tlemcen, the Islamist Occupation of Algeria: An Interview with Rabia Bekkar," *Middle East Report* Nov.-Dec. 1992: 11–15; Alan Cowell, "Muslim Party Threatens Turkey's Secular Heritage," *New York Times* 30 Nov. 1994: A14; John Darnton, "Discontent Seethes in Once-Stable Turkey," *New York Times* 2 Mar. 1995: A1, A8. See also Ansari, "The Islamic Militants in Egyptian Politics."

23. In all the twenty Arab countries surveyed, with the exception of Kuwait, the percentage of the labor force in agriculture declined, in some cases considerably, between 1970 and 1989. In industry, the majority either showed a decline or remained relatively unchanged. A few, mainly oil-producing countries, registered some minor increases. See Arab Monetary Fund, Index 11/12: 173.

24. Arab Monetary Fund, 56.

25. Hourani, *A History of the Arab Peoples,* 437.

26. Quoted in Linda G. Jones, "Portrait of Rashid al-Ghannoushi," *Middle East Report* July-Aug. 1988: 20.

27. Ajami, "The Battle for Egypt's Soul," 44. In the past ten years, Egypt's population has increased by fourteen million, a number greater than the aggregate population of Israel, Lebanon, Jordan, and the Palestinians on the West Bank and in Gaza. Also, close to 95 percent of its people live on less than 5 percent of the land, creating one of the highest population densities in the world.

28. On this theme, see Mamoun Fandy, "The Tensions behind the Violence in Egypt," *Middle East Policy* 2.1 (1993): 25–34. The policies of *infitah* marked a departure from the proclaimed "distributive justice" of the Nasserist socialist state. The growing gap between the many poor and the few rich precipitated the bloody food riots of January 1977 in Cairo.

29. Fouad Ajami, *The Arab Predicament: Arab Political Thought and Practice since 1967* (Cambridge: Cambridge University Press, 1982), 185. On Sadat's *infitah* economic policies, see Fouad Ajami, "Retreat from Economic Nationalism: The Political Economy of Sadat's Egypt," *Journal of Arab Affairs* 1 (Oct. 1981): 27–52.

30. It is estimated that 500,000 new job seekers enter the market annually, including 100,000 university graduates. Also, it is estimated that a quarter of Cairo's unemployed have university degrees, and the fraction is even higher in provincial capitals. On these points, see Caryle Murphy, "Poverty Breeds Despair in Egypt," *Washington Post* 15 July 1994: A14; Stephen Hubbel, "True Belief's Grim Patience," *Nation* 28 Sept. 1992: 323. Both Gilles Kepel and Eric Davis maintain that the Islamic movement in Egypt is a response to the declining socioeconomic conditions, or what Davis calls "pressurization." See Gilles Kepel, *Muslim Extremism in Egypt: The Prophet and the Pharaoh* (Berkeley: University of California Press, 1986); Eric Davis, "Islamic Radicalism in Egypt," *From Nationalism to Revolutionary Islam*, ed. S. Arjomand (New York: Macmillan, 1984), 147. See also Michael M. Fisher, "Islam and the Revolt of the Petty Bourgeoisie," *Daedalus* 111

(1982): 101–25.

31. See Mahfoud Bennoune, "The Industrialization of Algeria: An Overview," *Contemporary North Africa*, ed. Halim Barakat (Washington, D.C.: Center for Contemporary Arab Studies, 1985), 178–213; John Entelis, *Algeria: The Revolution Institutionalized* (Boulder, Colo.: Westview Press, 1986).

32. Francis Ghiles, "Algeria Locked in a Vicious Cycle of Violence," *Middle East International* 9 July 1993: 17.

33. Bahgat Korany, "From Revolution to Domestication: The Foreign Policy of Algeria," *The Foreign Policies of the Arab States*, ed. Bahgat Korany and Ali E. Hillal Dessouki (Boulder, Colo.: Westview Press, 1991), 104.

34. Rachid Tlemcani, "Chadli's Perestroika," *Middle East Report* Mar.-Apr. 1990: 16.

35. By 1988, 5 percent of the population was earning 45 percent of the national income, and 50 percent was earning less than 22 percent. See Layachi and Haireche, "National Development and Political Protest," 75.

36. It is estimated that more than 300,000 young Algerians enter the labor market annually, but job opportunities are ever dwindling. By 1992, unemployment was well over 20 percent; average per capita personal income steadily declined, placing 14 million of Algeria's 25 million below the poverty line. And foreign debt reached a staggering $26 billion, the servicing of which annually costs almost 70 percent of Algeria's oil revenues. See Gary Abramson, "Rise of the Crescent," *Africa Report* Mar./Apr. 1992: 20; *al-Majalla* 22–28 Jan. 1992: 10; *Economist* 6 Aug. 1994: 4; Robin Wright, "Islam and Democracy," *Foreign Affairs* 71 (Summer 1992): 134. In June 1991, Prime Minister Sid Ahmad Ghozali shocked the nation with his proposal to sell shares of Algeria's vast oil and natural gas reserves to foreign oil companies in order to raise $6 to $7 billion in cash to enable the country to break out of the foreign-debt cycle and invest in the economy. See Youssef M. Ibrahim, "In Algeria, Hope for Democracy but Not Economy," *New York Times* 26 July 1991: A5.

37. Before the Gulf War, per capita income in the rich Arab Gulf states ranged between $10,000 and $20,000, but for the poorer majority-Arab countries, it was less than $1,500. See "Country Facts" in Colbert C. Held, *Middle East Patterns: Places, Peoples, and Politics* (Boulder, Colo.: Westview Press, 1989).

38. On this general theme, see Ghassan Salame, "Islam and the West," *Foreign Policy* no. 90 (Spring 1993): 22–37.

39. This is according to Ibrahim M. Oweiss of Georgetown University. See Barton Gillman, "One Year Later: War's Faded Triumph," *Washington Post* 16 Jan. 1992: A1.

40. See Lamis Andoni, "Jordan Seeks Greater Role in Middle East Changes," *Christian Science Monitor* 13 Oct. 1993: 3.

41. See Cockburn and Cockburn, "Royal Mess," 60. It was reported that, in 1993, Saudi defense purchases amounted to more than a third of the country's total budget of $52 billion. See Christine M. Helms, "Irked by Bad Credit Report, Saudi Arabia Reveals Deeper Sensitivities," *Energy Compass* 3 Sept. 1993: 12.

42. See Nora Boustany, "Traditional Saudis Take Dim View of Attempts to Modernize Islam," *Washington Post* 24 Aug. 1994: A22.

43. As a result of the global oil glut and the sharp decline in oil prices, it was reported that, in 1985–1986, Egypt incurred a 40 percent loss in expatriate remittances from the previous year. See Hermann Frederick Eilts, "Egypt in 1986: Political Disappointments and Economic Dilemmas," *Washington Quarterly* 10 (Spring 1987): 124.

44. See Helms, "Irked by Bad Credit Report," 11; Cockburn and Cockburn, "Royal Mess," 60. Also, it is reported that government debt ballooned from nothing in 1988 to more than

$50 billion in 1993. Additionally, Saudi financial reserves fell from more than $121 billion in 1984 to less than $51 billion in 1993. See John Rossant, "Are the Sands about to Shift under Saudi Arabia?" *Business Week* 15 Feb. 1993: 50–52; Stephen Engleberg, Jeff Gerth, and Tim Weiner, "Saudi Stability Hit by Heavy Spending over Last Decade," *New York Times* 22 Aug. 1993: 1, 12.

45. John Lancaster, "Discontent in the Kingdom of Saud," *Washington Post National Weekly Edition* 26 Dec. 1994–1 Jan. 1995: 18; Nora Boustany, "At Saudis' Rich Table, the Alien Taste of Austerity," *Washington Post* 13 Aug. 1994: A1.

46. Lancaster, "Discontent in the Kingdom of Saud," 17.

47. The government's declining revenues and mounting budget deficits have forced it to sharply reduce agricultural subsidies. This action has severely hurt rural areas and might engender political unrest. Such reductions have been linked to unrest in Burayda, a city where Muslim fundamentalists held a rare public demonstration in September 1994, which led to some 150 arrests. See John Lancaster, "Budget Deficits Imperil Saudia Arabia's Vast Wheat Export Program," *Washington Post* 25 Dec. 1994: A30.

48. See Chris Hedges, "Saudi Rulers Resisting Pressure from Two Sides," *New York Times* 14 Feb. 1993: 3; *al-Sharq al-Awsat* 14 Jan. 1996: 10. It is estimated that up to 25 percent of recent university graduates are unemployed; many come from the Islamic universities and have dismal employment prospects. See Lancaster, "Discontent in the Kingdom of Saud," 17; Boustany, "Traditional Saudis Take Dim View of Attempts to Modernize Islam," A22. There are approximately 4.5 million expatriate laborers in Saudi Arabia who keep the economy running. See Irwin Stelzer, "An Oil Crisis Knocks on Recovery's Door," *Sunday Times* 11 Dec. 1994: 7.

49. Contrary to Daniel Pipes's thesis linking Islamic revivalism closely to the oil boom and the influx of wealth from oil exports—which leads one to conclude that the phenomenon is bound to wane, or even fade away, with the declining fortunes of the rich oil states— it appears that fundamentalism has gained greater strength and zealousness following upon the decline in oil prices and the diminution of Arab wealth. See Pipes, *In the Path of God: Islam and Political Power* (New York: Basic Books, 1983).

50. "Islam, Democracy, the State, and the West," 55.

51. The Islamists' initial rallying to Iraq's side notwithstanding, they quickly turned against Saddam Hussein after the defeat. They denounced his regime as secularist and non-Islamic, characteristics that were responsible for the catastrophe. Thus, in their eyes, Saddam, "the sword of the Arabs," was no better than Nasser, "the hero of the Arabs," or the Ba'th in Damascus, "the beating heart of Arabism." On this general theme, see Muhammad 'Isam Dirbalah, *Azmat al-Khalij: Ru'ya Islamiyya* (The Gulf crisis: an Islamic perspective) (Cairo: Bayt al-Hikma, 1992).

52. On the general question of governments and opposition in the Middle East, see Lisa Anderson, "Lawless Governments and Illegal Opposition: Reflections on the Middle East," *Journal of International Affairs* 40 (Winter/Spring 1987): 219–32.

53. Ajami, *The Arab Predicament,* 181.

54. On the interrelationship between Islamic resurgence and the eclipse of communism, see Ali A. Mazrui, "The Resurgence of Islam and the Decline of Communism," *Futures* 23 (Apr. 1991): 273–88.

3

The Islamist Challenge in Egypt

Islamic tradition runs deep in Egypt's history and culture. Al-Azhar University mosque, which has graced the city of Cairo for a millennium, is eloquent testimony to the enduring strength of Islam. Since its founding in 972 and until the advent of the modern period in the nineteenth century, al-Azhar played a central role in shaping the country's religious, educational, and cultural life, preserving its essentially Islamic mold.[1] The focal religious institution for the study of law, theology, Qur'anic exegesis, and classical Arabic, it propagated religious conservatism and traditional values. It stood at the apex of an educational system at the bottom of which were the *kuttab* (mosque, or Qur'anic school), the *madrasa* (religious school), and the Sufi (mystical) orders.

The system was the sole disseminator of education and culture to uncounted successive generations and remained dominant in Egyptian life until the introduction of modern European ways by the father of modern Egypt, Muhammad Ali Pasha (1805–1848). However, the new secular educational system did not supplant, but existed alongside the old system, inculcating Western science and ideas. Eventually, the two educational tracks, with their divergent orientations, created a dichotomized culture that has persisted to the present.[2]

The onset of nineteenth-century modernism did not eclipse Islam, but rather precipitated an Islamic revivalist movement in the latter half of the century. Early Muslim reformers, such as Jamal Al-Din Al-Afghani and Muhammad Abdu, called for a revitalization of Islamic thought, institutions, and society through the adoption of modern science and education. These scholars were well versed in Islamic learning and had been equally exposed to European education and culture, some aspects of which they had come to appreciate and sought to incorporate into their own society. They argued that Muslims should be aware of progress elsewhere in the world and adapt to the new circumstances it imposed. A synthesis of Islam and modernity could be the medium whereby their society could advance within the Islamic context. The aim was a renewal of Islam as the only means to recovery and power in the modern age.

The assumption of the reformers was that true Islam is not in conflict with modern life and can be reconciled with science and progress. They called for the restoration of *ijtihad* (application of personal reasoning in the interpretation of Islamic doctrine) so that Islam could assimilate Western ideas and culture to the nearest equivalent of its principles. Thus, the reformers sought an awakening derived from religion. Indeed, they all consistently defended the essence of Islam and its relevance to *al-nahda* (renaissance). Once Islam was purified of the accretions that had corrupted its essence and led to *al-jumud* (stagnation), it would adapt to modernity. Further, it was deemed easier to institute reforms based upon religious revival than upon European secular rationalism.[3] Hence, change was given an Islamic justification, not an Occidental, empirical-utilitarian one.

Attempts to develop an Islamic synthesis turned out to be fragile and inconclusive and had limited appeal for the conservative *ulama* (religious leaders) and the traditional masses. Neither group was ready or willing to accept a liberalized Islam and all that it would entail. Not surprisingly, the Islamic reformation consequently failed to take root. In fact, it is even assailed by contemporary fundamentalists, who reject the idea of a compromise between Islam and the modern West as tantamount to an abandonment of culture and identity. This is manifest in their anti-Western stance, which, contrary to that of the early revivalists, dismisses the Western example as invalid and irrelevant to the Muslim context. Despite the tenuous nature of early reforms, the fact remains that the initial voices for an Islamic renaissance clearly show that the notion of Islamic revival is deeply entrenched in Egypt and has continued to express itself in one form or another under different Islamic movements until the present.

Concomitant with the Islamic call, modern nineteenth-century Egypt developed a liberal tradition and culture that suffused its political life. The course of modernization and an opening up to Europe, initiated by the modern Egyptian state under Muhammad Ali, proceeded steadily. The spread of Western cultural and educational influences promoted a semblance of modern liberal culture championed by a small, but growing Western-educated elite who wanted to incorporate Western ideas, values, and techniques into the predominantly traditional Islamic milieu in Egypt. Modernizers, such as Rifa'a al-Tahtawi, Qasim Amin, and Ahmad Lutfi al-Sayyid, looked to European thought, politics, and economics for *tajdid* (renewal). Forerunners of a liberal movement that sought an awakening not derived from religion, they never denounced religion or dismissed its essential role in society. They were simply more receptive to Western intellectual tradition than to earlier Islamic epistemology.

By the turn of the century, a growing infatuation with the European model made the modernist message all the more susceptible to European secular nationalist thought. The emergent liberal-nationalist group, imbued with Western liberal principles, led the struggle for independence from Great Britain (1918–1922) and dominated the political and cultural landscape.[4] Accordingly, Egypt's early encounter with modernity influenced its institutional and political development in accordance with the European example. Indeed, the modernization of Egypt and its opening and exposure to the West made it the cultural and educational lighthouse of the Arab world, transmitting liberalism and modernism.

Islamic revivalism in Egypt, then, was counterbalanced and tempered from its inception by the ascendant forces of liberalism and nationalism, which steered the country on a modern path, starting with Muhammad Ali and continuing during the British rule (1882–1922) and after independence under the monarchy. The monarchic period (1922–1952) ushered in liberal constitutionalism and nationalism, led by a Western-oriented liberal elite. The emphasis was on building an integrated modern national community. Revolutionary nationalism and socialism followed in the post-1952 revolution under Gamal Abdul Nasser, with its emphasis on populism and Arab radicalism. Anwar Sadat (1970–1981) shifted toward a more open and liberalized economic and political direction, leading to free entrepreneurial activity and limited democratization—which has continued, albeit slowly, under Hosni Mubarak. Throughout, all attempts by various Islamic groups to change the course of the Egyptian state proved to be unavailing.

Despite the ascendancy of the modernist-nationalists, the tradition of Islamic revivalism continued in the twentieth century with the establishment of Jama'at al-Ikhwan al-Muslimoun (the Society of the Muslim Brotherhood) in 1928 by Supreme Guide Hasan al-Banna.[5] It became the major mainstream Islamic fundamentalist movement and has remained so, with its adherents and branches in other Arab countries making it close to being a transnational pan-Islamic movement. Essentially, it is an indigenous Islamic protest movement against the forces of change and modernity, government corruption and social and economic injustice, and foreign influence. All these debilitating conditions were, in the words of its leader, plunging Egypt into a "pit of degradation" and defeat.[6]

Starting as a reform movement concerned mainly with religious activities and individual and social morality, the Ikhwan—or Brotherhood—grew in the 1940s into a populist Islamic movement with an activist political bent, advocating an Islamic polity based on Islamic norms and laws (*Shari'a*). The movement found its strongest support among the middle and lower-middle classes, who saw Islam as Egypt's salvation. Indeed, the Brotherhood spoke to the masses in their own language, the simple language of Islam, affirming the belief that "Islam provides thorough and sound solutions to all problems."[7] This is in marked contradistinction to the elitist intellectual discourse of nineteenth-century Muslim reformers, which did not penetrate the masses' sentiments and hence never moved them.

Further, the Brotherhood movement's popular appeal was greatly enhanced by the large-scale network of social, educational, religious, and charitable organizations it established in cities and towns across Egypt. Local volunteers and financial support from domestic and foreign (mainly Gulf area) pious wealthy Muslim philanthropists provided the backbone for these structures. They served as centers for dissemination of the Islamic message and recruitment of members. Equally, this network of service structures helped to institutionalize the movement in Egyptian life, giving it strength and durability to become practically an autonomous society—a society within the larger society.

Another significant feature of the Ikhwan that became a trademark of modern Islamic fundamentalism is that Hasan al-Banna and the successor leaders were intellectual laymen, products of modern Egyptian institutions and universities, not the traditional al-Azhar. (Al-Banna neither attended al-Azhar University mosque nor belonged to the *ulama* religious class; he was a graduate of the College of Sciences and a schoolteacher of Arabic.) And they sought to recruit young men of similar backgrounds. Indeed, with the rise of the Ikhwan, the Islamic movement came increasingly under the control of educated lay leaders, marking a shift away from the religious scholars' leadership of early Muslim revivalism. The shift reflects, too, the anticlerical attitude prevalent among modern fundamentalists. They accuse the official *ulama* of antiquated religious formalism and irrelevance and of political subservience as "the mouthpiece of the government." Actually, there is much current anxiety among the *ulama* about their diminishing role and authority in the society. Their position, which started to erode with the onset of modernization, is now being chipped at further by the young fundamentalists.

But the most important legacy of the Ikhwan is that it has politicized Islam and injected it with a new dynamism and activism, which thrust it to the forefront of public affairs, a status that paved the way for the rise of Islamic militancy in Egypt. Indeed, today's militant fundamentalist groups are rooted in the Muslim Brotherhood. At center stage during the 1940s—a period of increasing social and political turmoil and violence in Egypt—the Ikhwan saw the Egyptian state as a colony under British tutelage, despite official independence in the early 1920s, and ruled in conjunction with a privileged Westernized group. It sought both to rid the country of undesirable forces and to establish an Islamic system in accord with *al-salaf al-salih* (the early pious ancestors in the seventh century). Also, it took up the cause of the Palestinian Arabs in the fight against the Zionists by sending volunteers to take part in the Palestine war of 1948. Its growing power and popularity were viewed with considerable alarm by the Egyptian state, prompting the first government crackdown in 1948. This led to the assassination of Prime Minister Mahmoud Fahmi al-Nuqrashi by a member of the Ikhwan later the same year and the counterassassination of the leader of the Ikhwan—Hasan al-Banna—shortly thereafter.

But the Brotherhood survived and continued to function, though outside the law. In fact, during much of its history it was tolerated—but not legalized—as long as it neither undermined nor challenged the authority of the state. Historically, the centrality of the state in maintaining social and political order has always been pivotal in Egyptian life, and the state has always jealously guarded its prerogatives. Although the Brotherhood did not publicly espouse violence against the state, its secret paramilitary wing (*al-jihaz al-khas*, or special apparatus) occasionally committed destructive acts. Thus, on the few occasions the Ikhwan threatened the state, the latter moved forcefully to suppress it. Such was the case in the 1948 repression, in the 1954 banishment of the movement after the failed attempt on Nasser's life, and in the 1965 arrest and repression of the younger leaders who had unremittingly castigated Nasser's "Godless" nationalist-socialist state.

After a brief period of coexistence and maintenance of at least a pretense of cooperation with the new post-1952 revolutionary regime, the Ikhwan soon found itself in collision with the emergent nationalist state of Nasser, which it accused of deviating from Islamic principles and deteriorating into military dictatorship.[8] The military-state dictatorship was held responsible for the decline of Islam and the rise in the barbarity of *jahiliyya* (pre-Islamic paganism).[9] Over the next two decades, Nasser's severe repressive measures incapacitated the Ikhwan politically, with fateful consequences for the future of the movement in Egypt. Thousands of members were jailed and tortured, and several top ideologists were executed such as Abdul Qader Odeh in 1955 and Sayyid Qutb in 1966. The intensity of the crackdown, the harsh prison experience, and the prolonged underground existence radicalized the movement and gave rise to militant splinter groups that split from the Ikhwan.[10] Thus, a new breed of extremist Islamic groups was created, incubated in Nasser's prison cells and hatched under Sadat's policies of *infitah* (openness) in the 1970s.

Nearly two dozen radical groups emerged in the span of a decade, major among them the Islamic Liberation Party (the Technical Military Academy Group), Jama'at al-Takfir wa al-Hijra (the Apostasy and Flight Group), the Jihad Organization, and al-Jama'a al-Islamiyya (the Islamic Jama'a or Group). They charted a path of confrontation and violence against the state and its symbols, while the revived main body of the Ikhwan eschewed violence in favor of a strategy of change by peaceful means. The difference widened the division with the young zealots, who objected to the Ikhwan's moderation in seeking a modus vivendi with Sadat. But, despite the divergent strategies, they all remained deeply committed to the ultimate goal of bringing about an Islamic state system.

Shortly after coming to power in 1970, Sadat unleashed the Islamic movement and even encouraged establishment of Islamic groups on university campuses and in various professional associations and trade unions in an effort to stem the imminent threat to his regime posed by the leftist-Nasserist power centers. As well, he allowed the Ikhwan to operate publicly and to expand its social, educational, religious, and philanthropic service networks at a time of government retrenchment and retreat from state welfarism under the new economic policy of *infitah*. These moves paved the way for the Islamist forces to assume a substantial role in Egypt's public life and for the emergence of the cluster groups of the Islamic Jama'a.

Sadat went beyond his accommodation of and cooperation with the movement to embrace religious Islamic rhetoric and symbols in order to thereby gain respectability and buttress his position. His initiatives ranged from assuming the title *al-ra' is al- mou' min* (the believer-president) to using the first name Muhammad, invoking the name of God at the start of his public speeches, and wearing traditional dress (*jallabiyya*).[11] More important, the 1971 constitution declared *Shari' a* "a principal source of legislation" in Egypt, thus tying the legal system to Islamic law.

Sadat, then, helped to promote further the atmosphere of religiosity that had been in evidence since the 1967 war. Still, the use of Islam by a national leader for political purposes has its price. It can set in motion inimical forces that will come back to haunt him. In fact, the more Sadat stressed the religious theme and the more he associated his state with religion, calling it "the state of science and faith," the more he became vulnerable to the Islamic opposition—which came to pass. His initial policies, aimed at containing the leftist-Nasserist threat, eventually gave rise to a far greater Islamic challenge with the blossoming of the radical fundamentalist organizations as they expanded recruitment and training.[12] It was not long before the nascent Islamic formations of the early 1970s grew in strength and appeal, especially among the many disaffected young, to emerge later in the decade as the leading nay sayers to Sadat, rejecting his domestic and foreign policies and the legitimacy of his "un-Islamic" regime.

Meanwhile, the Ikhwan demonstrated its moderation by rejecting the militants' doctrine and tactics and keeping a working relationship with Sadat. It did so despite its opposition to his peace initiative with Israel and his general alliance with the United States as betraying the Islamic struggle and to some aspects of his economic and political liberalization as leading to neither greater welfare of the society nor wider participation and freedoms.[13] It continued to follow a peaceable course within the legal framework of the system, cooperating with other political forces. In particular, it concentrated on building wide-based networks of social-welfare, economic, educational, and medical services and on penetrating and controlling university bodies and professional associations. All were utilized to create a climate of Islamicity that was beneficial to mainstream Islamists.

Under Mubarak, the Muslim Brotherhood was drawn further into the system, taking an active part in the open social, economic, and political environment. In multiplying its economic and social welfare organizations, it gained a central role in public welfare eclipsing that of the dilapidated government agencies.[14] It operated its own publishing houses and newspapers, propagating freely its Islamist message. Above all, it participated in free elections within unions and professional associations and won control of such major associations as those of lawyers, physicians, pharmacists, and engineers. And it ran candidates in parliamentary races in alliance with secular parties such as the New Wafd Party in 1984 and the Socialist Labor Party in 1987.[15] It even repeatedly sought recognition as a political party itself, but was denied legitimacy because of the prohibition on religiously oriented parties.[16]

Thus, despite a rocky course that had taken the Ikhwan in and out of acceptability, coexistence has become a modus operandi. The Brotherhood by and large reconciled itself with the Egyptian state, using only legal means to move society and state in the desired Islamic direction. Although it remains "illegal," it has represented a viable alternative model of a just and orderly society juxtaposed to Nasser's and successor regimes. It acted as a real opposition intent on its role: opposing. Hence, Sadat was not willing, nor is Mubarak willing, to legitimize it. Mubarak, like Sadat, wants to temper its potential strength and keep it subject to government whims, while keeping whip in hand.

Contrary to the mainstream Ikhwan movement, the new, younger fundamentalist groups pursued a course of violent confrontation with the state, a course that has been the center of attention internally and externally since the mid-1970s. These groups represent the radical *jihadi* (invoking holy war) tendency in the Islamic movement: the holy warriors of Islam. Chief among them were the Technical Military Academy Group and the Apostasy and Flight Group in the 1970s and the two major cell groups that have proliferated since the 1980s: the Jihad Organization and the Islamic Jama'a. They have forsworn the Ikhwan because of its compromises and accommodation with the system; accused the state, or state and society, of being un-Islamic, living in a condition of *jahiliyya* (pre-Islamic unbelief, or apostasy); and declared *jihad* (armed struggle) as the means to bring about an Islamic transformation in accord with their rigid religious interpretation. Thus, all the new groups are against the post-1952 nationalist state because it is inimical to Islam. Ironically, these neofundamentalists are themselves the product of the Nasserist policies of open, free education, egalitarianism, and high job expectations.

The intellectual fountainhead and inspiration of the radical Islamic movement was Sayyid Qutb, the young chief ideologue of the Ikhwan in the 1960s. He elaborated an ideology of resistance (*jihad*) against authority based upon his doctrinal interpretation of the existing conditions of Muslim societies as vitiated by *jahiliyya* and their rulers as *kuffar* (un-Islamic, or apostates). And all those in the society who partake in this state of affairs are in the category of apostates. Qutb's conception of *takfir* (to apostatize, or to declare someone non-Muslim) and *jihad*, which sanctions the overthrow of corrupt rulers by force, established a dangerous precedent for future radical fundamentalists to follow.

In the same vein, the Jama'at al-Takfir wa al-Hijra (the Apostasy and Flight Group), led by veteran Ikhwan member Shukri Mustafa,[17] declared that the Egyptian state and society were infested by *jahiliyya*, which requires a complete moral overhauling to bring about a true Muslim society. To achieve that end, the group called for a retreat (*hijra*) by a nucleus of true believers to the desert and mountains to build a "model Islamic community" that could grow and ultimately lead in a victorious struggle (*jihad*) against the *jahiliyya* society. The strategy of retreat and reconquest is analogous to the Prophet's flight in A.D. 622 from Mecca to Medina, where he founded the first Muslim community, and his recapture of Mecca eight years later.

The group had a violent showdown with the authorities in July 1977 subsequent to the kidnapping and killing of a former minister of *al-awqaf* (religious endowments), Sheikh Muhammad Hussein Al-Dhahabi, a leading member of the *ulama*. Many of the militants were either killed or imprisoned, and the top leaders, including Shukri Mustafa, were executed in 1978. One can surmise that the group's action shows its rejection of and hostility to the official *ulama*, whom they termed "*ulama' al-sulta*" (being slavish to the government). Al-Dhahabi had a record of vehemently characterizing the militants as misguided, even deviant—a behavior that, for the group, cast him in the role of a state agent echoing the government line.

Similarly, the Islamic Liberation Party (the Technical Military Academy Group) and the successor groups of the Jihad Organization and its ideological associate the Islamic Jama'a saw the prevalent corruption and decadence in the society as rooted in its ruling elite.[18] To redeem the society, the elite would have to be transformed into an Islamic leadership that applied *Shari'a*. The transformation should be carried out not by the peaceable means of religious education and moral uplifting, but by direct action and open confrontation: an all-out *jihad*. In his ideological tract *Al-Farida al-Gha'iba* (The absent commandment), Muhammad Abdul Salam Farag, leader of the Jihad Organization in 1979, pronounced the government to be apostate and an entity to be fought through a holy war by believers; a return to *jihad* was the only way to redemption.[19] The stridency and aggressive stance of these groups brought them into open conflict with the state, starting with the bloody attempted takeover of the Technical Military Academy in April 1974 by the Islamic Liberation Party as part of a coup.[20] This was followed by the assassination of Sadat in October 1981 by members of the Jihad Organization. The conflict has continued throughout much of the 1980s and into the 1990s.

The assassination of Sadat and the abortive fundamentalist revolt that ensued in the city of Asyut in Upper Egypt (al-Sa'id) shook the Egyptian state to its foundation. Al-Sa'id, in southern Egypt—predominantly rural, traditional-religious, and poor—is the hotbed of the militant Islamic Jama'a, which spearheaded the sanguinary uprising.[21] (In fact, the extremism of the Jama'a is heavily conditioned by its southern circumstances: economic impoverishment and deeply rooted traditions, such as *tha'r*, or vendetta, that supersede the power of the law.) After a brief lull following Mubarak's accession and an initial attempt at a dialogue, the acts of violence were ongoing in the second half of the 1980s and escalated in the post–Gulf War period in the early 1990s. Led by the Islamic Jama'a and the Jihad Organization, militants killed top government officials and security officers, members of the Coptic Christian minority, writers, and foreign tourists in a relentless murderous cycle.

Assassinations and threats of assassination of prominent state symbols, public figures, journalists, writers, and artists comprised the intimidating strategy of choice. It eventuated in the murder of Dr. Rif'at al-Mahgoub, former speaker of parliament, in 1990; abortive attempts on the lives of Minister of Interior Hasan al-Alfi and his two predecessors in the early 1990s; an abortive attempt at shooting down journalist Makram Muhammad Ahmad in the late 1980s; the assassination of secularist writer Farag Foda in 1992; and the attack on Nobel Prize laureate Naguib Mahfouz in 1994, among others.[22]

Violence against the Christian Copts in particular reached unprecedented proportions. Anti-Coptic riots and assaults were instigated between 1979 and 1981 by extremists and popular religious preachers such as Sheikh Abdul Hamid Kishk, whose radical sermons on cassettes were widely circulated inside Egypt and out.[23] In al-Sa'id—where the Copts are the most numerous, constituting almost 20 percent of the area population compared to less than 10 percent of the overall population—the Islamic Jama'a vented its animus against the "Coptic danger." The militant fundamentalists waged a campaign of terror and intimidation against the Christian communities in various towns and villages in the south, sanctioning the robbing of businesses, attacks upon churches, evictions, and even the murder of those who opposed Muslim dictates. Muslim extremists saw the Coptic Christian minorities as alien subjects serving as agents of the West in the midst of Islam.[24] In a country that had traditionally prided itself on religious tolerance and social harmony, the actions of the extremists posed a tremendous threat to social order and stability, an affront to government authority.

Another target of high visibility and immense significance was tourism. Attacks on tourists were meant to damage the tourist industry, Egypt's main hard currency source of more than $3 billion annually; its loss or even diminution could aggravate the economic crisis in the country. It is estimated that the resultant drop in tourism cost between $700 million and $1 billion in 1992.[25] The attacks, then, are not only a show of rejection of the West, Westerners, and their repugnant ways, but also a means to undercut a resource helpful to the regime and to stifle foreign investment—both vital for the regime's economic development plans. The assumption of the fundamentalist militants is that the greater the economic hardships, the greater the prospects for popular revolt advantageous to their cause.

Equally important, the power of the Islamic militants flourished with the creation of "Islamized spaces" or zones, chipping away at the dominion of the state.[26] The militants grew so strong that they were able to control whole poor neighborhoods in Cairo, such as Ein Shams, Imbaba, Umraniyya, and el-Zawiya al-Hamra, and small towns and villages in Upper Egypt, such as el-Fayyum, Dayrut, al-Minya, and Sanabu. They had become virtually the principal domestic power in these geographic places—imposing their own social and moral code; running their own mosques with their own preachers; providing rudimentary social welfare services; and settling disputes and applying Qur'anic *hudud*, or sanctions, completely outside government authority. The government presence was hardly to be found. These Islamized spaces not only were moral puritan enclaves representative of the ideal future society, but also provided competing networks of social and economic support services that rivaled and even supplanted the inefficient government system. These Islamic strongholds have witnessed repeated violent clashes with the security forces since 1987.

As the Islamic opposition from below loomed large with its "frightening alternative,"[27] challenging openly and ferociously the power of the Egyptian state, the government launched an equally fierce and relentless counterattack. Its initial response was a combination of repression and accommodation. It sought to quell the militant opposition, while courting the moderate Ikhwan and orthodox Muslims generally. Starting in the summer of 1992, great force and mass arrests were used to break up the power of the fundamentalists in their strongholds in the Cairo slums and in Upper Egypt—there to restore government hegemony. Entire neighborhoods and villages were put under virtual siege, swamped by special police forces and kept under constant security watch. Further, a systematic campaign was instituted to "decapitate" the Jama'a and Jihad leaderships and deplete their ranks. In the ensuing clashes, more than six hundred people were killed.

With the escalation of the government's campaign, military courts and the death penalty (introduced under emergency laws in effect since the early 1980s) were utilized to deal swiftly and severely with "terrorist crimes." Mass executions of dozens of militants have occurred since, the largest number of Egyptian executions for political crimes in this century.[28] Such a singularity is particularly shocking for a society that has been known for its traditional moderation and tolerance; it is tantamount to a loss of innocence.

The unprecedented harshness and extent of the government blows evoked some domestic criticism and international protestation from human rights organizations. But the government, impelled to greater authoritarianism by what it deemed threats to domestic security, dismissed such talk as injurious to Egypt's efforts to maintain stability and establish law and order. The High Constitutional Court sided with the government over the legality of using military courts for trying civilians for acts of terrorism under the emergency laws. Also, the government refused to recognize the Egyptian Organization for Human Rights. It accused the organization of being foreign-supported and used by terrorist groups and dismissed it as a "voguish" enterprise run by a coalition of Nasserists and Islamists seeking publicity at home and abroad.[29]

Mubarak was emphatic: "I refuse to allow human rights to become a slogan to protect terrorists."[30] At the end of the day, the Muslim extremists were no match for the strong arm of the state.

The government's efforts to contain the radical fundamentalist threat extended to the foreign front. On one level, the Mubarak regime launched an international campaign to discredit and isolate Iran and Sudan as the two leading centers of Islamic radicalism, accusing them of supporting terrorism in Egypt and elsewhere in the region. Both countries have become favorite targets of governments facing intense internal fundamentalist opposition. It is true that these two countries have furnished the fundamentalists some general support, but the fact is that Egyptian fundamentalism is a home-grown movement embedded in Egyptian circumstances. Further, Sunni fundamentalists in Egypt do not see eye to eye with the Shi'a-based religious state in Iran.

On another level, Mubarak moved to cut off the militants' foreign sources of support, appealing to the rich Gulf Arab states, where the bulk of contributions from pious wealthy individuals and charitable foundations emanates, to control the outflow of money.[31] He also sought to promote regional security cooperation with Tunisia, Algeria, Saudi Arabia, and Pakistan (some militant Egyptian fundamentalists who had fought in the Afghan war maintained bases and training centers in Peshawar) in order to coordinate strategy in the fight against the radicals.[32]

Mubarak sought as well to place the issue of terrorism under the international spotlight following the bombing of the World Trade Center in New York City in early 1993. Sheikh Omar Abdul Rahman, spiritual leader of the Islamic Jama'a in Egypt, and some of his followers were charged and convicted as the perpetrators of that event. Mubarak called on the United States to play a "tough role" because terrorism is a source of problems not only for the Middle East, but also for other regions and countries.[33] Additionally, at the International Conference on the Prevention of Crime and the Treatment of Offenders, held in Cairo in early May 1995, Egypt pushed hard for adoption of a resolution equating terrorism with international organized crime and calling for a concerted international effort to combat it.[34]

Mubarak repeatedly emphasizes the theme of the international character and scope of today's terrorist acts. On this point, he seems to be in full agreement with the late Israeli Prime Minister Yitzhak Rabin, who viewed Islamic fundamentalism as a "global threat" that must be combatted the way the West contained the communist threat.[35] Casting the problem into the international arena serves to raise the stakes in the fight against violent groups, gain acceptance of his heavy-handed tactics against the Muslim radicals, and deflect attention from the serious Islamic challenge at home.

Equally adept in the strategy of containment, the Egyptian government at the outset cloaked itself in the mantle of Islam to appease the general public's religious sentiments and to enlist the *ulama*'s support. Indeed, because the grip of Islam at the popular level remains strong in Egypt, it has often been used by the state against opponents of the right and of the left—which has become a universal practice in the Muslim world, with governments of all manner of ideological persuasion resorting to it.[36] Nasser invoked Islam to equate socialism and nationalism with Muslim egalitarianism and strength. His twin policies had to be given Islamic garb to gain popularity and status among the masses. Sadat consistently promoted the image of the pious Muslim and used Islam to battle secular leftists and validate his peace policies with Israel. Now, under Mubarak, the aim is to brandish state-supported Islam to combat the militant fundamentalists.

The Mubarak government and the official *ulama* question the authenticity of the extremists' "foreign-backed" doctrine of violence as something un-Egyptian and against the true spirit of Islam. It is even suggested that the Egyptian fundamentalists acquired their increasingly violent tone during their long exile in Saudi Arabia in the 1960s. During that period, they were imbued with elements of Islamic Wahhabi revivalist thought, emphasizing traditionalism, puritanism, and militancy, which is different from mainstream Egyptian Islam. According to Ibrahim 'Isa, a former journalist for the liberal weekly *Rose al-Yusif*, the battle is between the Saudi Islam of the desert, characterized by harshness and austerity, and the Egyptian Islam, which is more open and moderate.[37] The government branded all militant groups as "deviant" and even "heretical," having no relationship to Islam as a balanced "middle-course" religion with a noble, universal mission.[38]

The *ulama* rejected as contrary to the commonly accepted interpretations of early Muslim jurists and Sunni tradition the extremists' use of their own dogmatic views and unorthodox interpretations of the Qur'an and prophetic traditions (*Sunna*) to justify violence against state and society. Muslim clerics have traditionally approached interpretation of Islamic doctrine with an eye toward consensus (*ijma'*). Consensus is always preferable to disagreement. The religious leaders accused the militant groups of ignorance—stemming from either a lack of systematic training in Islamic studies or, at best, a thin understanding of Islamic theology.[39] They labeled the groups as *ghulat* (excessive)—outside mainstream Egyptian Islam; the groups were committing heterodoxy in the tradition of the Kharijites (the seceders) of the seventh century, who stood outside the consensus of the Muslim community under the fourth Caliph Ali (A.D. 656–661), rebelling against him and killing him.[40]

To add to its appearance of Islamicity, the government allowed circulation of a plethora of mainstream Islamist publications; promoted Islamic programming on radio and television, beaming long hours of religious messages; and showed increasing deference to the *ulama*, soliciting opinions on a wide range of socioeconomic issues such as investment in government bonds, family planning, and even Salman Rushdie's request to visit Egypt to meet with Egyptian writers.[41] Further, the Islamists, using the constitutional stipulation that Islamic *Shari'a* is the foundation of Egyptian law, have in recent years pushed hard to extend the application of *Shari'a* to cover many aspects of the legal code and the drafting of new legislation. They introduced legislation in the People's Assembly seeking to incorporate the Islamic *hudud* (penal code) in cases of adultery, robbery, and the drinking of alcohol. They attacked the Personal Status Law of 1979, which granted women more liberal rights in matters of divorce, child custody, and alimony. The 1985 amendment to this law limited these rights, making it once again more difficult for women to initiate divorce or gain custody.[42]

The Islamists have also been able to freely penetrate the educational system, especially at the precollege levels, and influence the curriculum in an Islamic direction, turning schools into centers of indoctrination.[43] This is in addition to controlling important public enclaves and bodies such as mosques, professional associations and unions, and local councils.[44] Thus, with government acquiescence and even encouragement, the religious discourse has dominated public life and set the social and political agenda to foster even greater Islamization.

The state-sponsored Islamization to check Muslim extremists raised deep concerns among intellectuals about the future of secular liberalism in Egypt. Their fear was that it might turn "the average mind and discourse toward Islam" and even foster *tatarruf sha'bi* (popular extremism) that could backfire against the government.[45] But, of more immediate concern, the dominant Islamic discourse began to tilt the cultural balance against the tradition of liberalism that has been in place since the early nineteenth century. It could lead as well to further marginalization and intimidation of the liberal secularists, threatening the dynamic cultural and intellectual life of modern Egypt. Indeed, intellectual freedom and expression, literature and scholarship, and the arts became less and less tolerated and increasingly imperiled.

Suffice it to mention some of the prominent cases. The conservative *ulama* of al-Azhar banned some novels by the renowned Naguib Mahfouz, declaring them offensive to Islam. Mahfouz was later assailed for his outspoken stance against "intellectual terrorism." Similarly, Farag Fouda's books were nowhere to be seen at the Cairo book fair in 1993, one year after his assassination—they had been banned. (The annual book fair has become increasingly dominated by Islamic-oriented material.) Other prominent writers and artists, such as Said al-'Ashmawi, Fouad Zakariyya, Nawal Sa'dawi (a feminist author), Amina al-Said (a leading woman writer), and Adel Imam, were proclaimed "enemies of Islam" and received death threats.[46]

Dr. Nasr Hamid Abu Zeid, an academic at Cairo University, was denied promotion in 1993 because of his nontraditional writings on Islam, especially his *Naqd al-Khitab al-Dini* (Critique of religious discourse). Shortly thereafter, a court case was brought by a group of fundamentalist lawyers accusing him of apostasy and asking that his marriage therefore be annulled or that his wife be considered an adulteress subject to the death penalty. The mere fact that the case was allowed before the court shows the flagrant invasion of religion into Egypt's secular life. Dr. Abu Zeid is currently on the death list of the

Jihad Organization following a higher court ruling that nullified his marriage based on the apostasy charge.[47]

Finally, a key argument in the defense of those accused of killing the writer Farag Fouda was that an ad hoc committee of al-Azhar had declared Fouda's writings anti-Islamic; therefore, he was an apostate who should be killed. Testifying for the defense, the late Sheikh Muhammad Al-Ghozali, a leading mainstream cleric, declared that a secularist who opposes *Shari'a* is an apostate and hence must be killed by the state. If an individual carries out the punishment (extrajudicial killing) upon state failure to do so, that individual is a mere *mufta'it* (transgressor) upon the government authority, a violation for which there is no specific punishment in Islam.[48] Surely the message is loud and abundantly clear, and it has dangerous implications for Egypt's Muslim liberals. Equally, this religiously charged atmosphere may further jeopardize the Coptic Christian community, already under attack by Muslim zealots.

All this is evidence enough that in manipulating Islam to defuse fundamentalism, the government is running the risk of incubating a zealotry that could lead to further extremism and ultimately undermine its authority. To prevent such a dangerous outcome, the government, having gained confidence in dealing with the Muslim extremists,[49] has now expanded its authoritarian reach to the mainstream Islamist movement, the Ikhwan. The Mubarak regime has of late moved to clamp down on its various organized activities in order to contain the Ikhwan's growing influence in public life. New legislation changing counciliar election procedures in the unions and professional associations has brought the councils under the supervision of the judiciary. The purpose is to break the hold of the Islamists on these organizations and establish instead control by the ruling National Democratic Party. In a May 1995 Labor Day speech, Mubarak strongly denounced the Ikhwan's "power monopoly" over important unions and syndicates, accusing it of manipulating these organizations for its own political ends.[50]

Further, the government acted to stem the proliferation of private mosques and associated charitable foundations and to end their extragovernmental autonomy. Indeed, recognizing that private organizations could serve to enhance the potential for Islamic opposition, the government brought all civic organizations, already required by law to be registered and licensed by the authorities, under closer scrutiny and control.[51] Additionally, the government attempted to rid the educational system of the Islamist influences that had crept into it over the past twenty years. It transferred hundreds of teachers to administrative posts, removed Islamist tracts from library shelves, and tried to ban the imposition of the *niqab* and the *hijab* (veiling) on young schoolgirls.[52]

Equally, the Mubarak government continued to deny the Ikhwan legal party status, citing the constitutional prohibition of religion-based parties and national unity stipulation. In effect, it barred the Brotherhood from participating in Egypt's limited multiparty politics, which remains circumscribed by lack of a party institutional development and popular roots and by government controls of political life generally.[53] In fact, Mubarak has no qualms about banishing the Ikhwan, as a leading opposition group, from Egypt's political life. Successive governments have always suspected its motives and hence have kept the group in a semipolitical diaspora subject to the limits of government tolerance.

Today, despite a semblance of moderation and cooperation within the framework of the system, the Brotherhood is still mistrusted for continuing to chip away at the existing secular state institutions and to push for its Islamic agenda. In fact, since Sadat's initial attempt at co-optation of the Ikhwan in the 1970s, the relationship between it and the state has remained tenuous and uncertain. The Ikhwan never fully embraced the regimes of Sadat and Mubarak; despite its decision to adhere to the legal rules set by the state, it could not identify completely with either regime. Nor did Sadat or Mubarak feel comfortable enough to embrace the Ikhwan as a dependable ally, for their agendas are radically different. The Ikhwan remains committed to the goal of Islamization of state, society, and culture, something it shares with the militants, but pursues it with nonconfrontational means.

The strong fear of Islamic political parties as a "grave error" and a danger has been intensified by the Algerian experience, about which Mubarak had warned the Algerian leaders. Accordingly, as the government grew increasingly assertive and resolute in countering the Islamists, it launched a crackdown on the Brotherhood, arresting dozens of leading members and hounding many more, and ordered the closing of its headquarters in Cairo.[54] Also, the outlawed Ikhwan was barred from competing in the November 1995 national election in an effort to disenfranchise the group. The few members who ran as independents were subject to government restrictions, police harassment, and vote tampering that virtually eliminated them from the contest. Unable to win a single seat, the Ikhwan was totally excluded from participation as an oppositional force in parliament.[55]

Mubarak seems determined to escalate the level of repression against what he characterized as "the forces that work in the dark" and remain deep-rooted in violence: the Ikhwan.[56] Indeed, the government even suspects some association between the Ikhwan and the militants, for the Ikhwan is the father of all these splinter groups. Thus, the Islamic movement as a whole is now under attack, with no distinction between moderate and radical tendencies. Surely the Ikhwan, cognizant of the overwhelming power of the state, which it had encountered more than once in the past, is in no position to challenge the state. It would be folly to try to contest the historical, millennia-old state in Egypt.

Meanwhile, the growing state authoritarianism under Mubarak, which has increased proportionately with the longevity of the regime—now in its third six-year term—has raised fears among the liberals about the prospects of democratic reforms. But the regime remains unmoved by such liberal worries and is intent on staying the course under the pretext of maintaining "discipline and control," which in its view does not contradict democracy.[57] Mubarak is determined to avoid repeating the experiences of the Soviet Union's Mikhail Gorbachev and Algeria's Chadli Benjedid. Both are believed to have moved too fast toward democratization and were soon overthrown. Algeria, in particular, provided a bitter lesson against full openness and participation lest it lead to a similar breakdown. Thus, democracy in Egypt remains limited, subject to preserving public order, stability, and regime continuity.[58] And the government will continue its policy of barring the Islamic movement from the political arena.

Indeed, in the face of the mounting violence that has marred Egyptian life and threatened the cultural elite, the liberal intelligentsia have been hard-pressed to tone down its appeals for greater political liberalization. And, despite the apparent retrogression in democratization and the presence of rampant official corruption, the secularist liberals have no choice but to take cover under a disliked state apparatus to escape the menace of fundamentalism. Likewise, the Coptic minority finds itself in desperate need of protection and order, even at the expense of having to submit to a repressive regime. Both groups have more to fear from the ascendancy of the Islamists than from the assertive power of the state. Both constituencies surmise that a truly open political system could result in an Islamist victory, thus bringing to an end secular government in Egypt. Surely all this has played into the hands of the regime in slowing the pace of political reforms and in playing off the liberals against the Islamists. To regain the cultural balance, the state is now promoting the dissemination of secularist discourse, which is currently witnessing a new rally.[59]

Today, as Mubarak wades through his third six-year term, hardly anyone believes that the radical fundamentalists pose a fatal threat to the regime. Their leadership has sustained grievous blows, and their ranks have been smashed. As to the mainstream Ikhwan movement, it is equally subject to government heavy-handedness and is being discredited as a shadowy group with a violent past masquerading now as moderate. Certainly the task of containment is greatly facilitated by the absence of an organized movement tying together the diverse Islamic forces. In fact, the multiplicity of the Islamic groups, with their regional, social, and ideological divisions, rent the fundamentalists asunder and militated against an Islamic front in Egypt comparable to the Algerian Islamic Salvation Front.[60] Neither is there a unifying, charismatic Muslim cleric à la Khomeini.

Yet, the fundamentalists are far from disappearing and will probably go on committing intermittent acts of violence,[61] especially in the medium term, because socioeconomic conditions remain intractable—probably only manageable, at best—and will continue to chip away at the regime's standing, which at the start of Mubarak's third term in October 1993 reached lows almost reminiscent of Sadat's last days.[62] In the long term, the only way to stamp out the Islamic opposition is to remedy the painful economic conditions of the country. But, in the Egyptian context of overpopulation that is constantly pressing against limited resources and a mammoth inactive bureaucracy at the core of a centralized government that is lukewarm to reforms as too risky and explosive, the task is herculean.[63]

Still, despite mounting disaffection, the regime is not in imminent danger of collapse, as the fundamentalists had thought or wanted the world to believe. The state remains strong and is supported by large segments of the elite, especially the armed forces. And Mubarak, despite his lack of charisma and commanding leadership, will continue holding onto power by simply carrying on the business of managing public affairs in the usual Egyptian manner: by employing the power of the state.

Ultimately, the durability of the Mubarak regime will probably depend on the loyalty of the military, the mainstay of the Egyptian state since 1952 and the traditional beneficiary of its favors.[64] So far, the army has stood above the fray, as the regime has contained violence and even lessened it considerably. But should a calamity befall the government, and with no clear successor to Mubarak,[65] the military is most likely to step in as the strongest power center and the guardian of the state. The result would be a successor secular regime. The fundamentalists are not winning the day now, nor will they in the future; it is highly unlikely that they can overwhelm the power of the state. The traditional mastery of the state in this ancient land will continue. So will the nagging socioeconomic problems.

NOTES

1. Founded by the Fatimid dynasty (A.D. 909–1171) soon after its conquest of Egypt, the mosque of al-Azhar is the oldest existing Muslim university. It has become the premier institution of Islamic learning, receiving students from all parts of the Muslim world. See Daniel Crecelius, "Al-Azhar in the Revolution," *Middle East Journal* 20 (1966): 31–49.

2. On the history of modern education in Egypt, see J. Heyworth-Dunne, *An Introduction to the History of Education in Egypt* (London: Luzac, 1938); Mahmud A. Faksh, "Education and Political Modernization and Change in Egypt," diss., University of Connecticut, 1972, 16–57. See also Malcolm H. Kerr, "Egypt," *Education and Political Development*, ed. James S. Coleman (Princeton, N.J.: Princeton University Press, 1968), 169–94.

3. On the theme of Islamic reform in Egypt, see Malcolm H. Kerr, *Islamic Reform: The Political and Legal Theories of Muhammad Abduh and Rashid Rida* (Berkeley: University of California Press, 1966); Charles D. Smith, *Islam and the Search for Social Order in Modern Egypt: A Biography of Muhammad Husayn Haykal* (Albany: State University of New York Press, 1983).

4. See Albert Hourani, *Arabic Thought in the Liberal Age, 1798–1939* (London: Oxford University Press, 1962); Smith, *Islam and the Search for Social Order in Modern Egypt*.

5. On the Ikhwan movement, its history, and its ideology, see Richard P. Mitchell, *The Society of the Muslim Brotherhood* (Ann Arbor: University of Michigan Press, 1970); Ishaq Musa Husaini, *The Muslim Brethren* (Beirut: Khayat's, 1956).

6. Hasan al-Banna, *What Is Our Message?* (Lahore, Pakistan: Islamic Publications, 1974), 28.

7. Al-Banna, *What Is Our Message?* 27.

8. Some of the Free Officers who carried out the July 1952 revolution were either members of or sympathizers with the Ikhwan. In fact, the two groups shared similar aspirations and worldviews. Thus, when the Revolutionary Council disbanded all parties in 1953, it exempted the Ikhwan on the basis that it was a nonpolitical organization.

9. See Sayyid Qutb, *Ma'alim fi al-Tariq* (Signposts on the road) (Beirut: Matba'at al-Risala, 1966). Under Nasser, the *Shari'a* courts, which had hitherto administered the personal status laws, were practically abolished in 1957, when they were taken over by the state civil system. And al-Azhar came increasingly under government control and was effectively nationalized in 1961, becoming a state-run university.

10. On the Nasserist repression and harsh prison experience, see Jabir Rizq, *Madhabih al-Ikhwan fi Sujun Nasir* (Slaughter of the Ikhwan in Nasser's prisons) (Cairo: Dar al-I'tisam, 1977). Omar al-Tilimsani, the past leader of the Ikhwan, called the Nasserist rule "the era of inquisition"; he saw the new rising violence among the young Islamist groups as a direct outcome of the ruthless suppression by the regime. See *al-Musawwar* 22 Jan. 1982: 14–19.

11. On the symbolism, see Hasan Hanafi, "The Relevance of the Islamic Alternative in Egypt," *Arab Studies Quarterly* 4 (Spring 1982): 63. It is worth noting here that the Qur'an (49:14–17) appears to give a superior moral position to the "believers" (*al-mou'minoun*, those with inner faith and belief) compared to those who are just nominal Muslims. Surely, by taking up the appellation of believer, Sadat seemed to aspire to the morally superior station.

12. President Mubarak acknowledged that Sadat was responsible for the formation of the Islamic groups: "He was badly advised, and he made a big mistake." Quoted in Mary Anne Weaver, "The Novelist and the Sheikh," *New Yorker* 30 Jan. 1995: 68. See also David Butler, "Mubarak Haunted by Egypt's Past," *Middle East Economic Digest* 26 Mar. 1993: 2.

13. The Ikhwan's newspaper, *al-Da'wa*, constantly restated the theme of no peace with Zionism and all of Palestine is Islamic. On the relationship between the Ikhwan and Sadat, see Omar al-Tilimsani, *Dhikrayat la Mudhakkarat* (Reminiscences not memoirs) (Cairo: Dar al-Tiba'ah wa al-Nashr al-Islamiyya, 1985); Saad Eddin Ibrahim, "An Islamic Alternative in Egypt: The Muslim Brotherhood and Sadat," *Arab Studies Quarterly* 4 (Spring 1982): 75–93; Ibrahim Ibrahim, "Religion and Politics under Nasser and Sadat, 1952–1981," *The Islamic Impulse*, ed. Barbara F. Stowasser (London: Groom Helm, 1987), 121–34.

14. This was clearly evident during the October 1992 earthquake, when Islamist-controlled organizations were the first to appear on the scene to provide shelter and medical care for the victims, in contrast to the delayed government response.

15. The Muslim Brotherhood ran with the New Wafd Party in the 1984 elections and won 8 seats in the 444-seat national assembly. In the 1987 elections, it ran with the Socialist Labor Party and won thirty-six seats. See Barry Rubin, *Islamic Fundamentalism in Egyptian Politics* (New York: St. Martin's Press, 1990), 32–33. In November 1990, the Brotherhood and most opposition parties boycotted the national election, charging the government with using unfair rules that favored the ruling National Democratic Party. But the Brotherhood continued to run candidates in local and professional union elections.

16. See *al-Musawwar* 2 May 1986: 16–19; *al-Majalla* 5–11 May 1993: 38–39. In banning religion-based political parties, it is argued that Islam does not represent a particular constituency to the exclusion of others. Rather, it is a common heritage shared by all members of the community, and therefore no single group can claim *wisaya* (guardianship) over

it.

17. He was an agronomist, imprisoned and radicalized in the mid-1960s, who broke away from the Ikhwan in the early 1970s.

18. The chief theological guide of the Islamic Jama'a is Sheikh Omar Abdul Rahman. He is currently in jail in the United States, serving a life sentence for the bombing of the New York City World Trade Center in 1993 and other terrorist plots. See Peter Waldman, "Holy Terror: How Sheikh Omar Rose to Lead Islamic War While Eluding the Law," *Wall Street Journal* 1 Sept. 1993: A1, A6. See also Richard Bernstein, "Islamic Cleric's Lifelong Battle vs. Secularism," *New York Times* 8 Jan. 1995: 1, 28; *al-Majalla* 17–23 Mar. 1993: 23–26; Jane Hunter, "US Bomb Trial: Shaikh Gets Life," *Middle East International* 2 Feb. 1996: 12.

19. Muhammad Abdul Salam Farag, *Al-Farida al- Gha'iba* (The absent commandment) (n.p., n.d.). To Farag, the duty of *jihad* is regarded as a sixth pillar in Islam and should be reactivated. The five principal pillars of Islam are *al-shahada* (testimony of faith), *al-salat* (prayers), *al-siyam* (fasting), *al-zakat* (alms giving); and *al-hajj* (pilgrimage). He was later implicated in the assassination of Sadat in 1981 and executed.

20. The plan was to stage an assault on the headquarters of the Arab Socialist Union (the then ruling party in Egypt) during a speech by Sadat, seeking to destroy the leadership and install an Islamic state. With hardly any chance for success, they forged ahead with the plan, considering it to be *ghadba lillah* (a rage for God), which led to their destruction. More than sixty people were killed or wounded, and the top leaders of the movement, including its head, Salih Siriyya, were executed in 1975. He was of Palestinian origin, with a Ph.D. degree in science education. See Saad Eddin Ibrahim, "Egypt's Islamic Militants," *Merip Reports* Feb. 1982: 10; *al-Majalla* 10–16 Mar. 1993: 26.

21. On the regional southern character of the Jama'a, see Mamoun Fandy, "Egypt's Islamic Group: Regional Revenge," *Middle East Journal* 48 (Autumn 1994): 607–25. On the economic impoverishment and neglect of al-Sa'id, see *al-Majalla* 19–25 May 1993: 22-33, 26 May-1 June 1993: 34–38. See also Deborah Pugh, "Upper Egypt," *Christian Science Monitor* 4 May 1994: 12–13. In fact, the dominant majority of militants implicated in the assassination of Sadat came from al-Sa'id. See Hamied Ansari, "The Egyptian Militants in Egyptian Politics," *International Journal of Middle East Studies* 16 (Mar. 1984): 131.

22. See *al-Sharq al-Awsat* 27–28 Mar. 1993: 5, 6; *Middle East Economic Survey* 23 Aug. 1993: C1; Weaver, "The Novelist and the Sheikh."

23. See Gilles Kepel, *Muslim Extremism in Egypt: The Prophet and the Pharaoh* (Berkeley: University of California Press, 1993). For a good analysis of Muslim-Coptic tensions, see Nadia Ramsis Farah, *Religious Strife in Egypt: Crisis and Ideological Conflict in the Seventies* (New York: Gordon & Breach, 1986).

24. Waldman, "Holy Terror," A6. On the plight of the Coptic Christians in southern Egypt, see Chris Hedges, "Heaviest Cross for Egypt's Copts: March of Islam," *New York Times* 27 July 1992: A4. In May 1992, extremists' attacks on Copts in the southern village of Sanabu left fifteen Christians dead. See *al-Sharq al-Awsat* 25 June 1992: 1. See also Deborah Pugh, "Coptic Christians Caught between State and Islamists," *Christian Science Monitor* 4 May 1994: 12.

25. See Sarah Gauch, "The Risky Existence of an Egyptian Extremist," *Christian Science Monitor* 20 May 1993: 6.

26. On the concept of Islamized spaces, see Olivier Roy, "Le néofondamentalisme: des Frères musulmans au FIS Algérien" (Neofundamentalism: from the Muslim Brothers to the Algerian FIS), *Esprit* Mar.-Apr. 1992: 82.

27. It was President Mubarak who called it such. See Fouad Ajami, "The Impossible Life of Muslim Liberalism," *New Republic* 2 June 1986: 26.

28. See *Christian Science Monitor* 9 July 1993: 7; *New York Times* 15 Sept. 1993: A18.

29. See *al-Sharq al-Awsat* 28 Mar. 1993: 5. On the government attacks, see *al-Majalla* 12–18 Mar. 1995: 26–30.

30. Quoted in Stanley Reed, "The Battle for Egypt," *Foreign Affairs* 72 (Sept./Oct. 1993): 103.

31. The Saudi government banned the raising of money for charitable purposes inside Saudi Arabia without the permission of the Interior Ministry. See Youssef M. Ibrahim, "Saudis Crack Down on a Dissident Islamic Group," *New York Times* 14 May 1993: A3. On Mubarak's efforts to block the flow of outside funding from the Gulf states, see *al-Sharq al-Awsat* 5 Nov. 1993: 4.

32. On the efforts to establish regional security arrangements, see *al-Majalla* 31 Mar.–6 Apr. 1993: 34–35; *al-Sharq al-Awsat* 14 Apr. 1995: 4. Mubarak repeatedly called on Pakistan and Afghanistan to halt the activities of the Egyptian fundamentalists in their countries and to hand over their leaders. An extradition treaty was signed with Pakistan in 1994, which has resulted in the deportation of several Egyptian nationals from the country. Egypt pressed hard with its campaign against foreign-based terrorist groups following the bombing in November 1995 of its embassy in Islamabad, Pakistan. See "Suicide Bomber in Pakistan Kills 15 at Egypt's Embassy," *New York Times* 20 Nov. 1995: A3; *al-Sharq al-Awsat* 16 Dec. 1995: 4.

33. See Elaine Sciolino, "Egypt Warned U.S. of Terror, Mubarak Says," *New York Times* 5 Apr. 1993: A6.

34. See *al-Sharq al-Awsat* 8 May 1995: 5; Cherif Cordahi, "Egypt: Facilitating Extradition," *Middle East International* 12 May 1995: 12.

35. For a rebuttal of this view, see John L. Esposito, *The Islamic Threat: Myth or Reality?* (Oxford: Oxford University Press, 1992). Mubarak's call for an international campaign against terrorism finally found a receptive audience with the convening of an antiterrorist, pro-peace international summit in Sharm el-Sheikh, Egypt, in mid-March 1996, immediately following a rash of suicide bombings by the Palestinian militant Islamic movement Hamas, which killed about sixty Israelis. The summit, which was sponsored by the United States and Egypt and attended by almost thirty world leaders, including those from a dozen Arab countries and Israel, served to vindicate Mubarak's strong antiterrorist stance. See Todd S. Purdum, "Nations Pledge Effort to Halt Violence," *New York Times* 14 Mar. 1996: A1; Steven Erlanger, "Meeting's Message: Singular Show of Mideast Solidarity Puts Mideast Terrorists on Notice," *New York Times* 14 Mar. 1996: A10.

36. Today Ba'thist-nationalist Iraq is mounting a "religious campaign," under the guidance of Saddam Hussein, emphasizing religious education and values in public life. Surely religion provides a source of inner strength and some comfort for Iraqis in the face of increasing hardships in their daily lives resulting from the international sanctions. See *al-Sharq al-Awsat* 14 Apr. 1995: 2. Even supposedly secularist Turkey is using Islam for state purposes as it now faces a growing Islamic movement. The government-licensed and -operated religious schools (the *imam-hatip*) have mushroomed of late. See John Darnton, "Discontent Seethes in Once-Stable Turkey," *New York Times* 2 Mar. 1995: A1, A8. Turkey is even using Islam to counter the rising Kurdish nationalism there by asserting that the latter is fratricidal, serving only to split the Muslims of Turkey, and is therefore anti-Muslim.

37. See Albrecht Metzger, "Islamists Set the Social and Political Agenda in Egypt," *Middle*

East International 20 Jan. 1995: 16. For example, the fundamentalists' notion of *takfir wa qital* (declaring people as apostates and hence sanctioning their killing) is very prominent in Wahhabi thought and behavior, which is based on the strict Hanbali school of Islamic jurisprudence. See Mamoun Fandy, "The Tensions behind the Violence in Egypt," *Middle East Policy* 2 (1993): 32.

38. The Qur'an (2:143) describes the Muslim community as *umma wasat*, or a justly balanced and middle-of-the-road community.

39. The position of the mainstream Islamist leaders is best exemplified in the rebuttal and refutation of Abdul Salam Farag's book *al-Farida al-Gha'iba* by Muhammad 'Amara and the *fatwa* (religious opinion) of the late Sheikh al-Azhar, Jad al-Haqq Ali Jad al-Haqq. See 'Amara, *al-Farida al-Gha'iba* (The absent commandment) (Cairo: Dar Thabet lil-Nashr, 1982). On the *fatwa*, see Johannes J. G. Jansen, *The Neglected Duty: The Creed of Sadat's Assassins and Islamic Resurgence in the Middle East* (New York: Macmillan, 1989), 54–60.

40. The Kharijites developed as a result of the struggle between Ali and Mu'awiyya (governor of Syria) over the leadership of the Muslim community, which took place shortly after Ali's selection as caliph in A.D. 656. They faulted Ali for his acceptance of the principle of arbitration in settling the dispute with Mu'awiyya, declared his action un-Islamic, and killed him. The Kharijites were the first sectarian movement in Islam to establish the right to rebel against a ruler who deviates from the Qur'an and the *Sunna* (prophetic traditions). Such a ruler should be declared non-Muslim and therefore must be deposed and put to death.

41. Although the government-appointed Mufti (chief jurist–theologian), Muhammad Sayyid Tantawi—now Sheikh al-Azhar—issued a ruling (*fatwa*) legalizing interest on government investment bonds, his decision was strongly attacked. The then Sheikh al-Azhar, Isma'il Sadiq al-Adawi, called the Mufti's *fatwa* "a mistake leading to eternal doom." Quoted in Alan Cowell, "Stirrings of Capitalism Shake a Muslim Egypt," *New York Times* 7 Dec. 1989: A16. The *ulama* of al-Azhar also rejected the idea of Rushdie's visit because of his "blasphemous" book *The Satanic Verses*, and the visit was denied. See *al-Majalla* 31 Mar.–6 Apr. 1993: 16. They also strongly opposed the United Nations Conference on Population and Development in Cairo in September 1994, characterizing its agenda as contrary to Islam.

42. See Emmanuel Sivan, *Radical Islam: Medieval Theology and Modern Politics* (New Haven, Conn.: Yale University Press, 1990) 143–47; Fauzi M. Najjar, "The Application of Shari'a Laws in Egypt," *Middle East Policy* 1. 3 (1992): 62–73; Najjar, "Egypt's Laws of Personal Status," *Arab Studies Quarterly* 10 (Summer 1988): 319–44.

43. In an interview in 1994, Dr. Hussein Kamil Baha' al-Din, Egypt's minister of education, admitted the Islamists' wide penetration of schools all over Egypt: "I couldn't believe how many fundamentalist teachers we had in the schools." Quoted in Weaver, "The Novelist and the Sheikh," 64. See also Chris Hedges, "In Islam's War, Students Fight on the Front Line," *New York Times* 4 Oct. 1994: A4.

44. In the 1992 local elections, the Ikhwan–Socialist Labor Party alliance won 115 districts. See Fandy, "Egypt's Islamic Group," 624.

45. See Judith Miller, "The Islamic Wave," *New York Times Magazine* 31 May 1992: 42; Metzger, "Islamists Set the Social and Political Agenda in Egypt," 16.

46. See *al-Majalla* 4–10 June 1993: 20–25; Youssef M. Ibrahim, "Egypt Fights Militant Islam with More of the Same," *New York Times* 18 Aug. 1993: A3.

47. See *al-Majalla* 13–19 Feb. 1994: 23–36; *al-Sharq al-Awsat* 28 Jan. 1994: 1. See also Deborah Pugh, "Court Case Casts Doubts on Secularism in Egypt," *Christian Science Moni-*

tor 24 June 1993: 1, 4. In June 1995, after two years of controversy and rejection, Dr. Abu Zeid was finally promoted to professor. See *al-Majalla* 25 June–1 July 1995: 31; *al-Sharq al-Awsat* 23 June 1995: 4. In January 1996, an appellate court upheld the ruling against Dr. Abu Zeid and ordered the annulment of his marriage. The couple is now in the Netherlands, where Dr. Abu Zeid is on sabbatical. See *al-Sharq al-Awsat* 12 Jan. 1996: 4.

48. See *al-Majalla* 18–24 July 1993: 22–28, 1–7 Aug. 1993: 20–25. See also Ibrahim, "Egypt Fights Militant Islam with More of the Same."

49. According to the Cairo-based Ibn Khaldun Center, there was a 30 percent drop in acts of violence in 1994 compared to 1993. See Metzger, "Islamists Set the Social and Political Agenda in Egypt," 16.

50. See *al-Sharq al-Awsat* 13 Feb. 1995: 2, 1 May 1995: 4.

51. For further elaboration on this theme, see Dennis J. Sullivan, *Private Voluntary Organizations in Egypt: Islamic Development, Private Initiative and State Control* (Gainesville: University Press of Florida, 1994).

52. See Weaver, "The Novelist and the Sheikh," 64. The government was successful in banning the *niqab*, which covers the hair, neck, and face, but not the *hijab*, which covers just the hair and neck. A court ruling struck down the ban on the *hijab* as "an infringement on personal liberties." See Hedges, "In Islam's War, Students Fight on the Front Line."

53. According to Mubarak, only when parties have popular bases or foundations can we speak about alternating governments between parties through elections. See *al-Sharq al-Awsat* 14 May 1991: 5. Certainly this will not be easy to achieve in Egypt, where parties were originally constituted in 1976 by a government decree, not by popular will, and they remain subject to political whims. Also, the ruling party's customary hegemony has emasculated the opposition parties and stifled their development and institutionalization.

54. According to Human Rights Watch, the number of Islamists in Egyptian jails in 1994 topped 40,000; there were some 6,000 in 1993. This large number of political prisoners is something unprecedented in Egypt's modern history. See Weaver, "The Novelist and the Sheikh," 62. Since January 1995 more than 130 members of the Ikhwan have been arrested, and 54 leaders have been sentenced to prison terms by a military court. See Chris Hedges, "Mubarak's Challenge," *New York Times* 3 Apr. 1995: A2; Peter Waldman, "As Egypt Suppresses Muslim Brotherhood, Some Fear Backlash," *Wall Street Journal* 8 Dec. 1995: A1; Douglas Jehl, "In the Face of Criticism, Egypt Sentences 54 Muslim Leaders," *New York Times* 24 Nov. 1995: A11; *al-Sharq al-Awsat* 25 Nov. 1995: 4.

55. With more than 400 seats of the 444-seat parliament controlled by the ruling National Democratic Party and its supporters, opposition is practically nonexistent. This raised serious questions about the honesty and legality of the 1995 election and led to demands by the opposition parties for its nullification. See "Ruling Party in Egypt Wins Big Majority," *New York Times* 8 Dec. 1995: A6; *al-Sharq al-Awsat* 1 Dec. 1995: 1, 30 Dec. 1995: 1, 2; Douglas Jehl, "Egyptians Vote Today, but Islamic Opposition Group Is Barred," *New York Times* 29 Nov. 1995: A7; Waldman, "As Egypt Suppresses Muslim Brotherhood, Some Fear Backlash."

56. Quoted in *al-Sharq al-Awsat* 1 May 1995: 4.

57. See *al-Sharq al-Awsat* 1 May 1995: 4. In line with its heavy-handed policy, the Mubarak government passed a controversial strict law on journalism in the summer of 1995, stipulating a severe punishment of up to fifteen years in jail for libel against the president and cabinet members and their families. See Youssef M. Ibrahim, "Behind the Smiles, Egypt Tells Mubarak to Shape Up," *New York Times* 3 July 1995: 3.

58. Election rules are tailored to ensure one result: that Mubarak's National Democratic

Party will always be in the lead and thus stay in power. Opposition parties remain undeveloped and largely ineffective as instruments of opposition; they are not allowed full freedom to contest the government.

59. This is evident in the reprinting of liberal classics such as Ali Abdul Raziq's *al-Islam wa Usul al-Hukm* (Islam and the principles of government), Taha Hussein's *Fi Mustaqbal al-Thaqafa fi Misr* (The future of culture in Egypt), Naguib Mahfouz's banned novel *Children of Geblawi*, and Salama Musa's *Freedom of Expression*. All of these were attacked earlier by the conservative *ulama*, and some were even condemned as un-Islamic.

60. On this theme, see Fandy, "Egypt's Islamic Group," 607–25. See also Rifaat Sid Ahmad, "Al-Islamiyyun, al-Sulta, wa al-Irhab" (The Islamists, the authority, and terrorism), *Middle East Affairs Journal* 2 (Spring/Summer 1994): 71–82.

61. Such as the attempt on Mubarak's life in Addis Ababa, Ethiopia, in late June 1995. See Robin Wright, "History Points to Islamic Extremists in Attack on Mubarak," *Los Angeles Times* 27 June 1995: A12.

62. There is a general perception that official corruption is becoming endemic and that the government is growing more and more stale and unimaginative under the same cabinet members, some of whom have been in office since the early 1980s. Prime Minister Atif Sidqi, who stepped down in early January 1996, had been in office since 1986, the longest term in office in Egypt's modern history. And Mubarak, in office since 1981, ran for his third six-year term in 1993 and had no competition.

The new cabinet, formed in January 1996 under Prime Minister Kamal al-Ganzouri, is mostly a replica of the previous one. Only seven ministers out of thirty-two are new. The rest, including the premier, are holdovers who have been serving as ministers for the past ten to fifteen years. All this led some Egyptians to suggest comically that the old cabinet resigned for one day only to be back the next day. See Mamoun Fandy, "The Tension behind the Violence in Egypt," *Christian Science Monitor* 2 Dec. 1992: 18; Deborah Pugh, "Discontent Surrounds Start of Mubarak's Third Term," *Christian Science Monitor* 12 Oct. 1993: 6; Ibrahim, "Behind the Smiles, Egypt Tells Mubarak to Shape Up." See also *al-Sharq al-Awsat* 3 Jan. 1996: 1, 5 Jan. 1996: 5; Douglas Jehl, "Egyptians Get a New Premier and Hopes for the Economy," *New York Times* 5 Jan. 1996: A8.

63. Despite pressure from international agencies, such as the International Monetary Fund and the World Bank, to expedite the course of privatization, Mubarak is still wary of pressing ahead lest doing so exacerbate social tension and cause unrest, leading to a repetition of the January 1977 food-price riots. Indeed, much of Egypt's industrial structure (more than 70 percent) remains government-owned and inefficient.

The new government is not expected to augur a major shift in economic policy. In the words of Mubarak: "The government will change but not its programme." Quoted in Steve Negus, "Mubarak's New Government," *Middle East International* 19 Jan. 1996: 13.

64. In fact, more than half of the annual U.S. aid to Egypt ($1.3 billion out of $2.1 billion) is earmarked for the military. See John Lancaster, "Praised Abroad, Egypt's Ruler Faltering at Home," *Washington Post* 13 Mar. 1995: A12.

65. Mubarak has refused to name a vice-president as a successor, creating a volatile situation and one fraught with danger.

4

The Islamist Challenge in Algeria

Unlike Egypt, Algeria has no tradition of early Islamic revivalism. Nor does it have a deeply rooted history as a political entity or a well-defined national identity. The country was molded largely by France in the nineteenth century to suit its colonial purposes. The colonization of Algeria was both long (1831–1962) and intense, seeking the assimilation and incorporation of the country as an integral part of France: not a colony in the traditional sense, but a *département* or province. The aim was to Frenchify—to cast Algeria in the image of France culturally, linguistically, and even demographically—through the proliferation of the French *colones* (colonial settlements) and the associated displacement and restructuring of the native population.[1] French influences were thoroughly woven into the fabric of the society, diluting indigenous culture and identity. This powerful colonial legacy would leave an indelible mark on Algeria's quest for national community—one that persisted even when independence was achieved; the country continues to grapple with the deep Francophone-Arabist schism and the generally overlapping prevalent Berber-Arab cleavage.[2]

The pervasive French cultural and educational influences were ascendant throughout much of Algeria's colonial existence. A European-like secular culture developed and became predominant, especially in the urban centers. In the absence of a counterbalancing Islamic reform movement, Islam remained essentially marginal in public life, confined to the rural Sufi orders (the *marabout*, or cult of the holy men),[3] with their traditional ritualism, and to the few urban-based networks of the *ulama* (religious scholars) dealing primarily with religious and social issues and morals. Islam was largely devoid of a dynamic, activist spirit. Certainly the French would not have tolerated any form of Islamic revivalism that might have threatened their rule. Nor were the French-educated Algerians susceptible to a revivalist call in light of the fact that many of them associated religion with the rituals and backward practices of the *marabouts*.

The one exception to Islamic dormancy was the founding in 1931 by Sheikh Abdul Hamid Ben Badis (1889–1940) of the Association of the Algerian Muslim Ulama. Basically reformist, its purpose was to deliver Islam from the polluted and corrupt innovations of the Sufis through a cultural and educational revival, with emphasis on the original sources and the ways of *al-salaf* (the pious ancestors of early Islam). The movement championed a reformed, *salafi* (invoking ancestral heritage) Islam against the rural traditional Islam of the "holy" men. It also sought to renew interest in the Arabic language, which was falling into disuse, and to raise the standard of education among native Algerians through religious Qur'anic schools.

The movement soon became more involved in the initial nationalist demands for equal rights and preservation of a distinctive Muslim identity. While rejecting the notion that Algerian Muslims could become Frenchmen, the movement stopped short of challenging French rule. It remained essentially a reformist religious association, with no tradition of political activism. This was implied in Ben Badis's slogan, "Islam is my religion, Arabic is my language, Algeria is my homeland," the enunciation of a stance counter to Europeanization.[4]

The message of the reformers laid the foundation of an Algerian national Muslim consciousness and identity that would give stimulus to the revolution in 1954, which initiated the war of independence (1954–1962). As the revolutionary momentum swept the country, the Islamic reform movement became a constituent part of the wartime FLN (National Liberation Front), and by 1956, it was completely subsumed. The paramount position of the FLN, with its predominantly secularist-modernist orientation, established the supremacy of the mostly French-educated secular leaders and the subordination of the *ulama*. The FLN looked upon Islam simply as one important element of national and cultural identity. Its stance was far from a commitment to religion.

Thus, when Islam came to prominence during the struggle for independence in the 1950s, it was more as a Third World nationalist force than as a religious revivalist force. The emergent nationalist movement was a militant anticolonial movement that utilized Islamic sentiments to bring about the mobilization of the populace in the battle for liberation. Colonial France was rejected by the assertion of native Islamic culture and identity; religion was honored more for form than for substance. Hence, the initial declaration of the Algerian revolution in November 1954, calling for the establishment of an independent sovereign state "within the framework of Islamic principles,"[5] was an appealing linguistic construct that did not materialize in Algerian public life. The worldly FLN took control of the future Algerian state and shaped it in accord with its own secularist vision—in the French, not Islamic mold.

Accordingly, the tradition of secularism continued after independence in 1962. Over roughly the next thirty years, the National Liberation Front, which became Algeria's sole ruling political party,[6] steered the country in a modern socialist direction, depriving Islam of a public role and relegating it to the status of a cultural element in the makeup of Algerian nationhood and identity, with no legal or political implications.[7] The FLN-run state followed the logic of its own nationalist *raison d' état*, not Islamic doctrine. At best, it paid lip service to Islam, while strictly controlling the religious establishment and the interpretation of Islam. Thus, in 1966, the state constituted the Higher Islamic Council as the sole authoritative body to render *fatwa* (religious-legal opinion).[8] In fact, official Islam became part of the state bureaucracy under the supervision of the Ministry of Religious Affairs.

In the end, neither Islam nor Arabic—the language of Islam—enjoyed much esteem or status. Islam was used to justify state socialism, and Arabic (despite a crash program of Arabization in the 1970s) remained the language of the half-educated young urban poor—the disenfranchised—secondary to French for purposes of social mobility. Ironically, French became more widespread, due to the expansion of education and the continued use of French in the growing state bureaucracy, even after more than thirty years of independence.[9] Arabo-Islamic education was cast as inferior and therefore undesirable. Throughout much of the 1960s and 1970s, the Algerian state, under the European-molded party-military-bureaucratic elite, remained largely unaffected by the pull of Islam felt elsewhere.

Although Islam was generally dormant during these two decades, it underwent occasional revivifying moments before the rise of the Islamic Salvation Front (FIS) thrust Algeria into the throes of Islamic fundamentalism—political Islam. Early manifestations of Islamic dissatisfaction with the secularist course appeared shortly after independence, with the emergence of the first autonomous Islamic movement: Jam'iyat al-Qiyam al-Islamiyya (the Association for Islamic Values). Founded in 1964 by Sheikh Ahmad Sahnoun—a disciple of Ben Badis's reform movement—along with Muhammad Khider, a revolutionay war hero,[10] al-Qiyam advocated restoration of Islamic values and ethos and adherence to Islamic principles in social life generally. It was critical of destructive foreign cultural influences on the moral fiber of Islamic society. Though emphasizing mainly the societal-ethical dimension, its message was laced with antimodernism and antisecularism. Hence, despite its ostensibly apolitical nature, the movement was suppressed by President Houari Boumedienne[11] in 1966, and its leading figure, Muhammad Khider, was assassinated the following year. The movement was formally banned in 1970, but its ideas did not wither away.

Islamic revivalism surfaced again toward the end of the 1970s and in the early 1980s, the outcome, not surprisingly, of President Boumedienne's leftward socialist-Marxist revolution, state bureaucratic elitism, and cultural revolution. His nationalization policies extended to seizure of private small businesses and expropriation of farmland, and the consequent disaffection of great numbers of Algerians took an Islamic form against alien Marxist state socialism. The socialist state-run economy promoted a new class of modernists,

French-educated technocrats with special privileges and status that set them apart. A new caste of overlords—the nomenclature—ran the country as its fiefdom, singing the promises of socialism and living the lives of capitalism. The common people's resentment was increasingly expressed in terms of Islamic egalitarianism, preaching the values of social equality and justice.

Meanwhile, Boumedienne's cultural revolution—the Arabization program—which he pursued in earnest as a means to confirm the regime's Arab revolutionary credentials and to link with the populace at the cultural-emotive level, meant that many Algerians found themselves at a standstill. The Arabisants (Arabic-educated), with their Arabic-centered mediocre schooling, were at a distinct disadvantage when it came to social mobility in a system that continued—despite its Arabist rhetoric—to value French. The new urban migrants felt betrayed by a self-proclaimed socialist regime whose Islam was all pretense and who had little use for the Arabic tongue.[12] It was those multitudes of disillusioned—the underclass—who provided the legions of recruits for the Islamic movement in the late 1980s.

Although some of the regime's policies would foment, albeit indirectly, a future Islamic revival, no significant Islamic challenge was posed to the regime. Throughout much of the 1970s, state authoritarianism coupled with state welfarism—both fully developed and institutionalized under Boumedienne—served to stifle all opposition, Islamic and otherwise. The authoritarian state, resting on single-party (FLN) rule and supported by the military and the security apparatus, built and operated a comprehensive network of controls over all aspects of the nation's life. The state kept a tight rein on Islamic spaces—places of worship, religious education, and religious foundations—thereby effectively nationalizing Islam. Further, it turned official Islam into a "government mouthpiece," thereby monopolizing religion.

On the distribution level, the state welfare system was still solvent—thanks to substantial oil and gas revenues—and therefore able to meet the primary demands of the people.[13] Welfare services ranged from foodstuffs, education, and job opportunities to medical care. The promised development and prosperity were the substitute for political participation: a condition akin to the Stalinist model of development at the expense of freedom. Thus, the regime was able to maintain a semblance of legitimacy based upon an implicit social contract— "We take care of you, we rule over you"—an arrangement common to all other Arab authoritarian systems. In addition, despite rampant official corruption and economic mismanagement, it still could invoke the heroic revolutionary war—the liberation struggle and the role of the "historic chiefs" who launched it in 1954—to buttress its standing. The legitimacy formula anchored to oil, state welfare, and revolutionary mythology remained operational during the Boumedienne years and helped to halt Islamism.

Only after the death of Boumedienne in 1978 was there a sign of Islamic opposition, with the rise of Rabitat al-Da'wa al-Islamiyya (the League of the Islamic Call) in the early 1980s. In fact, the Islamic movement in Algeria is a

product of the worsening conditions in the 1980s. The effects of years of socialist economic mismanagement, official corruption, and bureaucratic fiat
came home to roost during the successor regime of Chadli Benjedid: high
unemployment, educational decline, agricultural failure and food dependency,
overpopulation, rural migration and the attendant urban bloat and decay, and
exorbitant foreign debt—and the list goes on. These crises were compounded
by the precipitous tumble in oil prices, inducing mounting deficits, general
economic stagnation, and deteriorating social services. Once the exemplar of
Third World development, Algeria was becoming more and more like Egypt.

With the country seemingly near the abyss, the old legitimacy formula began to unravel. Neither the authoritarian state nor the welfare system was able
to hold on under the heavy weight of hard times. The authoritarian structure
was cracking. Further, the mystique of the revolutionary war had virtually
dissipated as people were being swamped by the harsh realities of daily existence.

State dictatorship gave way to Benjedid's economic liberalization and political relaxation. One can conjecture that Benjedid, who had been the compromise presidential candidate of the ruling political-military establishment,
lacked his predecessor's power and stature. A colorless colonel, he had been
chosen more for his neutrality and malleability than for his audacity and
assertiveness. The regime's change in direction was reflective of his leadership style: less command and coercion and more openness and concession.

The shift did not alleviate, but instead aggravated the economic difficulties. Like Sadat's *infitah* (openness), Benjedid's moves promoted a "new class"
of entrepreneurs and middlemen made fat by the opportunities afforded by
the open domestic economy, by international companies, or by connections to
the ruling elite.[14] And the lives of the overwhelming majority of Algerians
continued to deteriorate; disparities between the haves and the have-nots grew
ever wider. To those who hurt most, the new openness seemed directed more
toward meeting the needs and requirements of integration into the global
economy—as stipulated by the international financial agencies, such as the
International Monetary Fund (IMF), or the foreign lending governments, the
Western powers and Japan—than toward ameliorating the economic pain of
Algerians.

These circumstances were fertile ground for the Islamic movement. Its
growth corresponded with the revelations of a tired and confused state socialism and corrupt authoritarianism. The Islamists came to public prominence in
the 1980s as a consequence of government failure and public discontent, not
of a burst of pietism. The emergence of the League of the Islamic Call early in
the decade set the stage for the challenge to the state by Islamic groups; this
opposition would reach its zenith late in that same decade with the birth of the
FIS.

Under the League, the Islamic movement was largely amorphous; it had no
organized structure, coherent program, or central leadership. And, most of all,

it was not a mass movement. It revolved primarily around a number of diverse leaders such as Sheikh Ahmad Sahnoun, Sheikh Abdullatif Sultani, Abbas Madani, Mahfouz Nahnah, and Abdullah Jab,[15] all of whom advocated a moral and social overhaul in accordance with Islamic principles. Therefore, adoption of these principles was a requisite to stem the detested modern *jahiliyya* (pagan) conditions—brought into being by Western values—and to achieve the nation's salvation. Though the message was not explicitly political, it pointed toward the exercise of political power to bring about the desired transformation.[16]

Still, at that early point, the Islamic movement did not overtly represent a national front with open political ambition. Instead, it was more in the mold of Muslim conservatism—demanding thorough Arabization, the implementation of Islamic personal status laws, a ban on alcoholic beverages, and enforcement of public morals—than an organized political movement. Thus, the Benjedid government did not see it as an imminent threat and even implicitly acquiesced in the proliferation of its activities: mosques, universities, charitable organizations, neighborhood social welfare services, and religious and moral propagation as enjoined in the Muslim dictum "to command that which is righteous and to forbid that which is reprehensible." Throughout the 1980s, the Islamists managed to build a network of independent mosques and religious centers, especially in city slums, small towns, and depressed rural areas—all outside the control of the government. In fact, Benjedid quietly abetted the Islamists early on so as to check the power of other contenders, mainly leftist students, hard-line Boumediennist socialists, Berberist (the Kabyle) forces,[17] and feminist groups, in an effort to consolidate his position and to carry out his reforms.

Despite the Islamic movement's growing power, throughout much of the decade it remained largely limited as a national force and rather manageable by the government. It was not yet a mass movement. Thus, when clashes between Islamists and leftist groups on campuses in the early 1980s escalated into violent confrontations, the government moved to control the Islamists. Some of their leaders were arrested and then released, and a few members were brought to trial—measures that fell short of completely silencing the movement. The government's indecisiveness and irresolution in dealing with the Islamists were a manifestation of its equivocal stance and the lax and fluid political context under Benjedid.[18] However, things changed when a militant faction led by Mustafa Bouyali—a former *mujahid* (holy warrior) in the war of independence—took up armed struggle in the mid-1980s. In this first open Islamic rebellion against the state, the government acted decisively to crush the group, killing its leader and many of his supporters and giving long prison terms to others.[19] For most of the decade, the government generally kept the Islamic movement within bounds.

What marked the metamorphosis of the Islamic movement into a mass movement and catapulted it center stage were the October 1988 riots, which swept the principal cities and gave rise to the FIS. The upheaval revealed the dismal failure of Benjedid's policies and the overwhelming popular rejection of the degenerate FLN-run state, demonstrating the rift between state and society. To many of those born following independence in 1962 (over 70 percent of the populace), it was apparent that the post-colonial state had failed them and was no longer legitimate. Calling in the army to restore order, which exacted a toll of 200 to 500 lives, was no remedy. A new social consensus was an imperative. Its achievement was Algeria's predicament.[20] The course and pace of change that followed—full and immediate democratization—soon plunged the country into chaos. A new constitution adopted in February 1989 terminated the power monopoly of the FLN and established a multiparty parliamentary democracy. Within a year, more than fifty parties materialized. Still, the appeal of democratization and political openness was short-lived. A civil polity under a new social contract remains elusive.

The FIS arose from the massive civil disturbances and crystallized, under the new constitutional changes, as the principal Islamist movement when Abbas Madani and a group of radical Islamists, such as Ali Belhaj, split from the League of the Islamic Call and formed their own organization in February 1989. It was officially recognized as a legal party in August 1989, despite the legal prohibition on religious, regional, or ethnic political parties[21]—a status that most Arab countries have resisted granting.

Unlike the new secular parties, the FIS's popular-protest origins and its fundamentalist Islamic doctrine put it on a collision course with the post-independence, secularist-nationalist structures and culture that had prospered under the military-political establishment. Although the FIS is an amalgam of divergent tendencies, especially moderate and radical groups, the movement in general is against the secular nation-state, calling for an Islamic system based on *Shari'a* (Islamic law). In its eyes, the Algerian state is not an Islamic state: it does not follow the commandments of God or the ethics of Islam. The FIS mission therefore is to bring about the re-Islamization of society, using the movement's extensive network of neighborhood mosques, social services centers, religious study groups, and health clinics to work its way into local and national governments.[22] Accordingly, with two diametrically opposed visions of society—secular versus Islamic—the fault lines in the Algerian struggle are deeper by far and more potentially destabilizing than their equivalent in Egypt.

The opening of the political process following the 1988 upheaval thrust the Islamic Salvation Front to the forefront in the struggle against the status quo. Its stunning victories in the June 1990 municipal elections (the first free elections in twenty-eight years) and subsequently in the December 1991 national election showed up the stark contrast of opposites: a losing ruling elitist party and a triumphant oppositional popularist party.

At the local level, the FIS captured more than 55 percent of the municipal councils and about two-thirds of the provincial assemblies.[23] In the first round of the national election, which included more than fifty parties, it came in first with 188 seats, only 28 seats short of a majority in the 430-seat National Assembly; the FLN was third (15 seats), trailing the Socialist Forces Front (25 seats).[24] It is ironic that the two leading parties were Islamist and Berberist—testimony to the lack of a rallying national movement to substitute for the pulverized FLN. Indeed, many of the new political parties were composed merely of personal followers of those leaders who were old FLN members, imbued with the same authoritarian political culture.

The magnitude of the victory gave the FIS a sense of empowerment in fulfilling its mission to deliver state and society from the decadent order. It stood as the only possible successor to the FLN and the secular elite and offered a coherent and appealing alternative. The general motto "Islam is the solution," in reference to the severe economic ills—but carrying little by way of specific remedies—is reflective of the notion of religious deliverance, something that many of the desperate and despondent young were ready to accept.[25] That belief was shared by most other fundamentalists throughout the Arab world, who hailed the Algerian Islamists' victories as harbingers.[26]

Indeed, the elections, which Abbas Madani, leader of the Islamic Salvation Front, was willing to try, only confirmed what he had always maintained: his party had a "mandate from God."[27] This was in concert with the party slogan: "To vote against the FIS is to vote against God."[28] Thus, the FIS, unlike any other party, presented itself as a divine expression of the popular will (the Muslim *umma*). As such, once in power, it would be inconceivable to dislodge it by voting it out. Surely this is far from a commitment to democracy; it runs contrary to the democratic assumption of the right of an electorate to vote for change in periodic elections.

The fact is that many votes were cast for the Muslim fundamentalists in protest against the corrupt rule of the National Liberation Front rather than in support of an Islamic state. The FIS was the vehicle of nay saying. Its two largest blocs were the believers who heeded the Islamic call and the host of Algerians disenchanted with thirty years of mismanagement, malfeasance, and impropriety.[29] The overwhelming fundamentalist victory nevertheless aroused the anxicty of many Algerians who feared the changes it portended. The Islamic Salvation Front's generally theocratic views were inimical to secular traditions and institutions. Its assured hegemony in parliament and its coveting of the presidency—Abbas Madani repeatedly demanded a presidential election, hoping to become Algeria's first Islamist president[30]—augured an altered constitution and the establishment of Islamic law.

Surely these prospects would have derailed the nascent democratic process, but the army was quick to step in and stymie the process in order to preempt the fundamentalists. The emergent fundamentalist-secularist dichotomy as to the vision of Algeria and the intervention of the military—the bastion of secularism—would ultimately plunge the country into its worst political violence since the war of independence.

Unlike Egypt's military, the Algerian military—the real power center of the state and the sole "kingmaker" of presidents since independence[31]—had taken the lead in the fight against the fundamentalists. In fact, the top echelon had been lukewarm, at best, to Benjedid's opening of the system, fearing that liberalization would divest the military establishment of its role. Rooted in a bloody and prolonged liberation struggle, the army has always had strong political proclivities and perceived itself to be the guardian of the Algerian national state. But, above all, its equally strong secularist orientation made it particularly wary of the FIS and deeply skeptical of the merits of sanctioning the Islamic party, a legally questionable move.[32] The military felt extremely threatened by the sudden surge of the Islamists, and, unlike Benjedid, who showed a willingness to deal with them and to work out "a framework for cohabitation,"[33] it was not amenable to sharing power, was vehemently opposed to the notion of Islamic rule, and was determined to stop it.

The first showdown occurred in May-June 1991, a year after the FIS won its impressive victories in the local elections; demonstrations and strikes protested changes in the election laws, introduced just before the national election (scheduled for late June 1991), that presumably would favor FLN candidates. With thousands of jobless youths on the streets of Algiers "on the barricades," clashes with the military resulted in dozens of deaths and the arrest of about 3,000, including the leader, Abbas Madani, and his top lieutenant, Ali Belhaj; the imposition of martial law for four months; and the suspension of the scheduled national election.[34] For the second time in three years, intervention demonstrated the army's special role as the protector of state security.

The army crackdown and the absence of leadership put the movement increasingly under the influence of the extremists, who sought to radicalize it. At the same time, moderate Islamic organizations, such as Hamas (the Movement for Islamic Society), under Sheikh Mahfouz Nahnah, and al-Nahda al-Islamiyya (the Islamic Renaissance), under Sheikh Abdullah Jab, declared a break with the FIS leadership,[35] but—contrary to the military's expectations of a weakening Islamic challenge—the ensuing divisions contributed to the proliferation of militant groups, and the situation worsened. This was especially so after the army coup of Defense Minister Khalid Nizar on January 11, 1992, which forced Benjedid's resignation (two years before the conclusion of his third term), set aside the results of the December national election, and cancelled the upcoming second round. The ongoing military-fundamentalist vicious cycle of violence did not abate.

Many radical elements subsequently left the FIS to form the rebellious groups that have since been battling the security forces. Chief among them were the Islamic Guards (former followers of Bouyali's insurgency); the Algerian Afghans (veterans of the Afghan *mujahideen* struggle against the Soviet occupation); the Apostasy and Flight Organization (a radical ideological group, with no relationship to its Egyptian namesake, that accused those who follow the democratic path of apostasy); and the Algerianized faction, al-

Jaz'ara (a group that started out as moderate, but that became radicalized in the wake of government repression).[36] These groups later coalesced to form two major militant clusters: the Armed Islamic Group (GIA) and the Islamic Salvation Army (the FIS military wing).

The Muslim insurgents, especially the GIA, strongly opposed Abbas Madani's moderate stance and vowed to bring down the government by force and install an Islamic state. They pursued a violent and bloody course, denouncing their opponents as *kuffar* (apostates), who therefore must be killed. Today it is clearly evident that the imprisoned FIS leadership is in charge of neither the GIA nor the Islamic Salvation Army, which together spearhead the relentless Islamic *jihad* (holy war) against the state.

Under the pretext of order and stability, the military suspended the nascent democratic process altogether. The newly instituted democratic procedures—elections, voting, parties, assemblies, and so on—could not assuage the intense fears evoked by the prospects of a fundamentalist parliament, with an agenda akin to that of some of the fundamentalist-controlled town councils. This was especially true in light of the excessive social code and agenda some of the Muslim municipalities imposed: closing down movie theaters, segregating coeducational schools, banning alcohol production and consumption, and harassing women in Western dress.[37] The problem was that Algerian democracy was introduced at a time of social upheaval and the simultaneous brewing up of a potent Islamic movement whose ideology raised the specter of social and political regimentation.

The question that arises, then, is: should democracy be equated with the formal act of free elections and majority rule regardless of the outcome? More than a century and a half ago Alexis de Tocqueville, in the classic *Democracy in America*, grappled with the issue of majority rule deteriorating into tyranny. The Algerian elections presented the Arab world with a similar quandary: how to implement democracy without risking a fundamentalist triumph that could conceivably turn state and society topsy-turvy and even vitiate the very notion of democracy.[38] This is especially vexatious in view of the Islamic Salvation Front's vague and inconsistent pronouncements in regard to democracy, which cause anxiety as to its actual intentions.[39] It is evident that, in the absence of rooted democratic traditions and values and in the presence of a lingering authoritarian subculture, the attempted transition to democracy was hazardous and tenuous.[40] Democracy easily gave way to fear and was undone by the specter of a fundamentalist sweep.

Shortly after the military takeover, a five-man High State Council (presidential council) was formed to fill the presidency, and Muhammad Boudiaf—a revolutionary war hero in exile in Morocco since 1965—was called upon to be its head. Essentially, the council was the handmaiden of the military, formed to provide a semblance of legitimacy for indirect army rule—Boudiaf and successor presidents were mere figureheads appointed by the military.

The government, acting under a declared state of emergency, then arrested more of the FIS leaders and detained thousands of its supporters in desert camps, banned the party as illegal, annulled both the national and the local elections, and dissolved the assemblies. The new regime also undertook drastic measures against the Islamists' autonomous networks centered mainly around their independent mosques, replacing thousands of imams (religious preachers) and closing down many private mosques.[41] (In Algeria, the FIS local power is centered around the neighborhood mosque: the command and operation center.) Meanwhile, entire neighborhoods in Algiers, mostly poor and pro-Islamist, were put under virtual siege by heavily armed security forces. The military rejected out of hand coexistence with or accommodation to fundamentalism. The strategy was confrontation and repression.

A countercampaign of vicious violence by extremist elements of the FIS and armed Islamist factions was the result. A holy war was proclaimed; senior government officials, army and security officers, and political figures were the first targets. Boudiaf was assassinated in June 1992, a killing shrouded with suspicion and still unresolved.[42] Later came a terroristic drive against intellectuals, judges, journalists, and academicians. Resort to violence led only to more repression and further fragmentation of the Islamic movement. The hard-core militant elements, thrust into the lead as "holy warriors," committed ever more horrific acts.[43]

Since 1993, Muslim militants, especially the Armed Islamic Group, have intensified the terror, bringing the country close to implosion. The escalating violence has targeted civilian professionals in all fields: artists and actors, popular singers and media personalities, schoolteachers and schoolgirls, university professors and students, prominent women, managers of state enterprises and public employees, policemen and soldiers, and foreign nationals. In addition, indiscriminate car bombings and explosions in city streets and residential centers have wreaked havoc. Even the infrastructure—bridges, central warehouses, public buildings, power stations, and schools and institutions of higher education—has not escaped the ravages of the fundamentalists.[44] The climate of fear has provoked the flight of thousands upon thousands of Algerian intellectuals and professionals who feel themselves at risk of assassination, as well as the exodus of the foreign community—thereby sapping significant societal resources and damaging the economy.[45]

The objective of the Muslim militants is to break the government's resolve and bring it down, but the government has responded as before—with repression. It hunts down armed zealots with special forces (commonly called "Ninjas" because of their masks); convenes special antiterrorist courts, which hand down death sentences and long prison terms;[46] conducts sweeping raids of pro-Islamic, poor sections of Algiers; and wantonly violates human rights and liberties under the guise of state security. The toll of violence, now at 40,000 to 50,000 victims, continues to mount.[47] The bloody conflict does not seem to be something foreign to the Algerian character; rather, it somewhat mirrors the revolutionary war. It is as if the country is caught in the grip of

violence. The struggle now is between two polarized indigenous forces battling for the future of post-colonial Algeria. For the Muslim fighters, it is an
extension of the revolution; they seek to implement its Islamic principles, which
were betrayed by the Francophile elite. For the eradicationists in the military,
it is a matter of rooting out the fundamentalists.

Most significant, the fundamentalists have singularly failed to ignite a popular revolution à la Ayatollah Khomeini's against the shah of Iran. This is largely
because notable blocs of Algerians, although not supportive of the coup or the
FLN, are adamantly opposed to a fundamentalist takeover, especially in light
of the Iranian example. They include professional and business groups; a large
number of intellectuals, academics, and journalists; civil administrators;
women's organizations; the Algerian trade union movement (UGTA); leftist
syndicates; and the various socialist-secularist parties. Such liberal and predominantly middle-class cohorts remain committed to a secular vision of the
state as opposed to the fundamentalist religious vision—these two perspec-
tives are in conflict over the very core of Algeria's national life. Although the
antifundamentalists equally wanted to change three decades and more of the
closed power structure, they did not see the Islamists as the change agent.
Equally relevant, they have been completely repulsed by the Muslim extremists' violence and nihilist tactics; they maintain that the fundamentalists simply cannot be entrusted with the reins.

Added to this cauldron is the all-important ethnic factor in the sociocultural configuration of Algeria. The Berber areas, containing 20 percent of the
population and concentrated mainly in the Kabyle region near Algiers, are the
strongholds of the leading secularist and socialist parties such as the Berber-
led Socialist Forces Front (FFS), headed by Huceine Ait Ahmad (a revolutionary war leader), and the Rally for Culture and Democracy (RCD), led by
Said Sadi. They advocate a society that is a secular, democratic, pluralist, and
multicultural—the antithesis of the fundamentalist agenda. Culturally, the
Berbers, although Muslims, are generally against Arabization, preferring
French over Arabic—a legacy of colonial policy. They are similarly against
the imposition of *Shari'a*, aspects of which contravene traditional Berber tribal
customs. Indeed, some Berbers have found themselves in the ironic position
of having to acquiesce to the very state power they have opposed in order to
escape the Islamic alternative. Others have taken up arms as part of the antiterrorist local militias, endorsed and supported by the government.[48]

Additionally, the FIS did not actually muster the mass support that it as-
serted. This is evident in the number of votes cast for each of the three leading
parties in the December 1991 national election. The number of seats won (FIS,
188; FFS, 25; FLN, 15) is disproportionate to the number of votes cast—
mainly because of the winner-takes-all or absolute majority rule. To illustrate, the FLN received 1.5 million votes and the FFS 0.5 million; yet, the two
combined got only forty seats, slightly more than one-fifth of the seats ac-
corded the FIS, which received about 3 million votes.[49] Further, seeing the

election largely as a contest between two undesirable choices, FLN versus FIS, almost 5 million people, or more than 40 percent of the 13.2 million registered voters, did not cast ballots.[50] With this low turnout, the three million voters for the FIS accounted for less than 25 percent of the total electorate, surely far less than a popular mandate. And, undoubtedly, many of these 3 million votes were cast more for change and reform than as expressions of party loyalty.

Regardless of these limitations, how to bridge the gap to the 3 million who voted for the FIS remains the greatest challenge facing the Algerian government in the long term as it gropes for a way out of its crisis of authority. This can be managed only by addressing the grievances that led to the vote for the Islamic movement. Since assuming office in February 1994, President Liamine Zeroual,[51] a reputed moderate in the power structure, has pursued a two-pronged strategy: economic reform and recovery, and political dialogue coupled with repression.

On the economic front, the cabinet—mostly technocratic-professional figures—under former Prime Minister Mokdad Sifi (April 1994–December 1995), an able administrator, who replaced the hard-liner Reda Malik, gave high priority to the ailing economy. Making internal reforms and seeking financial help from international institutions and foreign nations, it was hoped, would undercut the extremists' contention that the regime was doing nothing.

The government took a series of radical steps to meet the conditions set by the IMF. It cut the budget deficit from 9.3 to 5.4 percent of gross national product by eliminating state subsidies on a wide range of food items and by reducing social welfare expenditures, devalued the currency (the dinar) by more than 40 percent, freed prices in accordance with a market economy, and liberalized trade and investment codes. The government also sought to streamline, and possibly even privatize, the inefficient state-owned industries—a formidable undertaking given the political instability. All of this prompted the French director-general of the IMF, Michel Camdessus, to describe Algeria's performance as a "model for developing countries."[52]

In recognition of its efforts, Algeria received additional IMF loans and extended fund arrangements, as well as a rescheduling by the Paris Club of official lenders of the $14.5 billion owed to Western governments—almost half of the total foreign debt—thereby reducing annual debt service from $9 to $4.5 billion. Algeria continues to receive $1.1 billion a year in export credits from France. The government also held talks with the Export-Import Bank of Japan and other agencies to secure export credits for new major projects to expand its gas and oil export capacity. So far, the gas and oil industries have been largely protected from any violence. Surely the receptivity of the Western powers, especially France, to Algeria's economic plight is evidence that, despite assertions to the contrary, they do not want to see Algeria go under and thereby become susceptible to a fundamentalist takeover.[53]

Such economic measures are directed more toward long-term improvement than short-term relief. In fact, they may exacerbate immediate distress—unemployment, inflation, and quality of life—increasing the potential for further social dislocations and unrest. Therefore, a parallel strategy to bring about national equanimity is all the more imperative for the success of the reforms. Economic and civic health are inextricably linked.

The standoff in the protracted and vicious conflict among Algerians (despite some lowering of the level of violence), the growing powers exercised by a band of senior army officers, and the dimming prospects for democracy widened the chasm between the major secular political parties (including the FLN) and the regime. Such realities precipitated calls for a broadening of political participation to involve all Islamist groups that denounce violence. President Zeroual moved cautiously in search of a settlement. Thus, in addition to using force against the militants to placate the hard-liners in the military, he initiated dialogue with the opposition forces. Most significant, he opened direct contacts with jailed FIS leaders in an attempt to defuse the crisis. Senior government officials held repeated talks with Abbas Madani and Ali Belhaj in the late summer of 1994, after having released two prominent FIS figures, Sheikh Ali Jeddi and Sheikh Abdul Kader Boukhamkham, earlier in the year. These preliminary approaches came to an end in October, with no apparent outcome. The two sides remained far apart on the major issues: ending the Islamic armed rebellion, releasing the FIS leadership and members in detention camps, and lifting the ban on the party.

The initial setback notwithstanding, the Zeroual government kept the lines of communication open. Beginning in mid-January 1995, the Rome meeting of the Algerian opposition parties, under the auspices of the Sant' Edigio Catholic Community, rekindled the prospects for a negotiated settlement. The eight political parties—the leading among them being the FLN, the FIS, and the FFS, which together won about 85 percent of the vote in the December 1991 parliamentary election—agreed on a program called al-Aqd al-Watani, or the National Pact. Its agenda seeks the restoration of a democratic civil society under the rule of law and rejection of "all forms of dictatorship regardless of its nature or form"; adherence to constitutional principles and procedures, and state institutions based on the sovereign will of the people; respect for human rights and individual freedoms regardless of ethnic, religious, or linguistic differences; rejection of violence and indiscriminate killing of civilians and foreign nationals; and recognition of pluralism and multiculturalism in political and social life. It also asks for a lifting of the ban on the FIS and the release of all political prisoners, an end to the military's intervention in politics, and the convening of a national conference at which representatives of the government and of opposition parties would be empowered to prepare the groundwork for "free and pluralist" elections.[54]

The Rome agreement was a victory of sorts for the FIS. It gained legitimacy on a par with all other opposition parties and secured the adoption of demands it had made earlier as the basis for any future negotiations, thus boosting its position. At the same time, it did not have to renounce its goal of an Islamic state or call for an end to *jihad*, or armed opposition. On the other hand, the document marked a clear pledge, though on paper only, to tolerate political pluralism and power sharing, social and cultural diversity, and constitutional and legal norms. This is a significant transition in the Islamic movement's stance and could help promote future compromise. Equally, the new association between the FIS and the secularist opposition parties could facilitate further dialogue with the state as the FIS moves more toward mainstream opposition politics and away from the Islamic militants. The latter, especially the notorious GIA, came out openly against the Rome accord, decried the FIS role, and vowed to continue the armed struggle against the government.[55]

Although the government's initial response was to reject the Rome accord "totally and in [every] detail,"[56] it showed some flexibility and moderation in dealing with the opposition parties that endorsed it. The government did not clamp down on their activities, for instance, when their representatives, including the FIS, met in Algiers in late January 1995 to refine the proposals— a meeting that could not have taken place without government acquiescence.[57] Another sign of a shift was the government's allowing, for the first time in almost four years, a public rally by the opposition in early June 1995 in Algiers, with FIS participation. About 10,000 people called for an end to emergency rule and a return to democracy.[58]

The government even initiated contacts with the opposition that culminated in renewed direct talks with FIS leaders in the summer of 1995, but to no avail.[59] Consensus has proved to be elusive; differences are deep and contentious. Most contentious of all, political Islam—a religion-based ideology for sociopolitical change—is predicated on challenging the secular system, not coexisting. And the ruling establishment is determined to uphold the secular state.

Meanwhile, the government pressed ahead with plans for an early presidential election on November 16, 1995, to be followed by parliamentary and local elections in 1997.[60] President Zeroual described the presidential vote as the proper means to conduct a "direct dialogue with the people" and to establish a measure of legitimacy that would lead the way to normalcy. But such a vote falls short of the overall political settlement demanded by the National Pact parties, and they withheld their support. They were also against elections supervised by the military-controlled government, which continues to ban the FIS. Absent participation by the major opposition parties, the presidential election alone could neither bestow legitimacy nor restore political stability.

The 1995 presidential election did not induce a reconfiguration of the Algerian political elite. Rather, it confirmed the existing power structure, sustained by the military-technocratic-administrative alliance. In fact, the landslide victory of President Zeroual, the regime-backed candidate (winning over 61 percent of the vote), over the three minor contenders—Mahfouz Nahnah of Hamas, Said Sadi of the RCD, and Noureddine Boukrouh, a Muslim moderate and leader of the Algerian Renewal Party—probably strengthened the regime's determination to maintain the political structure and to exclude the outlawed FIS.[61] President Zeroual ran on a platform of reaching out to the secular and moderate Islamist opposition and suppressing the hard-line fundamentalists. And people voted more for peace, security, and order than for candidates in a levelled election field.

It appears, then, that the chance of finding a solution to the political crisis through dialogue is slim. Although the FIS, in an about-face, admitted the legality of the election results and the legitimacy of the newly elected president and appeared to concede to the regime by calling for a unilateral cease-fire and renewed talks with the government, its seemingly conciliatory gestures were completely ignored. In his inaugural speech, President Zeroual omitted any mention of the fundamentalists in any future negotiations. He seems more inclined to look at Muslim moderates, such as Hamas and the Algerian Renewal Party, who together won approximately 30 percent of the vote, as the only legitimate Islamic political movements on the national scene.[62] In fact, the cabinet formed in early January 1996 under Prime Minister Ahmad Ouyahya—President Zeroual's former office director—includes members of both groups.[63] Although the new cabinet is mostly a holdover from the previous technocratic one, with emphasis on continuing economic reforms and establishing social peace, the prime minister is considered close to Said Sadi—leader of the RCD—and his secular, anti-Islamist orientation.[64]

Further, the gap between the military and the Islamists is as wide as ever, and intense suspicions linger. Many in the army command, particularly the hard-liners, dislike the Islamists in the extreme and see them as a dangerous religio-political force bent on nothing less than total victory. If the application of *Shari'a* is an immutable principle in the projected Islamic state, then it is doubtful that the FIS will abide by constitutional rules, the Rome platform notwithstanding. Also, mindful of what befell the Iranian officers under Khomeini, Algerian officers are likely to continue to oppose lifting the ban on the FIS. They believe that now, having gained the upper hand in the conflict, they will be able to sustain intermittent, low-level violence, while keeping the FIS out. Equally, they feel bolstered by the high voter turnout (almost 75 percent) in the presidential election and the perceived popular mandate given to the military-appointed candidate, which they see as an endorsement of eliminating the FIS as a political force.

Others in the military hierarchy, especially the proponents of dialogue, are willing to live with a less dominant, less ideological, and more moderate FIS—one that does not seek hegemony or impose Islamic rule. Surely this will entail a softening of the FIS ideological stance on the issue of an Islamic state, and eventually even its surrender as a goal, and a renunciation of *jihad* as a legitimate means of struggle. Although the FIS has of late dissociated itself politically from the Armed Islamic Group, it has yet to stand against violence generally and call for an end to *jihad*.[65] It is doubtful that the FIS is willing to go that far to reconcile itself with the secular institutions and to accept the secular premises of the Algerian state in order to be integrated into the political life like any other party. Indeed, such a course would be tantamount to an abandonment of its core Islamic ideology and therefore the loss of its raison d'être. A reformed liberal FIS would not be the FIS.

But, above all, both groups in the military seem to agree on the necessity of preserving the state's institutions and its secularist structure. They also agree on the need to separate religion from politics, although the latter group is willing to use religious vocabulary in public discourse. Further, they are emphatic about not repeating Benjedid's mistake of legalizing the fundamentalist FIS, which led to Algeria's political morass.

Finally, regardless of the outcome of dialogue with the opposition, the army is not apt to relinquish, of its own accord, its power "behind the throne." Probably it will continue in its customary role as supreme arbiter of national politics and protector of the secular state. The military-bureaucratic-secularist power elites seem determined to prevail against the fundamentalist challenge. They have not lost confidence in their ability to survive and to manage Algeria's traditionally messy politics. This is especially so in the post-presidential election period, as the worst seems to be over for Algeria. In a show of self-confidence about the future, the government has announced a general amnesty for political prisoners and has called on Muslim rebels to put down their arms in exchange for pardon and rehabilitation.[66] Also, in an attempt to weaken the opposition parties, it abetted and supported a change in the FLN leadership, which moved the party away from the National Pact coalition and closer toward the government—thereby fracturing the opposition and nullifying the pact.[67]

Given the inability of the fundamentalists to tear down the existing power structure, the regime will doubtless continue to keep its hold on power, tolerate a measure of opposition and even allow some limited participation by secularist and Islamic moderate groups, and strike against Islamist violence. Meanwhile, as Muslim extremists intensify their terrorism and split into even more factions, they may weaken the Islamic appeal and ultimately diminish the FIS role in society and politics. In fact, the FIS influence seems to have lessened considerably due to the heavy toll of the struggle, mounting internal divisions, and rival armed factions.[68] Will more people begin to question whether Islam can provide a way out? The extremists' sanguinary cycle of violence, which is turning the Islamic dream into a living nightmare, could prove to be the antidote to Islamism. Indeed, some Algerian secularists saw in the high turnout for the November 1995 presidential election a sign of the retreat of fundamentalism.[69] In the end, Algeria will not be North Africa's Islamic republic. Nor will it be the model democratic "civitas" on the southern Mediterranean. With its polarized society and politics, Algeria seems unlikely to break away from its authoritarian past, based upon the belief that the state has primacy over the civil society.

NOTES

1. France made clear that it considered Arabic a foreign language in Algeria and that it should be taught as such. In fact, as recently as the 1970s, more than 60 percent of Algerians could not read Arabic. See Rachid Tlemcani, "Chadli's Perestroika," *Middle East Report* Mar.-Apr. 1990: 17. Also, French colonial policies induced destructive rural migration and disruption of urban life.

2. The lack of a coherent, well-defined Algerian nation led former liberal-secularist leader Ferhat Abbas to declare: "If I had discovered the Algerian nation, I would have become a nationalist." Quoted in Michael C. Hudson, *Arab Politics: The Search for Legitimacy* (New Haven, Conn.: Yale University Press, 1979), 368. For an excellent study of the life and struggles of Abbas, see Benjamin Stora and Zakya Daoud, *Ferhat Abbas: une Utopie Algerienne* (Paris: Editions Denoel, 1995). The Berber tribes were the original inhabitants of North Africa before the Arab conquest in the late seventh century. They represent 20 percent of Algeria's population of 28 million. Although they are Muslims, they have maintained their ethnic-tribal identity and pre-Islamic language, Imazigh, which is spoken in ten different dialects. See William E. Hazen, "Minorities in Assimilation: The Berbers of North Africa," *The Political Role of Minority Groups in the Middle East*, ed. R. D. McLaurin (New York: Praeger, 1979), 135–55; Chris Hedges, "Arabs, Too, Play the Ethnic Card," *New York Times* 5 Mar. 1995: 4.

3. There were roughly 350 such Sufi orders, with approximately 300,000 members. See Muhammad Kamal Jum'a, *Intishar Da'wat Muhammad ibn Abdul Wahhab Kharij al-Jazira al-Arabiyya* (The spread of Muhammad ibn Abdul Wahhab's message outside the Arabian peninsula) (Riyadh: Dar al-Hilal, 1981), 239.

4. See *al-Sharq al-Awsat* 27 May 1990: 5; Hugh Roberts, "Radical Islamism and the Dilemma of Algerian Nationalism: The Embattled Arians of Algiers," *Third World Quarterly* 10 (Apr. 1988): 560.

5. See *al-Sharq al-Awsat* 14 Jan. 1995: 4.

6. As a political party, the FLN was more an exclusivist than a national political body. It became progressively marginal in state affairs, with the locus of power increasingly centered in a military-bureaucratic elite.

7. The Algerian Constitution of 1963 declared Islam the religion of the state, but *Shari'a* (Islamic law) was not incorporated into the legal system of the state. See Mary-Jane Deeb, "Algeria," *Religion in Politics: A World Guide*, ed. Stuart Mews (Essex, England: Longman Group, 1989), 6.

8. See Olivier Roy, *The Failure of Political Islam* (Cambridge: Harvard University Press, 1994), 126.

9. For opposing views of two Algerian writers on the role of French in Algerian literature and culture, see *al-Majalla* 2–8 July 1995: 8–9. The continued dominance of French-speaking culture is manifest in the many newspapers published in French, not Arabic.

10. He broke with Ahmad Ben Bella shortly after the latter became the first president of independent Algeria in 1962.

11. Boumedienne became president in 1965, following his military coup against Ben Bella, which signified deep internal struggle within the FLN leadership. He remained paramount leader until his sudden death in 1978, while Ben Bella was kept languishing in prison until 1980.

12. For further elaboration on these points, see Bruno Etienne, *L'Islamisme Radicale* (Paris: Hatchette, 1987); John Entelis, *Algeria: The Revolution Institutionalized* (Boulder, Colo.: Westview Press, 1986).

13. With the quadrupling of oil prices in the 1970s, the GDP growth rate reached a high of 10.8 percent in 1978. See *Africa Record* 1980–1981: B13.

14. According to a survey in 1982–1983 of 1,331 new entrepreneurs, 40 percent were state companies' managers or military officers. See Tlemcani, "Chadli's Perestroika," 16.

15. The last three would become the leaders of the three Islamist parties that appeared subsequent to the introduction of multiparty democracy in 1989: Abbas Madani, Islamic Salvation Front (FIS); Mahfouz Nahnah, Movement for Islamic Society (Hamas); and Abdullah Jab, Islamic Renaissance Party (al-Nahda).

16. On this theme, see Etienne, *L'Islamisme Radicale*, 141–42.

17. The Berberist movement, centered mainly in the Kabyle mountainous region near Algiers, which has the biggest concentration of Berbers, is not nationalist inspired. It is unlike the Kurdish movement in Iraq or in Turkey, whereby the Kurds are waging a nationalist struggle for autonomy or for nationhood. Berbers generally are an integral part of the Algerian body politic and are represented in all aspects of national life. Their movement is motivated by differences with the government's policies. Essentially, it advocates multiculturalism, secularism, and pluralist democratic socialism, and hence it opposes Arabization or Islamization. The two leading Berberist political parties are the Socialist Forces Front (FFS), headed by Hocine Ait Ahmad (a revolutionary war leader), and the Rally for Culture and Democracy (RCD), led by Said Sadi. See Hugh Roberts, "The Unforeseen Development of the Kabyle Question in Contemporary Algeria," *Government and Opposition* 17 (Summer 1982): 312–34; Hazen, "Minorities in Assimilation: The Berbers of North Africa."

18. One indicator of the soft nature of the state under Benjedid was the widespread social unrest in the 1980s. On the average, there were about seventy strikes a month in the public sector during the decade. See Tlemcani, "Chadli's Perestroika," 16.

19. Two of Bouyali's associates who were jailed, Ali Belhaj and Abdulkader Chabouti, later became leading members of the FIS. The latter organized and led an armed resistance group in the tradition of Bouyali.

20. For a brief, but inspiring analysis of the Algerian predicament, see Fouad Ajami, "The Battle of Algiers," *New Republic* 16 July 1990: 12–13.

21. See *al-Majalla* 19–25 Feb. 1992: 28. According to Prime Minister Mouloud Hamrouche (September 1989–June 1991), allowing the FIS to function as a legal party served "to control the phenomenon, understand it, manage it, and hold discussions with it." *Foreign Broadcast Information Services* 29 Jan. 1990. Certainly developments in Algeria did not follow such rational, pragmatic direction.

22. FIS social services and medical care networks were able to furnish aid to thousands of earthquake victims in November 1989, well before government agencies appeared on the scene.

23. See Youssef M. Ibrahim, "Islamic Party in Algeria Defeats Ruling Group in Local Elections," *New York Times* 14 June 1990: A1; Ibrahim, "In Algeria, Hope for Democracy but Not Economy," *New York Times* 26 July 1991: A5; Robert Mortimer, "Islam and Multiparty Politics in Algeria," *Middle East Journal* 45 (Autumn 1991): 584.

24. See Youssef M. Ibrahim, "Islamic Movement Leads in Algeria," *New York Times* 27 Dec. 1991: A10; Ibrahim, "Islamic Plan for Algeria Is on Display," *New York Times* 7 Jan. 1992: A3; Robin Wright, "Islam and Democracy," *Foreign Affairs* 71 (Summer 1992): 134–35.

25. In particular, those voters in their twenties were the most prone to believe the FIS promise of salvation. Their dead-end economic circumstances and the fading mystique of

the FLN's revolutionary past made them all the more susceptible to the opposition message of the FIS.

26. Ibrahim, "Islamic Party in Algeria Defeats Ruling Group in Local Elections," A20.

27. See Francis Ghiles, "Algeria Locked in a Vicious Cycle of Violence," *Middle East International* 9 July 1993: 18.

28. Robert A. Mortimer, "Algeria: The Clash between Islam, Democracy, and the Military," *Current History* Jan. 1993: 38.

29. In 1988, former Prime Minister Abdul Hamid Brahimi charged that top Algerian officials embezzled about $26 billion over a twenty-year period by means of illicit commissions on trade transactions. See Emad Eldin Shahin, "Algeria: The Limits to Democracy," *Middle East Insight* July-Oct. 1992: 18.

30. The FIS considered the December 1988 election of President Chadli Benjedid—the sole FLN candidate—for a third five-year term as not representative of the popular will and therefore invalid. Abbas Madani called for early presidential elections before the conclusion of Benjedid's term at the end of 1993.

31. The military was the decisive force in the selection of Ahmad Ben Bella in 1962, the ascendancy of Houari Boumedienne in 1965, and the choice of Chadli Benjedid in 1979.

32. The July 1989 law regarding political associations specifically prohibited religion-based parties.

33. Quoted in Alfred Hermida, "Democracy Derailed," *Africa Report* Mar.-Apr. 1992: 15.

34. See Ibrahim, "In Algeria, Hope for Democracy but Not Economy," A1, A5; Ibrahim, "Islamic Strikes in Algeria: A Mistake, Then Arrests," *New York Times* 27 July 1991: A5.

35. See *al-Majalla* 8–14 July 1992: 25–27; Ibrahim, "Islamic Strikes in Algeria: A Mistake, Then Arrests."

36. See *al-Majalla* 12–18 May 1993: 50–54.

37. Indeed, somewhat analogous to conservative Saudi Arabia, the FIS came out against satellite dishes that bring Western television programs and messages to Algerian homes. On the excessive Islamic measures of the fundamentalist-controlled municipalities, see Roy, *The Failure of Political Islam*, 80–85.

38. Although Muslim fundamentalists exhibit divergent ideological tendencies, generally they all share certain beliefs: the veiling of women, whose proper place is at home rearing children; the segregation of women at work and in schools; the application of *Shari'a*, with all its penalties; the banning of alcohol production and consumption; and the exclusion of secularist thought.

39. In fact, many suspected the FIS commitment to a multiparty democracy in light of the party's proclamation: "No constitution, no law, only the Qur'an and the law of God." And Ali Belhaj, Abbas Madani's deputy, had no qualms about dismissing democracy as a "foreign concept." See Hermida, "Democracy Derailed," 14; Mortimer, "Islam and Multiparty Politics in Algeria," 586.

40. On the limitations of democracy in Algeria, see Michael C. Hudson, "After the Gulf War: Prospects for Democratization in the Arab World," *Middle East Journal* 45 (Summer 1991): 414.

41. It is reported that the government replaced about 40 percent of the *imams* of Algeria's 9,000 mosques. See Wright, "Islam and Democracy," 136.

42. Boudiaf, who dissociated himself from the old regimes during his twenty-seven years in exile, wanted to act independently of the military and not appear as a mere figurehead. He sought to build a national front (al-Tajamu' al-Watani, or the National Rally) of nation-

alist and liberal-democratic forces to lead the way out of the current crisis and establish national legitimacy and stability. He also launched a series of investigations on corruption within the power structure that could have proved to be embarrassing to the military-led regime. Thus, he had to deal with opponents on both sides, the military-political establishment and the Islamists. In fact, some Algerians suspect that the assassination of Boudiaf was the work not of the Islamists—even though a soldier espousing their ideas was charged with the act—but of the same military-political clique that appointed Boudiaf. On the same conspiracy thesis, see Noor al-Din al-Taheri, *Al-Jaza'ir bayn al-Khiyar al-Islami wal-Khiyar al-Askari* (Algeria between the Islamic and military alternatives) (al-Dar al-Baida': Dar Qurtuba, 1992). See also *al-Majalla* 8–14 July 1992: 20–24; Youssef M. Ibrahim, "President of Algeria Shot Dead at Rally," *New York Times* 30 June 1992: A8.

43. See "Algeria's Muslims Urged to Move 'To Rifles,'" *New York Times* 23 Apr. 1992: A5; Youssef M. Ibrahim, "Crackdown Seems to Lead Algeria into Chaos," *New York Times* 20 Aug. 1992: A5; Howard LaFranchi, "Algeria's Intellectuals Are Targets in Their Country's Civil Conflict," *Christian Science Monitor* 2 July 1993: 7; *al-Majalla* 22–28 Aug. 1993: 15; Flora Lewis, "The War on Arab Intellectuals," *New York Times* 7 Sept. 1993: A19; Ghiles, "Algeria Locked in a Vicious Cycle of Violence."

44. It is reported that, in 1994 alone, there were 2,725 terrorist acts, inflicting physical damage on the infrastructure to the tune of $2 billion. See *al-Sharq al-Awsat* 20 Feb. 1995: 4, 21 Mar. 1995: 5.

45. The fundamentalist pamphlets spewed terrorist threats at and instilled fear in intellectuals: "Those who criticize us with their pen must die by the sword." See Francis Ghiles, "Can Algeria Be Saved from the Dinosaurs?" *Middle East International* 4 Mar. 1994: 16. On the mounting violence and its consequences, see Colin Barraclough, "The Crisis in Algeria: No Positive Signs on the Horizon," *Middle East Insight* Jan.-Feb. 1994: 21; Jonathan C. Randal, "Islamic Front Steps Up Struggle in Algeria," *Washington Post* 6 June 1994: A1, A16; Christine Moss Helms, "Once Around the Middle East in 1994: Omen for 1995," *Energy Compass* 22 Dec. 1994: 13–14; Helms, "1995 Gets Off to a Bloody Start as NATO Refocuses on the Islamic Threat to Its South," *Energy Compass* 10 Feb. 1995: 11; Youssef M. Ibrahim, "As Islamic Violence Accelerates, Fears of a Showdown in Algeria," *New York Times* 22 Feb. 1995: A1, A6.

46. More than 10,000 people were tried before such special courts, which handed down about 1,000 death sentences. These courts were terminated in early 1995, partly in response to the strong protests of international and domestic human rights groups and also in response to apparent government successes in the fight against the militant groups. See *al-Sharq al-Aswat* 20 Feb. 1995: 4.

47. See *al-Majalla* 18–24 June 1995: 12.

48. On these self-defense military groups, see *al-Majalla* 23–29 Apr. 1995: 38–41. It is reported that there are about 80,000 armed members cooperating with the security forces. See *al-Sharq al-Awsat* 24 Nov. 1995: 3.

49. These figures are derived from *al-Majalla* 22–28 Jan. 1992: 11; and *Christian Science Monitor* 2 July 1993: 7.

50. See Hermida, "Democracy Derailed," 14; Mortimer, "Algeria: The Clash between Islam, Democracy, and the Military," 39.

51. Liamine Zeroual, an army general and a defense minister, succeeded Ali Kafi, head of the High State Council, upon expiration of the two-year interim period of the council and the termination of its mandate. He was appointed president by the military, presumably for a three-year transitional period, when the major political parties boycotted a conference

called by the government to name a civilian head of state in an attempt to preserve a facade of legitimacy. President Zeroual has also kept his position as defense minister, which he has held since July 1993, following the resignation of General Khalid Nizar—the coup leader— from the post. The latter retained his position in the all-powerful Supreme Security Council, which has charge of state security. Nizar remains a "hidden" influential figure in state political and security affairs. On the hidden power elite in Algeria, see Youssef M. Ibrahim, "In Algeria, Real Power Hides in the Shadows," *New York Times* 11 June 1995: A3.

52. Francis Ghiles, "Is Algeria Staring Disaster in the Face?" *Middle East International* 17 Feb. 1995: 16–17. Also see *Middle East Economic Survey* 12 June 1995: A7–A8; "Time to Help Algeria," *Economist* 18 Feb. 1995: 11; *al-Sharq al-Awsat* 11 Apr. 1994: 1, 25 July 1995: 9.

53. Western powers generally have security concerns about the southern Mediterranean flank of NATO, and France especially fears the influx of swarms of Algerian refugees (more than a million), which could have destabilizing social and political consequences for France. See Thomas Kamm and Peter Truell, "As Blood Spills in Algeria, Europe Churns," *Wall Street Journal* 31 Oct. 1994: A10.

54. For the Arabic text of the National Pact, see *al-Sharq al-Awsat* 14 Jan. 1995: 4. Also see Youssef M. Ibrahim, "Algerian Opposition Offers Plan for Peace," *New York Times* 14 Jan. 1995: 5; Alfred Hermida, "Algeria: Opposition Gets Together," *Middle East International* 20 Jan. 1995: 12–13; "Algerian Parties Agree in Rome," *Middle East Economic Survey* 16 Jan. 1995: C1.

55. See Youssef M. Ibrahim, "Hopes for Algerian Peace Fade as Rome Plan Is Rejected by Militants on Both Sides," *New York Times* 23 Jan. 1995: A6.

56. "Algerian Government Rejects Opposition Proposal for Peace," *Washington Post* 19 Jan. 1995: A26.

57. "Algeria Wavers on Rome Initiative," *Middle East Economic Survey* 30 Jan. 1995: C3.

58. See *al-Majalla* 26 June–1 July 1995: 17.

59. See Alfred Hermida, "Algeria: Secret Negotiations," *Middle East International* 23 June 1995: 11; "Talks with the FIS," *Middle East Economic Survey* 26 June 1995: C2; *al-Sharq al-Awsat* 19 June 1995: 1; *al-Majalla* 16–22 July 1995: 16.

60. The election was held one year before the expiration date of the transitional presidential period at the end of 1996.

61. With almost 75 percent of the 16 million members of the electorate voting, President Zeroual won a sweeping 61.34 percent compared to Mahfouz Nahnah, 25.38 percent; Said Sadi, 9.29 percent; and Noureddin Boukrouh, 3.78 percent. See *al-Sharq al-Awsat* 18 Nov. 1995: 3; William Drozdiac "Leader Wins in Algeria: Vote Dismissed by Losers," *Washington Post* 18 Nov. 1995: A24. The presidential election was held in an atmosphere of terror created by Muslim extremists, who threatened to send voters from the "ballot boxes into the coffins," and intimidation created by the government's deployment of 200,000 troops across the country, turning polling places into fortresses. See *al-Sharq al-Awsat* 12 Nov. 1995: 4; Youssef M. Ibrahim, "Terror Poses Threat to Turnout as Algerians Go to Polls Today," *New York Times* 16 Nov. 1995: A8; Ibrahim, "Huge Turnout Is Reported by Algerians in Election," *New York Times* 17 Nov. 1995: A6.

62. At first, the FIS spokesmen dismissed the election as "a farce staged by the military-dominated government" to stay in power. See Ibrahim, "Terror Poses Threat to Turnout as Algerians Go to Polls Today," A8; Ibrahim, "Algerian Militants Now Ready to Negotiate," *New York Times* 21 Nov. 1995: A9; Ibrahim, "New Algerian Chief Pledges 'Authentic De-

mocracy,'" *New York Times* 28 Nov. 1995: A7.

63. The new cabinet includes two members of Hamas and one of the Algerian Renewal Party—all in nonkey ministries. Also, a Muslim moderate, Ahmad Merani, who split from the FIS leadership in June 1990 and turned against the movement, has been appointed minister of religious affairs. See *al-Sharq al-Awsat* 5 Jan. 1996: 1, 6 Jan. 1996: 4.

64. Thirteen out of twenty-two ministers are holdovers from the previous cabinet. The majority are professional technocrats and career diplomats. Further, President Zeroual retained the key post of defense minister. On the composition of the cabinet, see *al-Sharq al-Awsat* 6 Jan. 1996: 4.

65. See *al-Sharq al-Awsat* 22 Dec. 1995: 2.

66. See *al-Sharq al-Awsat* 30 Nov. 1995: 4, 22 Dec. 1995: 2.

67. FLN Secretary General Abdul Hamid Mehri—a leading opposition figure—was replaced by Bouallam Ben Hamouda, a pro-government party official. See *al-Sharq al-Awsat* 16 Jan. 1996: 4, 21 Jan. 1996: 4.

68. On the divisions among the FIS leadership in exile, see *al-Sharq al-Awsat* 24 Nov. 1995: 3, 29 Dec. 1995: 1. On the internecine feuds between the Armed Islamic Group and the Islamic Salvation Army, see *al-Majalla* 17–23 Mar. 1996: 36–37.

69. According to Malik Ait Aoudia, spokesman for the Berber-based RCD, "If this election shows anything, it shows that the Islamic current has lost a great deal of steam." Quoted in Ibrahim, "Huge Turnout Is Reported by Algerians in Election."

5

The Islamist Challenge in Saudi Arabia

Saudi Arabia has had no historical experience with Western colonialism or liberal secularism. Unlike Egypt and Algeria, it has not been exposed to disruptive foreign control and influences, except for the Ottoman-Turkish suzerainty over the coastal areas on the Persian Gulf and the Red Sea. The country has been neither the recipient of modern cultural and ideological thought nor the transmitter of enlightened ideas. And also unlike the other two countries, Saudi Arabia has not been the source of significant inspiration and leadership (ideologically and intellectually) in the region.[1] It has long been shielded by a veil of traditional Islam. Its tribal and religious ethos has made it the least receptive to modern secular ideologies—these simply could not compete with established traditions for individual loyalty or national identity.

The Saudi system is the product of a desert culture marked by tribal division and conflict, harsh and austere living conditions, and religious piety and fanaticism.[2] Family and religion are the sources of its legitimacy. Despite the influx of abundant oil wealth in the 1970s and the onset of modernization, which wrought great physical and societal transformation and excessive materialism, with potential dangers for the established order, Saudi Arabia cloaks itself with the official Islamic mantle, as it has since its inception. Throughout, it has remained essentially true to its contextual roots, preserving its religious character and tribal-family tradition in an effort to maintain the status quo.

Founded in 1932 by the Saudi tribal patriarch Abdul Aziz ibn Saud, who became known as King Ibn Saud, the state is the culmination of more than a century and a half of unity between the Al-Saud tribal-warrior family and the Al-Sheikh tribal-religious family. The revivalist Wahhabi Islamic doctrine— propagated by the latter group—provided the answer to the quest for an Islamic fundamentalist state system. It is a state propelled by Islamic ideology and consolidated by Saudi power through *jihad* (holy war). The symbiotic relationship between state and religion, begun in an alliance between Prince Muhammad ibn Saud and Sheikh Muhammad ibn Abdul Wahhab in 1744, endures, sustained today by the new oil wealth.[3]

Orthodox Wahhabi Islam has become the raison d'être of the Saudi state, serving as a unifying force in the social and political cohesion of tribal Arabia and providing the basis of the royal family's legitimacy.[4] As the official ideology, it has been utilized to support the monarchy's authority. Thus, Wahhabism has always been kept, in form at least, in the service of the status quo and has been undergirded by the power and wealth of the state. The symbiosis between Wahhabi ideology and Saudi power remains the basis of state identity and national unity. To be sure, the process of national consolidation was greatly facilitated by the country's homogeneity: the population is predominantly Arab and Sunni Muslim, with a Shi'a Muslim concentration (8–10 percent) in the eastern al-Hasa region.

Wahhabism is a conservative expression, or modality, of orthodox Sunni Islam. It is neither a sect of Islam nor a school of Islamic jurisprudence apart from the four classical schools (Hanafi, Maliki, Shafi'i, Hanbali), which had crystallized by the middle of the tenth century.[5] Though it follows the teachings of the Hanbali school in its dogmatism and strict adherence to the primary sources—the Qur'an and the *Sunna* (prophetic traditions)—it has not repudiated the other three schools of Islam.

The spirit of Wahhabism exults in the ethos of piety, austerity, and egalitarianism as it is believed to have existed in the days of the Prophet. Its doctrine emphasizes a revivalist-fundamentalist-puritanical interpretation of Islam, calling for a return to the true religion of Islam as practiced by *al-salaf* (the pious ancestors at the dawn of Islam) by insisting upon a literal meaning and application of the original sources. In addition, the quintessential monotheism in Islam (*tawhid*) must be maintained against any elements of polytheism (*shirk*) or any practice even remotely suggestive of polytheism. Therefore, corrupting outside influences and innovations (*bid'a*) must be vigorously fought.[6]

As to governance, the envisioned Islamic polity should be ordered in accordance with the Wahhabi puritanical-revivalist view of religion, with its emphasis on divine transcendence, societal unity and conformity, and Islamic authenticity. It is incumbent upon Muslims, rulers and subjects alike, to order their lives according to the Qur'an and the *Sunna*, as did *al-salaf*. To that end, the Qur'an is the sole and absolute law of the state, whose primary duty is to implement the Qur'an in its most rigid Hanbali version, without any innovations that may have been introduced in the intervening centuries. "Obey the pristine law, fully strictly, and establish a society where that law obtains . . . all else is superfluous and wrong."[7] The Saudi rulers are entrusted with upholding the doctrine and establishing the rule of God in Saudi Arabia.

But the most important legacy of Wahhabism is its religious zeal, its militancy to spread the mission and cement Saudi dominion. Invoking the Wahhabi doctrine of *takfir wa qital* (fighting against apostasy), the Wahhabi partisans—comprising the Ikhwan—carried on a relentless *jihad* as a means of conversion and conquest in the early part of the twentieth century. Recruited by Abdul Aziz ibn Saud from among bedouin tribes and settled in paramilitary agricultural communes (*hijar*), the members of the Ikhwan made up a body of Muslim warriors—the true believers—dedicated to Wahhabi Islam and the Saudi state.[8] Early in the 1920s, their capture of Mecca and Medina, the two holy cities of Islam, gave the Saudi leadership a major boost by linking it with Islam to a degree that had no equal. Thereafter, the Saudi leadership's achieved status as "Keeper of the Faith" and King Fahd's assumed title of "Custodian of the Two Holy Places" have served as hallmarks of Saudi Islamicity.

State-sponsored fundamentalism is thus a tradition in Saudi Arabia. Armed with Wahhabi Islam as its official ideology, the state has always posed as the Islamic state *par excellence*. Its domestic and foreign policies purport to adhere to its Islamic vision: the Qur'an is its constitution;[9] *Shari'a* (Islamic law) is its legal system; public morals and social behavior remain its province, watched over by the religious-moral police (*mutawi'in*); international Muslim causes and organizations enjoy its strong support; and proselytization and sponsorship of Islamic activities and groups worldwide are high on its agenda. And, above all, it does not countenance religious diversity; the society wears a strait-jacket. Little wonder that the religious establishment (the *ulama*) generally has posed no threat to the Saudi state; rather, it has been a watchdog guarding against aspects of modernity deemed iniquitous. Also, contrary to what exists in Egypt and Algeria, there is no major ideological divide between the state and the people.

Until the 1970s, there was hardly any domestic dissidence on the essentials of the Saudi system: Islamic values and royal family authority. Attacks on Saudi Arabia were carried out primarily by outside secularist-nationalist forces, led by Nasser and the Ba'th during the height of the Arab cold war in the 1950s and 1960s. They viewed the Saudi monarchy as the epitome of antiquarianism and backwardness and called for its downfall. The monarchy withstood the challenge behind a barricade of Islam and *turath* (tradition). The Saudi rulers were able to use Islamic ideology and local tribal traditions to appeal to the loyalty of the people and to thwart the leftist ideological offensive. They dismissed Nasserism and Ba'thism as alien to Saudi soil and hence wholly incompatible with indigenous cultural values and religious beliefs. They also pointed out that the Arabian and Islamic heritage of Saudi Arabia made it the center of Arabdom—the most authentically Arab of all Arab states in the Middle East—and the focal point of Islamdom.

King Faisal (1964–1975) went even further in actively using Islam to promote Saudi leadership in the Muslim world and to thwart Nasserism and other leftist forces. He called for an international Islamic conference in 1965 as a means to supersede pan-Arabism and take the wind out of the sails of Arab nationalism. In addition, he energetically encouraged and supported funda-mentalist Islamic movements throughout the region in order to counter the ideological offensive of the Left. In the end, Faisal's initiative crystallized in 1970 as the Organization of the Islamic Conference (OIC), headquartered in Jedda, and numbering more than fifty states today.[10]

The shield of Islam has not kept the kingdom immune to the growth of Muslim extremism, which threatens now to undermine its legitimacy. Over the past twenty-five years, Saudi Arabia has undergone rapid change and mod-ernization pursuant to the Arab oil embargo in 1973. Income increased ten-fold in a year, making the kingdom a financial colossus and a major regional political force.[11] These immense changes posed a serious problem for the so-ciety: the conflict between indigenous values and modernity—"Mecca versus Mechanization."[12] High morals, religious piety, and austere living seemed ill-suited to the overwhelming affluence. Accelerated development, materialistic consumerism, and ostentatious lifestyles—particularly among members of the royal family—coupled with the perception of intimacy with and even subser-vience to the West, especially the United States, all took on a very un-Wahhabi-like cast. These phenomena have tainted the Saudi court and occasioned a rupture in Saudi society and mores, giving rise to a new fundamentalist or neo-Wahhabi opposition to the monarchy. The Saudis ultimately could not escape the social and political costs of modernity: social disruption and po-litical conflict, expressed in religious protest.

It is ironic that, in using Islamic ideological rhetoric as the medium of pub-lic discourse, the Saudi leaders have become vulnerable to religious opposi-tion now holding them accountable to the Wahhabi ideals and values they espouse. Surely the dissident voices tend to resonate widely in a religion-based culture where there is no other outlet for the expression of dissent. Par-ties, unions, and social and professional organizations are nonexistent in Saudi Arabia, a country devoid of group politics. In the Saudi milieu, where reli-gious doctrine and institutions are supreme, Islam is used simultaneously by state and opposition to advance and challenge positions. The Saudis had le-gitimized Islamic discourse in politics and in the process had lent some de-gree of legitimacy to opposing groups who spoke the language of Islam.[13] In effect, this catapulted the Islamic forces to the center of opposition and en-abled them to set the public agenda.

In the 1950s and 1960s, religious opposition was directed against what the traditional *ulama* viewed as the dangers of modernization policies, especially those emerging during the reign of King Faisal. This opposition strongly pro-tested the importation of modern education generally and the education of girls in particular; the introduction of television; and the establishment of the Ministry of Justice in 1970, which brought the legal system under the purview of the state: all threatened the *ulama*'s grip and position. The religious leaders feared that modernization would change the social and institutional founda-tions to the detriment of the men of religion. This did, of course, come to pass.[14] The "balance" in the joint venture between political power and religious ideology shifted in favor of the former.

Although the *ulama* have continued to play an important role in education (they control Islamic legal education and theology and supervise female education), the judicial system (they implement *Shari'a*), and religious affairs (they oversee mosques and direct Islamic missionary activities abroad), their mark on important administrative, economic, and foreign-affairs policy decisions is hardly noticeable. Although the Saudi leadership remains solicitous of religious opinion, the *ulama*'s status has been reduced to that of a religious bureaucracy in the pay of the state and is therefore subject to state supervision—a circumstance contrary to the pact of the founding leaders.[15] No longer autonomous and equal, official Islam generally is used for state purposes: it is Saudized.

This turn of events did not end religious opposition, but rather gave rise to more militant fundamentalist forces. In particular, the subordination of religion to the state alienated many young Wahhabi zealots. The most serious manifestation of the new Islamic challenge was the neo-Wahhabi, or neo-Ikhwan, uprising: the takeover of the Grand Mosque of Mecca in November 1979. Led by Juhayman al-Utaibi, the group (mostly men in their twenties and thirties, students at and graduates of the Islamic University of Medina) accused the royal family of betraying the ideals of Islam, of polluting the Islamic character of Saudi life, of being corrupt and immoral, and of failing to provide true religious leadership and true Islamic rule.

The basic premise of the neo-Wahhabi group was that the unworthiness of the House of Saud made emergence of a divinely ordained leader—the *mahdi*, or promised savior—inevitable. Juhayman's associate, Muhammad ibn Abdullah al-Qahtani, proclaimed himself to be the expected *mahdi*. As to governance of the Muslim community, in *Al-Imara, wa al-Bay'a, wa al-Ta'a* (Rule, allegiance, and obedience), Juhayman stated that the *khalifah*, or ruler of the Islamic state, must be a pious Muslim chosen by the people in a general *bay'a* (by popular acclamation) and must uphold the religion.[16] The most fundamental application of the Qur'an and the *Sunna* is the sine qua non for the good Muslim life; all else is rejected as illicit.

The neo-Wahhabi movement was basically a religious-militant response to modernism: a reaffirmation of the country's core religious doctrine. It was driven by a combination of austere piety, religious dogma, and messianic militancy in pursuit of its objective: a reconfiguration of society along the lines of a highly puritanical vision. In effect, Juhayman and the neo-Wahhabi zealots sought to transform Wahhabism into an ideology of revolt against established authority in order to bring about the promised millenarian order. They failed.

For one thing, Wahhabism is essentially a conservative religious ideology rooted in state authority and the traditions of family rule and therefore resistant to radical millenarian notions of change. It remains closely bound to the Al-Saud leadership and the traditional men of religion—committed to the status quo and to law and order and steadfast against incitement to *fitna* (civil disorder). Little wonder that the *ulama* did not escape the wrath of the young militants, who called them "court clerics" subservient to the corrupt state. Moreover, with only a few hard-core followers, the neo-Wahhabis were quickly isolated and condemned by the religious establishment as seditionaries and even deviants from Islam (*khawarij*), whom it was legal to kill. Saudi forces moved against the occupiers of the mosque with the full acquiescence of the *ulama*, who issued a *fatwa* (legal opinion) sanctioning the government's action.[17]

The neo-Wahhabi insurrection and its outcome are reminiscent of the revolt of the Ikhwan—a group of Wahhabi holy warriors—in the formative years of the late 1920s. The Ikhwan was comprised of several thousand Wahhabi partisans whose religious zealotry and violent militancy superseded loyalty to tribe or ruling family. Conceived originally in the early part of the century as an instrument of Saudi conquest and consolidation, they later acted independently of royal authority—imposing strict Wahhabi purity and austerity on the country by force and carrying out *jihad* against non-Wahhabis in neighboring Hashemite-ruled Transjordan and Iraq. In effect, they threatened the social order and the Al-Saud rule.[18] Ultimately, their crusade was declared excessive and fratricidal by the *ulama*, and Abdul Aziz crushed them in 1929.[19]

Although the traditional Ikhwan and the new Wahhabi militants were unsuccessful, they both represented a deeply ingrained religious current in Saudi life, asserting the purity of the faith against foreign accretions and innovations and upholding the primacy of religion over state command. With their antimaterialist, antiroyalist, and anti-Western ideas, the Islamic fundamentalists awaited their moment.

The Gulf War of 1990–1991 reignited the neofundamentalist Islamic challenge in Saudi Arabia and gave it added momentum and stridency. The decision to place U.S. and other Western troops on Islam's sacred soil, there to unleash them against another Muslim Arab country (Iraq), was deeply unsettling to many Saudis and aroused strong opposition in young fundamentalists.[20] The war exposed the regime's startling military vulnerability and dependence on foreign powers, despite billions spent on arms in the previous decade. It also divided the religious leadership between supporters of the action and its opponents, albeit few, who rejected it as being a source of *fitna*, or Muslim fratricidal infighting. Equally, the war strapped the country's treasury, thus further aggravating already difficult economic conditions caused by sharply declining oil revenues since the mid-1980s, as well as increasing awareness of the slipping Saudi prosperity. In fact, since the Gulf War, Islamic voices have become more numerous and assertive, protesting against royal elitism and calling for openness and participation; decrying state mismanagement and official corruption and demanding more efficient and responsible government; and condemning the embrace of Western powers and adoption of their ways, under the pretext of development, and insisting on a genuine Islamic policy and stricter application of *Shari'a*.

The ranks of the Islamic opposition have since multiplied to include mosque preachers, religious scholars, university lecturers, students, unemployed graduates, and marginalized city dwellers. But the surge in Islamic activism has been especially strong among the young.[21] (This is all the more noteworthy in view of the fact that more than 60 percent of the population is under the age of twenty, a group whose economic demands and economic disappointments are likely to be aggravated in the future.) The combination of the Gulf crisis and the looming economic hardships has touched this cohort particularly, turning many of its members to Islam. These young fundamentalists appear to be more than the usual malcontents unable to find their way within the confines of the kingdom's balance between tradition and modernity.[22] Rather, they are a product of the new era of social and educational modernization and rising expectations in the midst of abundant wealth. They are "far more sophisticated, brazen, and political"[23] than were their predecessors a decade ago in their quest to thrust state and society toward its Islamic Wahhabi roots.

Although the young fundamentalists in the 1990s share some common intellectual grounds with the neo-Wahhabis of the late 1970s who stormed the Grand Mosque in Mecca, they differ from them in the sophistication of their message and the moderation of their tactics. The Islamic ideology they propound is cast more in the modern vocabulary of politics: participation, representation, responsible government, equality, legality, and human rights. They sound more like liberal democrats than Muslim ideologues. But the agenda is much the same: social conservatism and strict Islamic rule. Surely theirs is a far cry from the incoherent millenarian doctrine voiced earlier.

Further, today's fundamentalists have been less prone to open confrontation, let alone violence, in their tactics. Instead, as products of modern education for the most part, they opt for the use of modern technology and information dissemination to propagate their message. Their weapons of choice are faxes, e-mail, and computer network bulletins.[24] Additionally, these activists do not in general openly and directly challenge the legitimacy of the Saudi regime or call for its overthrow. Rather, they want to reform the system, not topple it. Their objectives are to have a say in decision-making and to exercise power, and their vehicle is religion. In effect, this means instituting politics as a legitimate public discourse in running the affairs of state.

In a country where politics is nonexistent and public debate over policy is a taboo and where there are no organized civil structures outside the religious centers that could provide a countervailing force against the Saudi state,[25] the neofundamentalists lead the public opposition and dominate the social and political agenda—something heretofore almost unheard of in Saudi Arabia. Ironically, being the sole oppositional force in the field increases their popularity, making it more difficult for the government to suppress their agenda completely. Emboldened, the young fundamentalists have attacked virtually every aspect of Saudi domestic and foreign policy, raising questions and stirring up issues regarding the course of domestic politics and relations with the West. They have been increasingly vociferous in their opposition to the royal family's power monopoly, to its lack of Wahhabi religiosity in the conduct of its private and public affairs, and to its growing attachment to U.S. power and the U.S. regional presence. In addition, they have been very critical of economic policies as a source of mismanagement and abuse of public funds, corruption, and usury (interest banking) and of the legal system, which, to their way of thinking, does not fully apply *Shari'a*.

The young fundamentalists have become bolder in their willingness to confront the regime publicly—an attitude unprecedented in the kingdom—using mosque sermons, open petitions to the king, faxes, cassette-recorded homilies, and videocassettes to disseminate information about royal family abuses, programs for reforms, and messages of dissatisfaction. All such messages and appeals break with the Saudi tradition that advice to the king can be given only privately and that he must never be petitioned or criticized publicly.[26] As a consequence, they have caused much dissension and deepened fissures in the society, contrary to traditional Saudi consensus.

King Fahd was presented with the first public petition in December 1990—in the midst of the Gulf War—signed by forty-three Saudi "liberals." The petition did not attack the royal family; rather, it was soft in tone and deferential toward the House of Saud. It supported the establishment of a *majlis al-shura* (a consultative council), which had been promised by the king. It also called for institution of a basic constitutional system of government that would guarantee the full equality of all citizens before the law, an independent judiciary, free media, and the right to form professional associations. All were sought in the name of *islah* (reform), not to contest the "noble" family.[27]

The tame petition had little public impact. The small group of intellectuals was even attacked by Islamists as "dirty secularists," a label that is usually applied to persons whose practices are un-Islamic or those of an infidel (*kafir*). The failure of the petition is exemplary of the limits of the modernist-liberal appeal in the traditional Islamic Saudi context. The liberal opposition, weak and timid, has not been able to mount an effective challenge to the monarchy and hence has been more amenable to control than has the religious opposition.

The liberal secularists were quickly overshadowed by the Islamists, who submitted an open "letter" to the king in May 1991, signed by more than 400 religious figures, including Sheikh Abdul Aziz bin Baz—the preeminent Saudi cleric—and leading notables. It called for establishment of a *majlis al-shura* with a role in domestic and foreign affairs; the accountability of public officials to restore *amana* (trust) in government; a purge of corruption at all levels; social and economic justice in the distribution of wealth; elimination of the exaction of *riba* (interest) by all financial institutions; promotion of Islamic banking; Islamization of the mass media to serve the dissemination of Islamic values and culture; unification of the judiciary under the religious

Shari'a courts; creation of a supervisory body, presumably controlled by the *ulama*, to oversee the correlation of state rules and regulations with *Shari'a*; and protection of the people's "rights" and "dignity" within the limits of *Shari'a*.[28] Surely the broad spectrum of the Islamic petition was a source of worry to the monarchy.

Islamist public activism became more direct and challenging to royal authority with the issuance of a Memorandum of Advice in September 1992 and the founding of the Committee for the Defense of Legitimate Rights less than a year later. The memorandum, signed by 107 activist religious leaders, was severely critical of domestic, foreign, and economic policies. Among other things, the lengthy document rejected the kingdom's reliance on any foreign power, even for defense; attacked Saudi foreign policy for accommodating Western interests and its oil-production policy for being tailored to world economic stability rather than the national interest; and deplored corruption and favoritism, especially among the princely elite and high government officials.[29]

More specifically, the memorandum called for a large army and a defense industry; government accountability to a consultative council; a pro-Islamic foreign policy and a pro-Saudi oil policy; and, above all, total enforcement of *Shari'a* in all spheres of Saudi life. The last item entailed an independent religious establishment and a religious body—"a supreme *Shari'a* court"— with review power over the Islamic constitutionality of all laws, regulations, and treaties. This is somewhat analogous to Iran's Council of the Guardians.[30] In effect, the activists were trying to restore the parity between state and Wahhabi Islam that existed in the formative years, making religion a coequal sphere and giving the men of religion the power to check the government.

The Committee for the Defense of Legitimate Rights was founded by seven prominent Saudi Islamists in early May 1993. It was the first attempt ever to organize an autonomous "human rights" group to monitor government observance of *Shari'a* , to remedy injustice, and to defend the rights of citizens as defined by *Shari'a*.[31] The assumption is that there is no absolute monarchic rule in Islam outside the bounds of *Shari'a*. The committee was a flagrant challenge to the closed Saudi system, which does not tolerate opposition from any independent group or association in the public sphere. Indeed, it came close to being the nucleus of a political opposition. Its spokesman, Dr. Muhammad al-Mas'ari—a physics professor at King Saud University in Riyadh—fled the country in April 1994, despite the government's prohibition on travel abroad, and set up the committee's office in London, where he continued to disseminate its agenda within the kingdom by the electronic media.[32]

Although al-Mas'ari sought to portray the committee as a human rights organization in order to appeal to the West, it is basically an opposition movement with a strictly fundamentalist agenda: full imposition of Islamic law (*Shari'a*).[33] To al-Mas'ari, "Only a return to a pure Islamic state can eradicate princely corruption, share the oil wealth more widely and create a government worthy of its custody of Mecca and Medina."[34]

All these defiant fundamentalist voices denounced the royal family and its "Westernized" allies in government for deviating from true Islamic rule and falling into despised and decadent Western infidel ways. The extremists used their own reading of Islamic ideology, which is somewhat at variance with the official religious doctrine, to attack the Al-Saud family and question its right as "keeper and interpreter of the Islamic way."[35] Surely these activities threatened to undermine the very foundation of the Al-Saud rule over the peninsula: its Islamic legitimacy. It is this aspect that renders the Islamic challenge in Saudi Arabia more menacing than that in secularist-nationalist Egypt or Algeria.

At the same time, it is the religious basis of the Saudi state that makes the challenge more manageable. The longstanding symbiosis between state and religion helps to thwart the fundamentalist opposition. Indeed, as the official mantle of religious power, Wahhabism serves both to enhance the legitimacy of the regime and to provide a license for repression of opposition groups, Islamic or otherwise. Thus, the regime continues to wrap itself in the cloak of Islam, invoking piety and conservatism, as a means of weakening the emergent religious opponents. Concurrently, it is able to counterattack with impunity, knowing that it has sufficient religious legitimacy in reserve to meet the extremists' challenge.

The Islamic opposition has been kept in check by a combination of repression of the religious extremists and co-optation of the religious establishment (the *ulama*). Threats, intimidation, dismissals, and arrests of Muslim activists have been carried out by the government without much publicity or public outcry. In late December 1991, following a virulent campaign of vilification by the fundamentalists against the royal family and educated Saudi women, Prince Turki Al-Faisal, the Saudi chief of intelligence, took the offensive and warned the fundamentalists of possible consequences of their behavior.[36] Shortly afterward, King Fahd himself, in an unusual public statement, threatened severe measures against the militants if they persisted in challenging state policies. He declared: "I am following things with wisdom and patience, ... [but] if things cross all limits, there shall be another way."[37] With a sword in its hand, the government instilled fear and thus averted a possible confrontation.[38]

Government warnings were sometimes underscored by suppression such as the crackdown against the Committee for the Defense of Legitimate Rights immediately after its founding: five members were dismissed from their government positions, and two lawyers lost their licenses and their offices were closed.[39] In September 1994, two prominent Islamists were arrested: Dr. Safar al-Hawali, dean of Islamic studies at Um al-Qura Islamic University, and Sheikh Salman Al-Auda, a charismatic preacher dubbed "the Saudi Khomeini," whose taped sermons extended his influence beyond the country's borders. Both men were told to "cease and desist" from their inflammatory preachments.[40]

The arrests touched off mass demonstrations in the town of Burayda—Sheikh Salman Al-Auda's stronghold—in the conservative region of al-Qassim in the northwest. The government arrested more than 150 protesters, accusing them of plotting acts of "agitation," spreading "sedition," and attempting to destabilize Saudi Arabia. The crackdown was extraordinary for its scope and its disclosure by the government—contrary to the customary penchant for secrecy. The Interior Ministry, in a rare display of candor, admitted the arrest of only 110 people in the disturbances "after those who pledged to avoid dissension failed to respect their pledges."[41] Many of the detainees were later released, usually after signing a statement confessing to their "improper" behavior and promising to refrain from such behavior in the future.[42] Also, in an effort to lessen the significance of the demonstrations, Prince Nayef pointed at Iran as their instigator and supporter not only in Saudi Arabia, but also elsewhere in the Middle East.[43] (Now that Iraq is temporarily out of the picture, the Saudis look at Iran as their principal nemesis.) Although there is scarcely any direct Iranian involvement, Iran has consistently defamed the royal family rhetorically, while praising its radical opponents.

It is evident that the Saudi response is very much unlike that of Egypt and Algeria, where the state-religion schism is deep and where confrontation and repression are intense and bloody, especially the latter. In Saudi Arabia, despite the harsh treatment of radical fundamentalists, the preference is to avoid violent showdowns. Indeed, neither side has attempted an open clash. The bombing of the U.S. military training mission in Riyadh in November 1995 by four Saudi religious militants seems to mark an escalation—uncharacteristic of Saudi opposition.[44]

Saudis are generally uncomfortable with overt manifestations of conflict,[45] a policy that seems to suit the Saudi leadership's purpose: to enjoin conformity more by persuasion and consensus than by coercive power—the latter usually as a last recourse. Indeed, in Hanbali tradition—the basis of Wahhabi official Sunni doctrine—there is a strong emphasis on conformism and dogmatism and an aversion to dissension, lest it lead to disunity. Further, the radicals, cognizant of the overwhelming power of the state, are averse to direct confrontation, which could seal their fate. The crushing of the Ikhwan in the late 1920s, the suppression of religious zealots in the 1960s, and the destruction of the neo-Wahhabis in the late 1970s are testimony to the fate of extremists: extinction. The logic of state authority and civil order have always triumphed over religious dogma and zealotry.

In addition, to fend off the fundamentalists, the government has enlisted the support of the religious establishment. Its longstanding alliance with the House of Saud has subjected the *ulama* to vitriolic attacks by the fundamentalists, who accuse them, among other things, of selling out to the royal family. The official *ulama* have always defended Al-Saud rule as in accord with *Shari'a* and condemned those who challenge its legitimacy. Further, their *fatwas* (legal opinions) have sanctioned all major policy decisions in public affairs and in the conduct of the Gulf War.[46] Their loyalty has been cultivated and sustained by the state's generous financing of their positions, institutions, and centers and by its acknowledgment of their status as an important constituency that is often consulted, especially in crises.[47] Indeed, their increasing dependence on the state closely links the men of religion to the regime; they are courted and controlled for reasons of legitimation.

No religious challenge has yet managed to break the bond between the Al-Saud and the religious establishment. Contrariwise, coming under increasing attack and fearing loss of position, the *ulama* veered closer to the government in the battle with religious radicals. Sheikh Abdul Aziz bin Baz, the leading official cleric, attacked the militants and denounced their public behavior as scandalous, fratricidal, and "against the will of God," counseling them "to repent and to desist."[48] Further, the Council of Senior Ulama (*Hay'at Kibar al-Ulama'*), which he heads, condemned the radicals' 1992 Memorandum of Advice to the government, accusing the signers of practicing sedition and "serving the interests of the enemies of Saudi Arabia." Seven elderly members of the eighteen-man council who refused to endorse the condemnation were "retired" by King Fahd in December 1992—an assertion of government dominion over the religious establishment.

During his meeting with the senior *ulama* that month, the king accused the petitioners of acting in a manner contrary to the Saudi way of *tanasuh* (mutual advice and consent) and of propagating foreign-inspired ideas—an allusion to Shi'a Iran's complicity.[49] In so doing, he maintained the right of the Saudi state to define its Islamic path within the "Saudi context"—a stance that has the support of the *ulama* as the official interpreters of Saudi Wahhabi Islam. Surely, to the senior *ulama*, the Committee for the Defense of Legitimate Rights was an "illegitimate body that cannot be approved because Islamic *Shari'a* is the law of the land and religious courts are available to seek justice."[50] This paved the way for the government to move quickly and dismantle the group.

Finally, amid the rising dissidence, the official *ulama* in 1994 launched a campaign in the media and in mosques and religious centers that stressed the importance of *ta'a* (obedience) to rulers, even when they err or deviate from strict Islamic teachings.[51] This is in line with mainstream Sunni Islamic jurisprudence—traditionally giving preference to state power and control over civil strife and chaos—a form of Sunni statist doctrine used to sustain traditional rulers in the Middle East.

Meanwhile, the government showed greater vigilance in the application of Islamic norms, albeit selectively: censorship of the press was tightened, the importation of satellite dishes was banned, rigid standards of public morals were enforced, and the *hudud* (the Muslim penal code) was imposed[52]—all to add the appearance of piety and orthodoxy. It sought wider consultation with the *ulama*, heeding their concerns and giving them a greater sense of participation. The government boycotted the United Nations Conference on Population and Development in Cairo in September 1994 at the urging of the Council of Senior Ulama, which vehemently attacked it as anti-Islamic.[53] Likewise, the government did not participate in the Fourth World Conference on Women in Beijing in September 1995. The senior *ulama* repudiated the conference's agenda as contrary to Islamic *Shari' a* and destructive to the family.[54]

Also, the Saudis have been reluctant to sign a defense agreement or to hold joint military exercises with the United States partly in response to the conservative *ulama*'s disquietude over close embrace of the West.[55] In addition, the government designated a number of mainstream theologians to the recently appointed sixty-one-member Consultative Council.[56] Further, it tolerated the revival of the conservative religious Department for the Preservation of Virtue and the Prevention of Vice, operated by the *mutawi' in* (salaried religious police who are in charge of enforcing strict public morals and religious observances), but it discouraged acts of zealotry by young militant volunteer *mutawi' in* as contrary to the teachings of Islam.[57] So long as the fundamentalist challenge keeps knocking on the doors of the House of Saud, the Al-Saud family will continue to position itself behind official Islam.

Simultaneously, the Saudi state instituted tighter controls over religious life in the kingdom by adding two new supervisory religious bodies in October 1994 to the Council of Senior Ulama: the Higher Council of Islamic Affairs, headed by Defense Minister Prince Sultan bin Abdul Aziz and staffed by ranking family members and technocrats, and the Call and Guidance Council, chaired by Dr. Abdullah al-Turki, minister of Islamic affairs, endowment, and propagation.[58] They are designed to streamline the activities of religious centers and organizations at home and abroad, to increase the government's supervision of religious interpretation, and to limit the dissemination of dissident ideas under the cover of Islam. All in all, they reassert the right of the authorities to oversee religious affairs in the country.

To balance the conservative *ulama*, the Saudi monarchy has sought to co-opt the Western-educated modernists, many of whom are its governmental allies. Indeed, the proliferation of modern education since the early 1970s has resulted in a new technocratic-administrative elite—mostly a salaried group employed by the state—tied to the power elite (the royal family) and serving to enhance its capability and control. Although some of the modernists have antiroyalist sentiments, advocating modern social and political structures and popular participation, they have not posed a threat to the regime. Neither have they coalesced into a politically active, independent opposition force. Rather, many modernists seem to find some common ground with the princely elite when it comes to protecting their positions and privileges.[59] Also, liberal modernists generally share with the Al-Saud family and the religious leadership— the traditional Saudi establishment—a dislike of the neofundamentalists, who have constantly vilified them as secularist atheists.[60]

To appeal to the modernists, in March 1992 the king decreed the establishment of a basic system of government (a constitutional framework for the state), the Consultative Council (an appointive national assembly), and a system of regional government (thirteen appointive provincial councils).[61] Although these initiatives appear to present a semblance of openness, they occurred within the bounds of monarchic paramountcy and Islamic tradition. The much-heralded Consultative Council has neither a legislative nor a supervisory role: it is strictly an advisory body. In fact, "legislative" power is precluded, for *Shari'a* remains the basic law of the land. Thus, the council has not truly expanded the range of participation in terms of wielding power in policy making. Real power rests in the king, who is still the ultimate arbiter on matters of state; the appointed regional governors—all members of the royal family—are an extension of monarchic authority; and the provincial councils are paper tigers.

Still, the Consultative Council, which includes many (more than 70 percent) from the modernist ranks —bureaucratic-technocratic elite, professionals, academics, and businessmen[62]—provides a measure of reform, albeit limited and short of meaningful participation. It partially fulfills the modernists' desire for openness without jeopardizing royal authority. The tilt toward the liberal modernist serves the monarchy's effort to balance the traditionalists' influence in public life, while still emphasizing its Islamic foundation. By no means does it guarantee liberal ascendancy, for the council is severely constrained by its rules and procedures and by royal family whims.

Equally important, the *majlis* can serve to counter the fundamentalists by providing a veneer of "popular participation" through co-optation, but short of representation, behind which the royal family can take cover. Indeed, the *majlis* helps to legitimize royal family rule under the guise of "broadening" participation by and sharing responsibility with council members.[63] At the same time, it is a means to preempt participatory politics by enabling a selected group to render *mashwara* (opinion and advice) without permitting political structures and debate.

It is evident, then, that in the short term, the Saudi state is in no imminent danger from the fundamentalists. Nor is it headed toward a possible future revolutionary explosion and a fundamentalist takeover. The leadership has been exceptionally adept at balancing divergent social forces by manipulating tribal-family loyalties (*asabiyya*) and religious affinities, subtly using patronage and co-optation, and playing group against group—all the while making sure to maintain the preeminent position of the royal family. In so doing, it has successfully contained the Muslim extremists and minimized their potential danger. In the midterm future, the extremists are likely to continue on the Saudi scene as a fringe group, unable to upset the social balance.

In the long term, so long as the oil flows at a relatively moderate rate and at stable prices, the government enables the majority of the middle and professional-technocratic classes to continue their comfortable lifestyles, and the business community—the government's usual ally—is afforded greater opportunities for economic expansion, the Saudi leadership will be able to keep a lid on societal tension and thereby diminish further the prospects of Muslim malcontents. Recent financial strains notwithstanding, the country that is "blessed" with 25 percent of the world's proven oil reserves is not about to go broke anytime soon.[64] Rather, it ranks among the wealthiest nations in the world—its big honeypot will go on being used for domestic stability and external security. The largely rentier economy still serves to shelter the population from the burdens of taxation and import duties.[65]

The Saudi monarchy has demonstrated a remarkable aptitude for survival. Over the past half century, it has withstood the Arab nationalist sweep, the Iranian Islamic revolutionary wave, and the Iraqi military threat. And it will certainly prevail against today's Islamist challenge. The monarchy will be able to sustain itself as the custodian of power and faith by using a mix of moderate political reforms tempered by religious conservatism and modest state welfarism coupled with expanding economic entrepreneurship. In the end, Saudi Arabia will be neither a modern liberal constitutional monarchy nor a revolutionary Islamic republic. Benevolent authoritarian monarchy will probably persist into the twenty-first century.

NOTES

1. On this theme, see James E. Akins, "The New Arabia," *Foreign Affairs* 70 (Summer 1991): 40.

2. On the tribal structure of Saudi Arabia, see Roy Lebkicher et al., *ARAMCO Handbook* (Netherlands: Arabian-American Oil Co., 1960).

3. The current Saudi state is the third such state in recent history. The first, originating in the second half of the eighteenth century, was destroyed by Egypt's Muhammad Ali in 1818 at the behest of the Ottoman sultan, who wanted to keep control of the holy places of Islam in Mecca and Medina and the Gulf sea lanes. The second, originating in 1824, was soon marred by turbulence and fratricidal fighting among competing princes and ended in 1890. But the eclipse of Saudi power was brief. Led by Abdul Aziz ibn Saud, the Al-Saud family returned from temporary exile in Kuwait to regain control in the early part of the twentieth century and ultimately establish the kingdom. See Ahmad Assah, *Mu'jiza fawg al-Rimal* (Miracle above the sands) (Beirut: al-Matabi' al-Ahliyyah, 1971); Sheikh Hafiz Wahba, *Arabian Days* (London: Arthur Barker, 1964); Christine Moss Helms, *The Cohesion of Saudi Arabia* (Baltimore: Johns Hopkins University Press, 1981).

4. On this theme, see Helms, *The Cohesion of Saudi Arabia.*

5. The four classical schools of Islamic jurisprudence have always practiced mutual tolerance and acceptance.

6. For further analysis of Wahhabism, see Bayly Winder, *Saudi Arabia in the Nineteenth Century* (New York: St. Martin's Press, 1965); George Rentz, "Wahhabism and Saudi Arabia," *The Arabian Peninsula: Society and Politics*, ed. Derek Hopwood (London: George Allen & Unwin, 1972), 54–66; Helms, *The Cohesion of Saudi Arabia*; Ayman al-Yassini, *Religion and State in the Kingdom of Saudi Arabia* (Boulder, Colo.: Westview Press, 1985).

7. Wilfred Smith, *Islam in Modern History* (New York: New American Library, 1957),

49.

8. On the Ikhwan, see Helms, *The Cohesion of Saudi Arabia*; al-Yassini, *Religion and State in the Kingdom of Saudi Arabia*.

9. The newly instituted basic system of government (March 1992) states that the Qur'an is the constitution of the kingdom and that the basic system is in accord with Islamic principles. Therefore, the kingdom has no need for a formal constitution.

10. Pan-Arabism remains a myth; once forced into reality during the brief Egyptian-Syrian union (1958–1961), the result was a mess. See Mahmud A. Faksh, "Withered Arab Nationalism," *Orbis* 37 (Summer 1993): 425–38.

11. Michael C. Hudson, *Arab Politics: The Search for Legitimacy* (New Haven, Conn.: Yale University Press, 1979), 168–69.

12. Morroe Berger, *The Arab World Today* (Garden City, N.Y.: Doubleday, 1964), 414–15.

13. On this point, see F. Gregory Gause III, *Oil Monarchies: Domestic and Security Challenges in the Arab Gulf States* (New York: Council on Foreign Relations, 1994), 32.

14. For a discussion of the theme of marginalization of the *ulama*, see Alexander Bligh, "The Saudi Religious Elite (Ulama) as Participants in the Political System of the Kingdom," *International Journal of Middle East Studies* 17 (Feb. 1985): 37–50.

15. On this general theme, see Lisa Anderson, "Absolutism and the Resiliency of Monarchy in the Middle East," *Political Science Quarterly* 106 (Spring 1991): 1–15.

16. See Juhayman al-Utaibi, *Al-Imara wa al-Bay'a wa al-Ta'a* (Rule, allegiance, and obedience) (n.p., n.d.).

17. See *al-Riyadh* 25 Nov. 1979: 1.

18. Abdul Aziz feared that the Ikhwan's excesses would embroil him with Great Britain in Transjordan and Iraq and would alienate his moderate Muslim subjects in the urban centers.

19. Abdul Aziz had to obtain a *fatwa* from the *ulama* before he could move to crush the Ikhwan. The *ulama* ruled that it is the *Imam* (ruler) who could declare *jihad*.

20. During the Gulf crisis, taped speeches by Safar al-Hawali (dean of Islamic studies at Um al-Qura Islamic University), denouncing U.S. deployment in Saudi Arabia as a "Western crusade against Islam," circulated throughout the kingdom. The tapes attacked the Al-Saud family and those in the official clergy for condoning the joining in battle of non-Muslims against Muslims. See Mamoun Fandy, "The Hawali Tapes," *New York Times* 24 Nov. 1990: A21.

21. See Youssef M. Ibrahim, "The Saudis Are Fearful, Too, as Islam's Militant Tide Rises," *New York Times* 31 Dec. 1991: A1.

22. See Caryle Murphy, "Fundamentalists Shaping Politics of Saudi Arabia," *Washington Post* 17 Dec. 1992: A33.

23. Tony Horwitz, "Two Years after War, Many Saudis Behave as If It Never Occurred," *Wall Street Journal* 13 Jan. 1993: 1.

24. See Robert Fisk, "Saudis Attack Rulers by Tape and Fax," *Independent* 21 June 1993: 12. This is unlike the Egyptian militant Islamic groups, "who have to break into jewelry shops to raise money" to finance their operations against the government. See Leslie Cockburn and Andrew Cockburn, "Royal Mess," *New Yorker* 24 Aug. 1994: 66.

25. Parties and unions are rejected as contrary to the notion of *umma* (community) unity. They lead to *tahazzub*, or factionalism and fratricide, to the detriment of the public welfare *(al-maslaha al-'ama)*. The only organized groups that are sanctioned and somewhat autonomous are the local chambers of commerce in the different regions of the country.

26. See *al-Sharq al-Awast* 2 Sept. 1994: 14.

27. On the petition, see "Empty Reforms: Saudi Arabia's New Basic Laws," *Middle East Watch* May 1992: 59–61. See also Judith Caesar, "Liberals and Conservatives Press Riyadh," *New York Times* 5 July 1991: A21.

28. See "Empty Reforms," 61–62.

29. See Caryle Murphy, "Conservative Clergy Attack Saudi Government," *Washington Post* 28 Sept. 1992: A12.

30. Iran's Council of the Guardians acts as the protector of the Islamic principles of the Iranian constitution and sees to the constitutionality of all laws and regulations. See the Islamic Constitution of the Islamic Republic of Iran, Articles 91–99.

31. See *al-Sharq al-Awsat* 14 May 1993: 1; Dilip Hiro, "Saudi Dissenters Go Public," *Nation* 28 June 1993: 906–9.

32. See Caryle Murphy, "Exiled Saudi Dissidents Launch Media Campaign," *Washington Post* 1 June 1994: A24.

33. One of the committee members, conservative cleric Sheikh Abdullah al-Jibrin, publicly branded the Shi'a minority in Saudi Arabia as *kuffar* (apostates), a charge that carries the death sentence in Saudi Arabia. Another prominent member, Abdullah al-Tuweijri, called for stiff penalties against the women who drove in public in 1991 to protest the customary ban on women's driving as a form of segregation against women and referred to them as prostitutes. See Youssef M. Ibrahim, "Saudis Crack Down on a Dissident Islamic Group," *New York Times* 14 May 1993: A3.

34. Quoted in Michael Sheridan, "Saudi Rulers Learn to Live with Fewer Millions," *Independent* 13 Dec. 1994: 16.

35. See Michael Sheridan, "Islamists' Challenge Stirs the House of Saud," *Independent* 12 Dec. 1994: 11.

36. Ibrahim, "The Saudis Are Fearful, Too, as Islam's Militant Tide Rises," A1.

37. Quoted in Youssef M. Ibrahim, "Saudi King Takes on Islamic Militants," *New York Times* 30 Jan. 1992: A3.

38. For example, a protest demonstration scheduled by the fundamentalists in late January 1992 was called off after the government issued a warning against the act and put the security forces on alert, with orders to arrest all demonstrators. See Ibrahim, "Saudi King Takes on Islamic Militants."

39. See *al-Sharq al-Awsat* 14 May 1993:1; Caryle Murphy, "Saudis Move against Rights Unit," *Washington Post* 16 May 1993: A27; "Saudis Detain Human Rights Advocate," *Christian Science Monitor* 17 May 1993: 6; Ibrahim, "Saudis Crack Down on a Dissident Islamic Group." Sheikh Abdullah al-Jibrin, a prominent member of the committee, later renounced association with the group, stating that he had been "misled." See *Arabia Monitor* August 1993: 15. Dr. Muhammad al-Mas'ari, the spokesman of the committee, sought refuge in London. Under Saudi government pressure, implicit in the statement of Prince Nayef (interior minister) that "any activities against the government of Saudi Arabia will be a key element of our interests," the British Home Office refused his application for asylum. See Sheridan, "Islamists' Challenge Stirs the House of Saud." In early January 1996, the British government ordered the deportation of Dr. al-Mas'ari—his presence represented a peril to British business interests in Saudi Arabia. Dr. al-Mas'ari appealed the order in court, and in April 1996, the appeals court ruled against the government. See *al-Sharq al-Awsat* 1 Jan. 1996: 1; Richard W. Stevenson, "Saudi Gadfly and the British Embarrassment," *New York Times* 30 Jan. 1996: A1; John Darnton, "Britain, Facing Setback in Court, Won't Deport Saudi Dissident," *New York Times* 19 Apr. 1996: A11.

40. See Cockburn and Cockburn, "Royal Mess," 69; Leslie Plommer, "Royal Family Vulnerable to Islamists," *Guardian* 28 Nov. 1994: 24.

41. See Youssef M. Ibrahim, "Saudi Arabia Arrests 110 in a Crackdown on Muslim Militants," *New York Times* 27 Sept. 1994: A12.

42. But the ministry's warning remains: "People who act against religion or the security of the country through writing or in any other way will face appropriate measures of deterrence." See Charles Snow, "Saudis Set Up New Religious Bodies," *Middle East Economic Survey* 31 Oct. 1994: C4.

43. See *al-Sharq al-Awsat* 17 Dec. 1994: 2.

44. Initially, two obscure Islamic groups—the Islamic Movement for Change and Tigers of the Gulf—claimed responsibility, but there was little evidence to support these claims. Early in the summer of 1995, the Islamic Movement for Change had sent faxes around the kingdom, calling for the withdrawal of U.S. and British troops by the end of June and threatening to attack U.S. military personnel if they did not comply. See John Lancaster, "Five Americans Killed by Car Bomb at Military Building in Saudi Capital," *Washington Post* 14 Nov. 1995: A1; Elaine Sciolino, "Bomb in Saudi Arabia's Capital Kills 4 Americans," *New York Times* 14 Nov. 1995: A1; *al-Majalla* 19–25 Nov. 1995: 24–29.

In April 1996, the Saudi government announced the arrest of four Saudi nationals, who confessed to the car bombing. In late May 1996, they were beheaded according to Saudi *Shari'a*. The four stated that they had fought in Afghanistan and had been influenced by radical Islamic groups outside the kingdom, including Muhammad al-Mas'ari and Usama bin Laden. The latter is a Saudi millionaire and a self-styled revolutionary Islamist who helped finance Arab-Muslim fighters in Afghanistan, as well as other militant Islamic factions elsewhere. He was stripped of his Saudi citizenship in April 1994 and is currently in exile in Sudan. See "Four Confess on Saudi TV to Bombing of U.S. Center," *New York Times* 23 Apr. 1996: A13; *al-Sharq al-Awsat* 8 Apr. 1994: 1, 23 Apr. 1996: 1, 5; "Saudi Arabia Beheads Four in Bomb Attack," *New York Times* 1 June 1996: 4.

The second bombing of a U.S. target in late June 1996 in Dhahran shows that Saudi Arabia cannot remain insulated from intermittent acts of terrorism by determined extremist fringe groups seeking to destabilize the Saudi monarchy. See Elaine Sciolino, "Bombing Attack Raises Questions about Stability of Saudi Government," *New York Times* 27 June 1996: A11; Douglas Jehl, "Saudi Islamic Council Condemns Bombing," *New York Times* 2 July 1996: A5.

45. See Frank J. Mirkow, "The Nature of Saudi Arabian Strategic Power: Implications for American Foreign Policy," *Fletcher Forum of World Affairs* 17 (Winter 1993): 162.

46. Among the many *fatwas* were those regarding the accession of King Faisal in 1964, displacing King Saud; the attack on the Grand Mosque in 1979; and the stationing of foreign troops on Saudi soil during the Gulf War.

47. On the role of the *ulama* in Saudi Arabia, see Joseph A. Kechichian, "The Role of the Ulama in the Politics of an Islamic State: The Case of Saudi Arabia," *International Journal of Middle East Studies* 18. 2 (1986): 53–71.

48. Quoted in Ibrahim, "The Saudis Are Fearful, Too, as Islam's Militant Tide Rises," A10.

49. See Kathy Evans, "Petitioners Press Saudi Leaders," *Guardian* 23 Sept. 1992: 9; *al-Sharq al-Awsat* 18 Sept. 1992: 1; Youssef M. Ibrahim, "Saudi Denounces Fundamentalists," *New York Times* 22 Dec. 1992: A10.

50. See *al-Sharq al-Awsat* 14 May 1993:1.

51. For example, see *al-Sharq al-Awsat* 2 Sept. 1994:14.

52. It is reported that, since January 1995, there has been a noticeable increase in the number of beheadings carried out in Saudi Arabia. Nearly 100 convicted criminals have been executed in public squares, found guilty of rape, murder, and drug trafficking. See "Paper Money from Saudi Arabia," *Foreign Report* 11 May 1995: 6.

53. See Youssef M. Ibrahim, "Saudi Arabia Cracks Down on Islamic Militants, Seizing Many," *New York Times* 22 Sept. 1994: A5.

54. For the full text of the declaration of the Council of Senior Ulama, see *al-Sharq al-Awsat* 3 Sept. 1995: 8.

55. Elaine Sciolino and Eric Schmitt, "Saudi Arabia, Its Purse Thinner, Learns How to Say 'NO' to U.S.," *New York Times* 4 Nov. 1994: A1.

56. King Fahd named Sheikh Muhammad bin Ibrahim bin Jubeir as president of the council in September 1992. See *al-Sharq al-Awsat* 18 Sept. 1992: 1. A year later, in August 1993, he appointed the sixty members of the council and set out its rules, procedures, and powers. Six of the members were religious leaders. On the composition of the council, see *al-Majalla* 29 Aug.–4 Sept. 1993: 25–27.

57. Nabila Megalli, "'Enforcers' Step Up Drive to Keep Saudis in Line," *Los Angeles Times* 19 Jan. 1992: A27.

58. Snow, "Saudis Set Up New Religious Bodies." See also "Prince Sultan Outlines Duties of Higher Council of Islamic Affairs," *Saudi Arabia* Dec. 1994: 3; Youssef M. Ibrahim, "Saudi King Trying to Dilute Islamic Radicalism," *New York Times* 6 Oct. 1994: A5.

59. On the rising technocratic-professional middle class and its relationship with the ruling family, see William Rugh, "Emergence of a New Middle Class in Saudi Arabia," *Middle East Journal* 27 (Winter 1973): 7–20.

60. A case in point is the accusation of *'ilmani* (secularist) and *kafir* (apostate) levelled against Ghazi al-Qusaibi—a leading modernist who was minister of industry and electricity and is now Saudi ambassador to the United Kingdom—by the Islamists during the height of the Gulf War. See R. Hrair Dekmejian, "The Rise of Political Islam in Saudi Arabia," *Middle East Journal* 48 (Autumn 1994): 632.

61. The regions of Mecca, Medina, and Riyadh have twenty-member councils; the other ten regions have fifteen-member councils. See *al-Majalla* 9–15 Jan. 1994: 19.

62. On the composition of the council, see *al-Majalla* 29 Aug.–4 Sept. 1993.

63. King Fahd described the members of the *majlis* as the "cream of the crop" (*nukhba mukhtara*), who have the knowledge and wisdom needed to render proper advice. See *al-Majalla* 9–15 Jan. 1994: 18.

64. See Andrew Cunningham, "Saudi Arabia Bites the Financial Bullet," *Middle East International* 14 Mar. 1994: 17.

65. Although the government announced early in 1995 major price hikes for gas, water, electricity, telephones, and air travel as necessary measures to ease the budgetary imbalance, King Fahd went out of his way to underscore the temporary nature of these measures. Meanwhile, subsidies of domestic fees were maintained for the poor. See *al-Sharq al-Awsat* 1 Jan. 1995: 5; "Paper Money from Saudi Arabia," *Foreign Report*; "Saudi Arabia's Future," *Economist* 18 Mar. 1995: 21.

6

Future Prospects:
The Limits of Islamic Fundamentalism

As the Middle East approaches the dawn of a new millennium, it appears that, after twenty-five years of revival, struggle, and government containment, militant Islamic fundamentalism is now running its course. Its fortunes have peaked, and currently it seems headed toward decline. The invincible legions of God—the revolutionaries of Islam—no longer pose a fatal threat to the region. Thus, "doomsdayers" notwithstanding, the Middle East is not about to be torn asunder by the fundamentalists at any time—now or in the future. An Islamic fundamentalist explosion, especially in the post–Gulf War period, has proved to be an overstated threat. It has not materialized—certainly not in the dimensions envisaged.

Although Islamic fundamentalism has become a social force, raising Islamic cultural consciousness and influencing the attitudes and actions of many, especially the young and the poor, it has been far less successful as a political force seeking change. In fact, fundamentalism has failed to translate its ideological rhetoric into political power. Today only the rhetoric remains.[1] The regimes that have faced up to the Islamist challenge have fared well in the contest and are deeply entrenched. And, contrary to fundamentalist expectations, the Gulf War even augmented the U.S. position in the region, which is stronger now than ever. Indeed, Islamic fundamentalism has yet to march out of the mosques and into government office.

Today pauperized Sudan is the only Arab country where a military-backed fundamentalist system is in place—and has been since 1989—but for reasons unrelated to the Gulf crisis. The National Islamic Front came to rule by means of an army coup, not a popular Islamic revolution. The dictatorship that displaced the democratically elected government of Prime Minister Muhammad Sadiq al-Mahdi (1986–1989) has behaved entirely in character, despite the government-staged parliamentary and presidential elections of March 1996. Although Hasan al-Turabi, the National Islamic Front's chief ideologue, has always tried to present the regime as valid and exemplary, Islamic Sudan could hardly serve as a model for other Arab countries. The country's military dictatorship, impoverishment, prolonged ethnic-tribal conflict between the Arab-Muslim north and the black African Christian and pagan south over issues of citizenship and equality, a dismal human rights record, and international isolation as a supporter of terrorism all make it wholly unappealing as a prototype.[2] As a peripheral isolated case in the Arab world—the first and only militant Sunni fundamentalist state—it is somewhat akin to formerly Marxist South Yemen: an aberration.

Outside the Arab circle, Iran stands alone since 1979 as the revolutionary fundamentalist state *par excellence*. But, here again, the early luster that bedazzled many and frightened some soon dissipated in the ensuing political turmoil, the Iran-Iraq war, and social and economic failure. The Shi'a model of the rule of the *imams*, a heterodox theoretical-juridical exercise throughout much of Islamic history, remains confined to Iran. The model failed to catch on in orthodox Sunni Arab lands, partly because of historical Sunni Arab–Shi'a Persian antipathy. Other than its close ties with its coreligionists in the Hizbullah of Lebanon and its general support of Muslim militants, Shi'a Islamic Iran has little direct influence over the Islamic movements in the Middle East.

Now, after more than a decade and a half of Islamic rule, Iran's worsening economic difficulties, its repressive social and political environment, the incessant power struggle between its moderates and radicals, and its loneliness as a pariah nation render it an unappealing archetype.[3] Indeed, Iran under the rule of the *mullahs* is a state still in the throes of revolutionary confusion and factionalism. All these circumstances do not bode well for the Islamic regime, which has yet to find solutions and achieve a sense of security and permanence.[4]

Neither Sudan nor Iran provides an inspiring Islamic example, but the Afghan experience truly illustrates an Islamic fundamentalist movement run amok. Once in power, the Islamists did not abstain from internecine feuding and infighting along tribal-ethnic and religious-doctrinal lines, plunging the country into disintegration and chaos. The seemingly endless civil war since the withdrawal of Soviet forces in 1989 has pushed Afghanistan closer to "a primal state." Human torment is particularly evident in the south, which is controlled by the militant fundamentalist Taliban.[5] In fact, Afghanistan is another example of Islamic governance gone awry.

It is evident, then, that other than the rallying cry "Islam is the solution," there is neither a guiding center nor a coherent ideological structure to lead the Islamic movement, as there was once, for instance, in communism. Instead, there are diverse Islamic groups, even within a single country, with a wide range of objectives and tactics and a partial articulation of "the solution." The multiplicity and diversity of Egypt's Islamic groups and the amorphous Islamic opposition in Saudi Arabia render the Islamic course incoherent and chaotic. Even the Algerian Islamic Salvation Front (FIS) is a composite of groups and ideological tendencies that is far from being unified sufficiently to speak in unison. This also applies to the Islamic movements in Syria, Jordan, and Lebanon, among others. Even in Iran, the religious leadership is not as one regarding the course of the regime; factional disputes are endemic.[6]

It can be said as well that today's fundamentalism is "all cause and no programme."[7] The fundamentalists are more preoccupied with restoring the religious-moral order as they believe it to have existed in the early days of Islam (*salaf*) than with offering an elaborate blueprint for a future order. Thus, like many other revolutionaries, they direct their struggle against "un-Islamic" regimes rather than toward planned change that goes beyond slogans promoting "true" Islam as the "solution." In the long run, their single-mindedness will severely limit the Islamic movement and considerably diminish its prospects. In the quest for the future good life, imposed morals and values alone are no substitute for programmatic approaches.

Equally important, there are certain inherent limitations that could impede the march of Islamic fundamentalism. The fundamentalists' vision of state and society is in contradistinction to existing conditions, making it appear too radical an alternative. The ideological formulations of Muslim fundamentalism are wholly inadequate in today's regional and international contexts. Indeed, the fundamentalists' premise of total Islamic self-sufficiency—Islam as a complete system of life, permanent in time and place—runs contrary to modern conditions of global interdependence, world interactivity, and universal cultural awareness. Unwittingly, it even lends credence to Samuel Huntington's thesis of a forthcoming "Clash of Civilizations."[8]

Socially, the fundamentalists seek to establish greater societal uniformity and conformity according to their rightist religious dogma— a societal corporatism, with a highly integrated and regimented way of life, based on religion. Society becomes a holistic, wholesome Muslim body that is resistant to foreign impurities and domestic *assimiles*. This conception has been manifest in Iran's persecution of the Bahá'í religious minority and of members of the Western-educated elite and intellectuals. Among the first victims of revolutionary Shi'a Islam, as propagated by Ayatollah Khomeini's Islamic republic, were the modernist liberals. It is also evident in Sudan's holy war on the Christians and animists in its south and in its repression of modern thinkers and academics, and in Egyptian fundamentalists' attacks on Christian Copts and in their intimidation and even assassination of leading secular writers, thinkers, and artists. It is also seen in the Algerian fundamentalists' opposition to Berber cultural identification and in their assassination of scores of prominent intellectuals, journalists, and professors as *laico-assimilationistes*. FIS publications have strongly condemned the advocates of Berber culture and language as racialist- and colonialist-inspired against the unity of the Algerian Muslim nation.[9] In Pakistan, the Jama'at-i-Islami has shown deep intolerance of members of the Ahmadiyya sect, accusing them of being heretical or "un-Muslim," characteristics that should prohibit their participation in public life.[10] Indeed, the rise of Islamic fundamentalism has occasioned a growing isolation of and hostility toward ethnic and religious minorities across the Middle East. Little wonder that these minorities tend to look at the Islamists as an even greater threat to their survival than the disliked regimes that always have tried to suppress them.

All the foregoing are clear cases of intolerance and terror precipitated by a narrow, collectivistic view of society that is contrary to the sociocultural, religious, and ethnic mosaic of the Middle East. Pluralism, multiculturalism, secularism, and all other notions associated with modern liberalism are rejected in favor of religious nationalism and exclusivism, wherein religious loyalty becomes the focal point of identity. Islamic fundamentalism is a fierce and virulent reaction to secular liberalism, which disavows the notion of a "pure" and regimented society based upon religious certainty. It is an attack on the modernist-secularist incline of the past 100 years, seeking its reversal and a return to Islam. It is "a new religious totalitarianism" wanting to move society along a divine providential path[11] and exalting the power of the primordial collectivistic mass—the *umma*—guided by a divine schema. It is exclusivist, with religion as the hallmark of membership, yet holistic—exalting the collectivity—and therefore repressive. Its rejection of societal and ideological diversity and pluralism is tantamount to religious "Bolshevism." But the fact is that the Arab peoples are much too diverse to be compressed into a uniform entity.

Politically, the fundamentalists see the state as an extension of religion, and hence the fusion of the two spheres becomes for them a cardinal principle. In their schema, politics is reduced to morals, and political power is the means to constitute the moral community, not the management of political and social predicaments or conflicts.[12] Their view clashes with the political realities in the Middle East today in that it denies the notion of secular-national politics and delegitimizes national governments in all forms in the Arab world. But to remold Arab politics along such a religious conception would, in effect, entail the wholesale exclusion of some important segments, groups, and organizations in the societies that for different reasons support the national state as the source of independence, strength, identity, or material benefit. Iran is an early warning: the ruling Islamic hierarchy has charted the country on a religious-totalitarian course, banning all "non-Islamic" groups, including moderate nationalist elements. The clergy have absolute power. With politics mutated into a religious discourse, superimposed as a totalitarian ideology, the *mullahs* are not the vanguards of liberation and freedom; rather, they are the new forces of oppression and absolutism.

Despite the ideological rhetoric about the future ideal Muslim community (the *umma*), the Islamic movements, in their varied contexts, have not been able to transcend the bounds of the modern nation-state. Indeed, the fundamentalists across the Muslim lands have failed to produce a genuine Islamic alternative to the Western-based state paradigm. But, here again, Islam has never spelled out a specific political organization model; instead, it offers more general principles, values, and standards of governance.[13] Further, neither Islamic universalism nor Arabian tribalism is conducive to the rise of an indigenous, territory-based state system. In fact, both contexts are the antithesis of the nation-state. (This is unlike medieval agriculture-based Continental feudalism, whose units provided the nuclei for the European nation-state system in the sixteenth century.) And Muslims today seem unable to extricate themselves from the Western model: "From Casablanca to Tashkent, the Islamists have molded themselves into the framework of existing states."[14] Thus, the aspired Muslim *umma* has not replaced distinctive national states' solidarities. The Islamic *umma* remains only a theoretical ideal, wholly detached from the reality of political and territorial divisions in a world of nation-states.

The most controversial and worrisome aspect of the Islamization of political life is the proposed broad application of Islamic *Shari'a* (law). The fundamentalists see *Shari'a* as the basis of community life, valid for all times and places, and call for stricter observance of its rules. This would have major implications for the social and economic realms. For education, it would entail the end of coeducation and the expansion of religious propagation in schools: the ascendancy of dogma over reason. For women, it would mean imposed segregation and exclusion from public activities. For economic and financial fields, it would result in a ban on "un-Islamic" business pursuits such as the production and sale of alcohol and entertainment, forbid the payment of interest as "usury" (there is no place for "the miracle of compound interest" in Islam), and scorn materialism and the corruption of wealth generally. All this would not square easily with modern conditions in the Middle East, which would defy imposition of a puritan-like order. It could even bring about societal inaction and stagnation.

In fact, the majority of Arab-Muslim peoples do not desire a theocratic state, nor do they wish the wholesale imposition of *Shari'a*, including the Qur'anic *hudud*, or penal code, which provides penalties such as public lashing, amputation of limbs, beheading, and stoning to death, practices considered medieval. But most threatening under the Islamic penal code are the charges of blasphemy or apostasy, actions punishable by death.[15] The charges are widely invoked by today's fundamentalists against modern thinkers and intellectuals: Islam's new "heretics."[16] The death verdict (*fatwa*) issued by Ayatollah Khomeini against author Salman Rushdie in 1989 for an "anti-Islamic" work, *The Satanic Verses*, is a ghastly illustration of the current plight of freethinkers in the lands of Islam: they are besieged by traditional conservatism and fundamentalist antirationalism.

Further, an Islamic state ruled by the Qur'an greatly marginalizes the role of women in the society, relegating them to motherhood and confining them to the household, inactive and unproductive in public life. Such "gender apartheid" assumes a traditional economy—mainly agriculture and commerce—

not conducive to female economic independence, which is not the case in many Muslim countries today.[17] Additionally, a Qur'anic state disenfranchises non-Muslim minorities, casting them as unequal *dhimmi* (people under Muslim trust or protection). Whatever rights they may have are not a function of legal equality, but a gesture of Muslim benevolence under *Shari'a*. Thus, their status is subject to the whims of Muslim rulers, who are deemed inherently superior and therefore to be entrusted with their protection. Such a status does not solve the minority question, but rather is bound to exacerbate it by denying full inclusion in the body politic. All this suggests that the growth of Islamic fundamentalism is invariably accompanied by a diminution in the status of women and minorities. In fact, the impact of Islamization is usually felt first by women and non-Muslims, as is the case in Saudi Arabia, Iran, and Sudan.

Equally important, the religion-based collectivistic-totalitarian world outlook of the Islamic fundamentalists is in sharp contradiction to the current dynamic proliferation of global cultural, educational, material, and technological forces—all promoting the expansion of progress and modernity. The juxtaposition is a case of "Jihad vs. McWorld": totalitarianism and exclusivism against openness and globalism.[18] The Islamist religious utopia will not be able to withstand the lures of a material McWorld. Even while the fundamentalists persist in vilifying the "evil" West, they and the majority of the population aspire to its fruits and comforts.

The Islamists are not "traditionalists," but products of urban life and a consumerist-oriented climate. They desire consumer goods and services, but are frustrated by being unable to obtain them. Indeed, the failure of the social and economic modernization policies in the Middle East is partly responsible for the surge of fundamentalism. The out-of-reach modern accouterments are a principal cause of the people's deep anger toward and resentment of their rulers and the West generally, whom they see as the authors of their misfortunes.[19]

But for the fundamentalists to reject the West and its ways in the name of preserving Islamic cultural authenticity and identity is to doom their societies. Muslim societies can no longer isolate themselves from cultural influences and technological advances elsewhere. (Ironically, at a time when Muslim fundamentalists go on attacking foreign secularism and corruption and preaching cultural "purity," the invasion of satellite television is opening the region to new vistas of world culture.) The Muslim homeland is no longer the purified cultural place it is thought by some to have been earlier. Nor can Muslims lay claim to a superiority in a technology-based, fast-moving, interconnected world system. Indeed, the challenge that will face the Arab world at the beginning of the twenty-first century is not how to deal with Islamism; rather, it is how to foster modern societies, how to integrate them into the world economy, and how to achieve a level of development that will sustain a stable social order.

Above all, the conceptions ingrained in fundamentalist thought and behavior raise the larger question of the compatibility of Islamic ideology with liberal democracy.[20] Individualism, liberalism, constitutionalism, the rule of law, and the separation of church and state—the quintessentials of democracy in the West—are simply not the language of Islam and have not found wide expression in the Arab-Muslim milieu. Muslim political thought and behavior, anchored to religious dogma and communal traditions, do not promote a culture of pluralism and democracy. Past and present Arab rulers generally have exercised their power capriciously and beyond the scope of the law—rule by whim. The practice of democracy in the Middle Eastern Muslim states has for the most part been tenuous, precarious, and uneasy, at best; evidently, the traditions of democratic life are weak, if not nonexistent.

Middle Easterners are not truly committed democrats, and their concern for democracy remains low.[21] A survey study of ten Arab countries showed that, in 1980, only 5.4 percent of the respondent sample listed democracy as a major problem in the region; in 1990, the figure was merely 11 percent.[22] Little wonder that the history of the Middle East has been largely a history of leftist-authoritarian or rightist-traditionalist autocratic rule. And calls for democracy to make the push toward democratization credible or effective have been rare.

Moves toward multiparty politics and free elections, such as in Jordan and Yemen, among others, are still too recent to tell us much about the prospects of their routinization and institutionalization. Further, the scope of democratization in these experiments is limited to power sharing with new groups under the hegemonic rule of the existing elites—an arrangement that certainly does not include relinquishing control. Today virtually no Arab country adheres to the principle of a peaceful transfer of power to an opposition in accord with true democracy. (In Arab politics, even to entertain such a notion is tantamount to a subversive, antistate act.) Additionally, these hesitant steps have been largely directed and controlled from the top, more in response to international requirements than to popular demand: democracy by decree. Clearly, there is "a democratic deficit" in the world of Islam.[23]

Still and all, the fundamentalists like to boast about Islamic concepts, such as *shura* (consultation in public affairs) and *bay'a* (popular acclamation of rulers), as their model of "Islamic democracy." But these concepts are relics of early Islam that have never developed a coherent theoretical or structural foundation. They were based upon general Qur'anic principles and Arab traditions and were practiced in the Medina Muslim-tribal society of fourteen centuries ago, in which Muhammad and his first disciples lived before the advent of the great dynastic Islamic empires. The empires marked the end of the ideal religious state and the beginning of imperial transgressions.[24] The ensuing chasm between the ideals and the realities in Muslim political life has inhibited the growth and institutionalization of those early Islamic principles of governance.

Further, Muslims have failed to produce modern adaptations of these Islamic ideals and to give them meaning and substance to fit modern times. The Islamic principle of *shura* is limited to consultation and advice without actual participation in final decision-making, which rests solely with the ruler. It connotes neither representation nor supervision of government action or legislation. Indeed, there is no tradition of a deliberative legislative assembly in Islam. The source of law is revelation, the *ulama* (religious scholars) are entrusted with its interpretation, and the rulers are charged with its application. (In principle, there is no legislative power in Islam.) Throughout much of Muslim history, *shura* had remained merely an ad hoc practice of consultation by rulers, confined to an inner circle of advisers, and had never developed into a regularized, structured body.

The principle of *bay'a* is a theoretical ideal, stipulating a contractual relationship between the ruler and the ruled: the subjects' duty is to obey, and the ruler's obligation is to adhere to *Shari'a*. Yet, it provides no specific mechanism or procedure for remedy if a ruler fails to abide by the law. (In fact, a constitutional theory to delegitimize rulers has not emerged in Sunni Islam.) In practice, the contractual basis of the ideal was preempted as dynastic rule and military power became the norm. Throughout many of the lands of Islam, the relationship of the individual to authority had been one of submission, in accord with the Islamic principle of *ta'at uli al-amr* (obedience to those in command), not participation or government responsibility. Hence, *bay'a* has not yielded a social contract-like theory, with the assumptions of government accountability and popular sovereignty manifest in regular representation—the essence of democracy.

Today, despite incipient limited movement toward political liberalization, there is hardly a single Arab country that is consistent with the democratic principles of government responsibility and power transfer through popular elections. Saudi Arabia, which declares that it adheres to the Islamic ideals of governance, is the least compatible with popular will. There the Islamic mantle is used to cover an autocratic, dynastic rule that reduces the populace to petitioners, not participants. King Fahd rejects the notion of representation through elections—and parliamentarianism in general—as contrary to traditions and custom in Saudi Arabia.

In revolutionary Islamic Iran, where parliamentary elections are held and parliamentary debates are frequent, all candidates for the *majlis*, or parliament, are screened for Islamic worthiness, personal uprightness, and commitment to the revolution. (Indeed, all the candidates in the March 1996 parliamentary election had to profess their allegiance to Islamic rule.) Also, no one can speak out against the Islamic regime or its leaders.[25] In the process, all potential oppositional elements, secular or Islamic, are shut out. (Even the grand ayatollahs who are opposed to the involvement of the clergy in politics and to state control of the religious establishment are under virtual house arrest in the holy city of Qom.)[26] Surely the Islamic regime will not allow itself to be voted out of office or allow power to change hands.

Today's Muslim fundamentalists are not the harbingers of a new era of democracy in the Middle East, notwithstanding their populist rhetoric. Indeed, the application of *Shari'a*, *shura*, and *bay'a* as an Islamic hybrid of democracy seems incongruent with liberal democracy and its emphasis on individualism (the individual as the measure of all things), pluralism (freedom of associations and groups), equality, and representation—all anchored to popular sovereignty and its twin, secularism. Given their ideological assumptions—all rooted in divine conceptions—Muslim fundamentalists, like Muslim reformers of a century ago, are highly unlikely to play the same positive role that sixteenth- and seventeenth-century Protestant fundamentalist reformers played in paving the way for the development of modern political and economic institutions in Europe—as Max Weber argued in *The Protestant Ethic and the Spirit of Capitalism.*

The sixteenth-century Protestant Reformation was an attack on the Catholic Church's hierarchy, authority, and orthodoxy, which established dictatorships of popes and bishops, stifled religious interpretation and participation in church matters, and imposed doctrinal rigidity. The reformers called for individual empowerment and independent initiative against the church's doctrine and structure. The penchant for the role of the individual was best manifested in the Protestant concepts of self-governance and free participation in the running of local congregations—all derived from the Protestant idea of the ability of the individual to speak directly to God.

The Protestant values of religious freedom and individual initiative and autonomy sparked the power of individualism—every individual is capable of shaping the conditions of his or her participation in the society—which, following the onset of the Enlightenment and secularism in the seventeenth century, became the driving force behind capitalism and democracy. The Enlightenment marked the triumph of reason and science over religious certainty, and secularism brought about the end of religious imposition on public life and the inception of popular legitimacy. Fueled by the engines of the Industrial Revolution in the eighteenth century, these ideas and values put Europe over the next 200 years on the path of economic capitalism and political liberalism.

These landmark developments in the transition to modernity in Europe have no relevance to Muslim historical experience or to Muslim fundamentalist thought. Today's Muslim fundamentalists are not the hidden hands of Islamic reformation. They have not set out to reform Islam: to take it away from doctrinal rigidity and uniformity and to break the hold of religious orthodoxy. Rather, they have emphasized power and politics more than theology and reform, and here is where they have failed. Although the fundamentalists oppose the traditional *ulama*, for being the sycophants of the powers that be (which is the basis of their anticlerical elite mode), doctrinally they have no major quarrels with the *ulama*, except in the degree of emphasis on total and forceful application of *Shari'a*. The fundamentalists insist on their dogmatic interpretation of Islamic precepts, emphasize the necessity of full implementation, and stress uniformity and conformity in the social and religious spheres—all to restore the old vigor and purity of early Islam. Thus, contrary to Protestantism, Islamism is not a rebellion against dogma; it is an embrace of dogma—orthodoxy is its hallmark.

This doctrinal view of the "Islamic order" does not augur emergence of a democratic civil society that tolerates individuality, autonomy, and multiplicity, with no one single authoritative answer.[27] Indeed, the Islamists cannot fit within the liberal, pluralist mold of civil society, wherein the sacred meets and coexists with, but does not sacrifice the secular. Their agenda is not democracy; it is power based upon divine authority, which renders democracy moot. Meantime, they are willing to demand and exploit opportunities associated with democracy to achieve their goal.

Finally, the fundamentalists are out of step with history as events unfold in the Middle East. They have staked a claim as the champions of the Palestinian cause and Islamic dignity in total obliviousness to past lessons and present changing conditions and attitudes. They hold onto the old Palestinian and generally Arab view that peace and negotiations with Israel are tantamount to heresy (as Anwar Sadat's assassination demonstrated) and press the unworkable strategies of a bygone era: armed struggle and confrontation until total victory is achieved. To them, "true peace means Israel does not exist."[28] But the facts of history point in the opposite direction: the Arabs were deluded by the myth of the armed struggle and victory against Israel—they were defeated.

Today, as the Middle East moves toward peace and accommodation, especially since the signing of the historic Israeli-Palestinian autonomy accord in September 1993 and the establishment of the Palestinian National Authority in Gaza and the West Bank cities and villages, coupled with the signing of the Israeli-Jordanian peace treaty in the summer of 1994, the fundamentalists keep marching to the drumbeat of *jihad* (holy war) and the destruction of Israel, as if nothing has changed. They are virtually the only "champions" left in the Arab "rejectionist front," along with remnants of leftist-nationalist ideologues, who continue to say no to Israel and to reject it as a Zionist entity based upon "dispossession and usurpation."[29]

Fundamentalist groups, such as Hamas and Jihad in Gaza and on the West Bank, the Islamic Action Front (IAF) in Jordan, and Hizbullah in Lebanon, among others, are strongly opposed to the peace process and seek to end it. They view it as a "pax Americana," imposed on weak and defeatist Arab regimes in order to serve U.S.-Zionist interests and hegemony. But neither Hamas nor Jihad inside the Palestinian territories nor Hizbullah and other radical groups in the region are able to stop the march of peace.[30] And the Arab regimes that have opted for peace are still in place, determined to press forward. Even the latecomer, Syria, is now seeking peace with Israel as a "strategic choice" and is seemingly willing to distance itself from the radicals in the region. This will probably result in reining in Hizbullah and putting it under strict Syrian controls.

Ultimately, with strong international and regional endorsements and support—as demonstrated by the immediate and firm response to the series of deadly suicide bombings by Hamas and Jihad inside Israel in late February and early March 1996 and the subsequent convening of an international summit on terrorism in Sharm el-Sheikh, Egypt, later in March—and with no other viable alternative to the ongoing negotiations, the peace process will continue, to the detriment of the fundamentalists.[31]

Even among the Palestinians, as long as the climate of peace continues, the culture of militancy and martyrdom of the *intifadah* (uprising) will gradually fade, giving way to nation-building.[32] This was manifested in the heavy turnout (more than 85 percent of the electorate) in the January 1996 elections of the eighty-eight-member Palestinian Council and of Yasir Arafat (with more than 88 percent of the vote) as its president, despite the call for boycott by the militant Islamic movement Hamas.[33] The Palestinian mass participation is a vindication of Arafat's historic peace with Israel and a confirmation that there is no turning back. The commitment to peace is all the more evident in the ideological changes to the Palestinian Covenant made by the Palestinian National Council, the old Palestinian parliament-in-exile, in April 1996, which removed those articles originally calling for an "armed liberation struggle" and the elimination of the "Zionist presence" in Palestine.[34]

These limitations notwithstanding, Islamic fundamentalism will not soon go away. Although it is under siege and sliding, its moment is not completely over. Its cultural and moral attraction for young Muslims still holds. Its societal impact persists through the dissemination of the ethos of Islamization in the societies. And its discourse continues to serve as a medium of protest against social injustice and inequality, which is in accord with the deeply rooted ethic of Islamic egalitarianism. The religious symbols and values of Islam are deep and enduring. But as a militant political force, Islamism has been so weakened by the wear and tear of struggle and the blows sustained that it no longer constitutes an imminent danger. In the long term, as a revolutionary ideology or "ism," the current Islamic revivalism will not endure, much as Arab nationalism and communism have not endured.

NOTES

1. On this theme, see Olivier Roy, *The Failure of Political Islam* (Cambridge: Harvard University Press, 1994).

2. Sudan was listed by the United States in 1993 as a country supporting international terrorism. See Milton Viorst, "Sudan's Islamic Experiment," *Foreign Affairs* 74 (May/June 1995): 45–58. Also, in early January 1996, the United Nations Security Council passed a resolution demanding that the Sudanese government turn over to Ethiopia the three Egyptian extremists suspected in the assassination attempt on Egyptian President Hosni Mubarak in June 1995 or face the threat of punitive measures. Subsequently, the United States with-

drew all of its diplomatic personnel, effectively closing the embassy in Khartoum. See Barbara Crossette, "Featuring Terrorism, U.S. Plans to Press Sudan," *New York Times* 2 Feb. 1996: A6; Douglas Jehl, "Sudan Pays High Price for Ties to Islamic Militants," *New York Times* 13 Feb. 1996: A3. Later, the United Nations Security Council imposed some limited sanctions on Sudan such as reducing its diplomatic missions and restricting the travel of its government and military officials. See Paul Lewis, "Mild Sanctions on the Sudan Approved by U.N. Council," *New York Times* 27 Apr. 1996: 3.

3. The U.S. sanctions imposed on Iran in the summer of 1995 made a bad situation worse. The United States accused Iran of supporting terrorism, opposing the Middle East peace process, and entertaining nuclear ambitions. Also, in early 1996, it was revealed that the United States adopted a plan devised by Speaker of the House of Representatives Newt Gingrich for a covert operation to destabilize and possibly change the Iranian Islamic regime. See Tim Weiner, "U.S. Plan to Oust Iran's Leaders Is an Open Secret Before It Begins," *New York Times* 26 Jan. 1996: A1.

4. For an assessment of the Iranian Islamic revolution after fifteen years, see Hazhir Timourian, "Iran's 15 years of Islam," *World Today* 50 (Apr. 1994): 67–70.

5. See John F. Burns, "From Cold War, Afghans Inherit Brutal New Age," *New York Times* 14 Feb. 1996: A1.

6. There are those grand ayatollahs who want to continue the Shi'a practice of separating religious authority, especially the position of *marji' al-taqlid* (supreme religious exemplary), from the state domain. This is in opposition to Ali Khamenei—Supreme Guide of the Islamic Republic—who has sought to combine it with his office. See *al-Sharq al-Awsat* 18 Feb. 1996: 2.

7. S. Parvez Manzoor, "The Future of Muslim Politics: Critique of the 'Fundamentalist' Theory of the Islamic State," *Futures* 23 (Apr. 1991): 298.

8. Samuel P. Huntington, "The Clash of Civilizations?" *Foreign Affairs* 73 (Summer 1993): 22–49.

9. See Mustapha K. al-Sayyid, "Slow Thaw in the Arab World," *World Policy Journal* 8 (Fall 1991): 729.

10. Members of the sect were declared a non-Muslim minority because of their nonadherence to the Islamic belief that Muhammad is the final prophet: "the seal of prophets."

11. Marty Martin, "Cultural Foundations of Ethnonationalism: The Role of Religion" (Paper presented at the conference on Race, Ethnicity, and Nationalism at the End of the Twentieth Century, University of Wisconsin–Milwaukee, 30 Sept.–2 Oct. 1993).

12. On this theme, see Lahouari Adi, "Islamist Utopia and Democracy," *Annals of the American Academy of Political and Social Science* no. 524 (Nov. 1992): 120–30.

13. See Mahmud A. Faksh, "Basic Characteristics of the Islamic State System," *Journal of South Asian and Middle Eastern Studies* 5 (Winter 1981): 3–16. Indeed, of roughly 6,200 verses in the Qur'an, only some 250 are generally prescriptive in nature, and of these, only 10 or so deal with politico-economic issues. See G. H. Jansen, "Islam and Democracy: Are They Compatible?" *Middle East International* 29 May 1992: 18.

14. See Roy, *The Failure of Political Islam*, 18–20.

15. This is based on a *hadith* (a saying of the Prophet Muhammad): "He who commits apostasy must be killed." Also, a precedent was set by the "apostasy wars" (A.D. 632–634), fought by the first caliph, Abu Bakr, against the tribesmen who reneged on their commitment to Islam following the death of Muhammad in 632.

16. See "Save Islam's Heretics," *Christian Science Monitor* 27 Oct. 1993: 18. Also see Ethan Bronner, "Arab Intellectuals in Crisis as Few Dare Discuss Religion," *Boston Sunday*

Globe 3 Mar. 1996: 8.

17. On the isolation and exclusion of Saudi women, see Jan Goodwin, "From the Valley of the Chador," *Mirabella* (Apr. 1994): 106–10.

18. See Benjamin R. Barber, "Jihad vs. McWorld," *Atlantic* (Mar. 1992): 53–63.

19. On this theme, see Roy, *The Failure of Political Islam.*

20. On the general theme of Islam and liberalism, see Leonard Binder, *Islamic Liberalism: A Critique of Development Ideologies* (Chicago: University of Chicago Press, 1988).

21. For further elaboration, see Ghassan Salame, ed., *Democracy without Democrats* (London: I. B. Tauris, 1994).

22. See John Waterbury, "Democracy Without Democrats: The Potential for Political Liberalization in the Middle East," *Democracy without Democrats*, ed. Ghassan Salame (London: I. B. Tauris, 1994), 33.

23. "Islam and the West," *Economist* 6 Aug. 1994: 12.

24. On this theme, see Faksh, "Basic Characteristics of the Islamic State System."

25. In fact, attacking Ayatollah Khomeini or his successor, Ali Khamenei, is a crime punishable by death. See *al-Sharq al-Awsat* 30 Nov. 1995: 1.

26. Among those leading ayatollahs are Muhammad Rouhani, Hussein Ali Montazeri, and Muhammad Shirazi. See *al-Sharq al-Awsat* 10 Dec. 1995: 2.

27. See Edward Shils, "The Virtue of Civil Society," *Government and Opposition* 26 (Winter 1991): 3–20.

28. These are the words of Fathi Shiqaqi, leader of Islamic Jihad, who was assassinated in late October 1995. Quoted in Barton Gellman, "Islamic Jihad Likely to Avenge Its Slain Leader," *Washington Post* 1 Nov. 1995: A21.

29. See "Interview With Sheikh Hussein Fadlallah of Hizbullah," *al-Majalla* 11–17 June 1995: 26.

30. In fact, rather than halting the peace process, the fundamentalist threat in the region and the fear of the adverse regional consequences of failure to reach a settlement have moved the process forward. On this theme, see Richard W. Bulliet, "The Israel-PLO Accord: The Future of the Islamic Movement," *Foreign Affairs* 72 (Nov. 1993): 38–44.

31. The decline in fundamentalist strength was clearly evident in the November 1993 national election in Jordan, which marked a victory for the king's peace policies. The Islamic Action Front (IAF), which is headed by the Ikhwan and is strongly opposed to the peace process, lost ground, dropping from 33 seats in the last assembly to 16 seats. See Peter Ford, "Jordanian Vote Marks a Victory for the King and the Peace Process," *Christian Science Monitor* 10 Nov. 1993: 3. Later, in July 1995, the Islamic Action Front lost in important municipal elections to a pro-government slate that supported peace with Israel. See Thomas L. Friedman, "Muffled Militants," *New York Times* 19 July 1995: A19. This is also manifested in the decreasing influence of the Islamic movements of Hamas and Jihad as Palestinian self-rule continues to expand in Gaza and on the West Bank under the control of Palestinian Liberation Organization leader Yasir Arafat, now president of the Palestinian National Authority. On the recurrent terrorist bombings, see Serge Schmemann, "4th Terror Blast in Israel Kills 12 at Mall in Tel Aviv; Nine-Day Toll Grows to 59," *New York Times* 5 Mar. 1996: A1. See also Todd S. Purdum, "Nations Pledge Effort to Halt Violence," *New York Times* 14 Mar. 1996: A1. A poll in Gaza and on the West Bank found "a sharp decline in support for violence" among Palestinians generally over the last year. See John Kifner, "Alms and Arms: Tactics in a Holy War," *New York Times* 15 Mar. 1996: A9.

32. On this theme, see Joel Greenberg, "On the West Bank, 'Martyrs' Lose Their Mystique," *New York Times* 21 Dec. 1995: A12.

33. See Serge Schmemann, "Palestinian Vote: Down for Most, Legitimacy for Arafat," *New York Times* 22 Jan. 1996: A3.

34. See Serge Schmemann, "P.L.O. Ends Call for Destruction of Jewish State," *New York Times* 25 Apr. 1996: A1.

Selected Bibliography

Ajami, Fouad. *The Vanished Imam: Musa al-Sadr and the Shia of Lebanon.* Ithaca, N.Y.: Cornell University Press, 1986.

_____ . *The Arab Predicament: Arab Political Thought and Practice since 1967.* Cambridge: Cambridge University Press, 1982.

Arjomand, Said Amir. *The Turban for the Crown: The Islamic Revolution in Iran.* New York: Oxford University Press, 1988.

_____ , ed. *From Nationalism to Revolutionary Islam.* New York: Macmillan, 1984.

al-'Awwa, Muhammad. *On the Political System of the Islamic State.* Indianapolis, Ind.: American Trust Publications, 1980.

Ayubi, Nazih. *Political Islam: Religion and Politics in the Arab World.* London: Routledge, 1991.

al-Banna, Hasan. *What Is Our Message?* Lahore, Pakistan: Islamic Publications, 1974.

Berger, Morroe. *Islam in Egypt Today: Social and Political Aspects of Popular Religion.* Cambridge: Cambridge University Press, 1970.

_____ . *The Arab World Today.* Garden City, N.Y.: Doubleday, 1964.

Binder, Leonard. *Islamic Liberalism: A Critique of Development Ideologies.* Chicago: University of Chicago Press, 1988.

_____ . *The Ideological Revolution in the Middle East.* New York: John Wiley, 1964.

Dekmejian, R. Hrair. *Islam in Revolution: Fundamentalism in the Arab World.* Syracuse, N.Y.: Syracuse University Press, 1985.

Dessouki, Ali E. Hillal, ed. *Islamic Resurgence in the Arab World.* New York: Praeger, 1982.

Enayat, Hamid. *Modern Islamic Political Thought.* Austin: University of Texas Press, 1982.

Entelis, John. *Algeria: The Revolution Institutionalized.* Boulder, Colo.: Westview Press, 1986.

Esposito, John L. *The Islamic Threat: Myth or Reality?* Oxford: Oxford University Press, 1992.

_____ . *Islam: The Straight Path.* Oxford: Oxford University Press, 1991.

_____ , ed. *Voices of Resurgent Islam.* New York: Oxford University Press, 1991.

Etienne, Bruno. *L'Islamisme Radicale*. Paris: Hatchette, 1987.

Farah, Nadia Ramsis. *Religious Strife in Egypt: Crisis and Ideological Conflict in the Seventies*. New York: Gordon & Breach, 1986.

Gause, F. Gregory, III. *Oil Monarchies: Domestic and Security Challenges in the Arab Gulf States*. New York: Council on Foreign Relations, 1994.

Gibb, H. A. R. *Islam: A Historical Survey*. Oxford: Oxford University Press, 1978.

_____ . *Modern Trends in Islam*. Chicago: Chicago University Press, 1947.

Gilsenan, Michael. *Recognizing Islam: Religion and Society in the Modern Arab World*. New York: Pantheon, 1983.

Haddad, Yvonne Y., Byron Haines, and Ellison Findly, eds. *The Islamic Impact*. Syracuse, N.Y.: Syracuse University Press, 1984.

Helms, Christine Moss. *The Cohesion of Saudi Arabia*. Baltimore: Johns Hopkins University Press, 1981.

Hiro, Delip. *Holy Wars: The Rise of Islamic Fundamentalism*. New York: Paladin, 1989.

Hopwood, Derek, ed. *The Arabian Peninsula: Society and Politics*. London: George Allen & Unwin, 1972.

Hourani, Albert. *A History of the Arab Peoples*. New York: Warner Books, 1991.

_____ . *Arabic Thought in the Liberal Age, 1798–1939*. London: Oxford University Press, 1962.

Hudson, Michael C. *Arab Politics: The Search for Legitimacy*. New Haven, Conn.: Yale University Press, 1979.

Hunter, Shireen T., ed. *The Politics of Islamic Revivalism: Diversity and Unity*. Bloomington: Indiana University Press, 1988.

Husaini, Ishaq Musa. *The Muslim Brethren*. Beirut: Khayat's, 1956.

Jansen, Godfry H. *Militant Islam*. New York: Harper & Row, 1979.

Jansen, Johannes J. G. *The Neglected Duty: The Creed of Sadat's Assassins and Islamic Resurgence in the Middle East*. New York: Macmillan, 1989.

Keddie, Nikki R. *Religion and Politics in Iran: Shi'ism from Quietism to Revolution*. New Haven, Conn.: Yale University Press, 1983.

Kedourie, Elie. *Democracy and Arab Political Culture*. Arlington, Va.: Washington Institute for the Near East Policy, 1992.

_____ . *Afghani and Abduh: An Essay on Religious Unbelief and Political Activism in Modern Islam*. London: Frank Cass, 1966.

Kepel, Gilles. *Muslim Extremism in Egypt: The Prophet and the Pharaoh*. Berkeley: University of California Press, 1993.

Kerr, Malcolm H. *Islamic Reform: The Political and Legal Theories of Muhammad Abduh and Rashid Rida*. Berkeley: University of California Press, 1966.

Korany, Bahgat, and Ali E. Hillal Dessouki, eds. *The Foreign Policies of the Arab States*. Boulder, Colo.: Westview Press, 1991.

Kramer, Martin. *Shi'ism, Resistance, and Revolution*. Boulder, Colo.: Westview Press, 1987.

Lawrence, Bruce. *Defenders of God: The Fundamentalist Revolt against the Modern Age*. New York: Harper & Row, 1989.

Lerner, Daniel. *The Passing of Traditional Society: Modernizing the Middle East*. New York: Free Press, 1958.

Lewis, Bernard. *Islam and the West*. Oxford: Oxford University Press, 1993.

_____ . *The Political Language of Islam*. Chicago: University of Chicago Press, 1991.

_____ . *The Middle East and the West*. New York: Harper & Row, 1964.

McLaurin, R. D., ed. *The Political Role of Minority Groups in the Middle East*. New York: Praeger, 1979.

Mitchell, Richard P. *The Society of the Muslim Brotherhood*. Ann Arbor: University of Michigan Press, 1970.

Mortimer, Edward. *Faith and Power: The Politics of Islam*. New York: Random House, 1982.

Nasr, Seyyed Hossein. *Ideals and Realities of Islam*. Boston: Beacon Press, 1972.

Pipes, Daniel. *In the Path of God: Islam and Political Power*. New York: Basic Books, 1983.

Piscatori, James P. *Islam in a World of Nation-States*. Cambridge: Cambridge University Press, 1986.

———— , ed. *Islamic Fundamentalism and the Gulf Crisis*. Chicago: Chicago University Press, 1991.

———— , ed. *Islam in the Political Process*. Cambridge: Cambridge University Press, 1983.

Rahman, Fazlur. *Islam and Modernity: Transformation of an Intellectual Tradition*. Chicago: University of Chicago Press, 1982.

Rahnema, Ali, ed. *Pioneers of Islamic Revival*. London: Zed Books, 1995.

Roy, Olivier. *The Failure of Political Islam*. Cambridge: Harvard University Press, 1994.

Rubin, Barry. *Islamic Fundamentalism in Egyptian Politics*. New York: St. Martin's Press, 1990.

Safi, Louay M. *The Challenge of Modernity: The Quest for Authenticity in the Arab World*. Lanham, Md.: University Press of America, 1994.

Salame, Ghassan, ed. *Democracy without Democrats*. London: I. B. Tauris, 1994.

Sivan, Emmanuel. *Radical Islam: Medieval Theology and Modern Politics*. New Haven, Conn.: Yale University Press, 1990.

Smith, Charles D. *Islam and the Search for Social Order in Modern Egypt: A Biography of Muhammad Husayn Haykal*. Albany: State University of New York Press, 1983.

Smith, Wilfred. *Islam in Modern History*. New York: New American Library, 1957.

Stora, Benjamin, and Zakya Daoud. *Ferhat Abbas: une Utopie Algerienne*. Paris: Editions Denoel, 1995.

Stowasser, Barbara F., ed. *The Islamic Impulse*. London: Groom Helm, 1987.

Sullivan, Dennis J. *Private Voluntary Organizations in Egypt: Islamic Development, Private Initiative and State Control*. Gainesville: University Press of Florida, 1994.

Voll, John Obert. *Islam: Continuity and Change in the Modern World*. Boulder, Colo.: Westview Press, 1982.

Wahba, Sheikh Hafiz. *Arabian Days*. London: Arthur Barker, 1964.

Waterbury, John. *The Egypt of Nasser and Sadat*. Princeton, N.J.: Princeton University Press, 1983.

Watt, W. Montgomery. *Islamic Fundamentalism and Modernity*. London: Routledge, 1989.

———— . *Islamic Political Thought*. Edinburgh: Edinburgh University Press, 1968.

Winder, Bayly. *Saudi Arabia in the Nineteenth Century*. New York: St. Martin's Press, 1965.

Wright, Robin. *In the Name of God: The Khomeini Decade*. New York: Simon & Schuster, 1989.

al-Yassini, Ayman. *Religion and State in the Kingdom of Saudi Arabia*. Boulder, Colo.: Westview Press, 1985.

Zubaida, Sami. *Islam, the People and the State: Political Ideas and Movements in the Middle East*. London: I. B. Tauris, 1993.

Index

Abbas, Ferhat, 82n.2
Abbasid Caliphate, 4, 18n.11
Abdu, Muhammad, 17n.4, 20n.45, 41
Abdul Rahman, Sheikh Omar, 16, 51, 59n.18
Abdul Raziq, Ali, 17n.4, 19n.28
Abu Zeid, Nasr Hamid, 53–54
al-Adl wa al-Ihsan (Justice and Charity Group, Morocco), 36n.5
Advice, Memorandum of (Saudi Arabia), 97, 100
al-Afghani, Jamal al-Din, 17n.4, 18n.9, 20n.45, 41
Afghanistan, 35, 60n.32, 106, 110
Ahmad, Huceine Ait, 76, 83n.17
Ahmadiyya sect, Islam, 111–12, 120n.10
Ahmad Khan, Sir Sayyid, 17n.4, 20n.45
Ahmed, Eqbal, 17n.1
Algeria, 9, 26, 30, 36, 39, 55, 56, 65–82. *See also* FIS; FLN
Algerian Renewal Party, 80, 87n.63
Ali, Ameer, 17n.4
Ali, Fourth Caliph, 21n.72, 52, 61n.40
Ali Pasha, Muhammad, 41, 42, 43, 103
Amin, Qasim, 42
Aoudia, Malik Ait, 87n.69
Apostasy, 47, 53, 54, 73, 74, 91, 107n.60, 113, 120n.15
Apostasy and Flight Group (Egypt), 45, 47, 48

al-Aqd al-Watani (National Pact, Algeria), 78
Arab Afghans, 35
Arabization, 67, 68, 70, 76
Arab nationalism, 10, 24, 91, 119
Arafat, Yasir, 119, 121n.31
Armed Islamic Group (Algeria), 74, 79. *See also* GIA
al-Asad, Hafiz 34
Association for Islamic Values (Algeria), 67
Association of the Algerian Muslim Ulama, 66
Ataturk, Mustafa Kemal, 1, 19n.28
al-Auda, Sheikh Salman, 16, 98, 99
al-Azhar University, 19n.28, 41, 44, 53, 54, 57n.1, 58n.10, 61n.41

Baha' al-Din, Hussein Kamil, 61n.43
al-Bahi, Muhammad, 8
al-Banna, Hasan, 43, 44
Ba'th/-ism, 9, 20n.54, 24, 33, 34, 40n.51, 60n.36, 91
Bay'a (allegiance), 93, 115, 116, 117
Baz, Sheikh Abdul Aziz bin, 96, 100
Beheadings, in Saudi Arabia, 106n.44, 107n.52
Belhaj, Ali, 16, 71, 73, 78, 83n.19, 84n.39
Ben Badis, Sheikh Abdul Hamid, 66, 67
Ben Bella, Ahmad, 82nn.10–11, 84n.31

Francophone-Arabist split, Algeria, 65, 82n.1

al-Ganzouri, Kamal, 63n.62
Gaza, 16, 118
al-Ghannouchi, Rachid, 16, 28
al-Ghozali, Sheikh Muhammad, 54
Ghozali, Sid Ahmad, 39n.36
GIA (Armed Islamic Group, Algeria), 74, 79
Gingrich, Newt, 120n.3
Gorbachev, Mikhail, 56
Grand Mosque, Mecca, 93, 95
Gulf War, 24, 30, 31, 32, 49, 94, 96, 100, 106n.46, 109

Hakimiyya (divine sovereignty), 6, 11
Hamas (Algeria), 16, 73, 80, 83n.15, 87n.63; Palestinian, 118, 119
Hamrouche, Mouloud, 83n.21
Hanafi juridical tradition, 90
Hanbali juridical tradition, 90, 99
Hassan, king of Morocco, 34
Hassan, martyr, 14, 15
al-Hawali, Safar, 16, 98, 104n.20
al-Hawwa, Said, 8, 16
Heikal, Muhammad Hasanein, 25
Higher Council of Islamic Affairs (Saudi Arabia), 101
Higher Islamic Council (Algeria), 67
High State Council (Algeria), 74
Hijar (para-military agricultural communes), 91
Hijra (migration or retreat), 48; of the Prophet, 36n.1
Hizbullah (Lebanon), 16, 110, 118, 119
Hizbullah (party of God), in writings of Maududi, 12
Holy war, 12, 27, 35, 47, 48, 74, 75, 90, 111, 118. *See also Jihad*
Hudud (Islamic sanctions), 50, 53, 100, 113
Huntington, Samuel, 111
Hussein, king of Jordan, 34
Hussein, martyr, 14, 15, 21n.73
Hussein, Saddam, 32, 33, 34

Ibn Khaldun, 17n.6

Ibrahim bin Jubeir, Sheikh Muhammad bin, 107n.56
Ijma' (consensus), 52
Ijtihad (individual doctrinal interpretation), 3, 42
Ikhwan (Brotherhood), 91, 93, 94, 99, 104nn.18–19; Egypt, 43–56 *passim*, 58n.8, 58n.13, 58n.15, 62n.54
Al-Imara, wa al-Bay'a, wa al-Ta'a (al-Utaibi), 93
IMF (International Monetary Fund), 63n.63, 69, 77
India, 11
Industrial Revolution, 117
Infitah (openness), 28, 45, 46, 69
Inqilab Islami (Islamic transformation), 7, 11
Intifadah (uprising), 119
Iran, 1–15 *passim*, 35, 51, 76, 99, 110–16 *passim*, 120n.3
Iran-Iraq war, 110
Iraq, 24, 31, 32, 34, 94, 99, 110
'Isa, Ibrahim, 52
Islam: Ahmadiyya, 111–12, 120n.10; political, 2, 3, 10, 16, 19n.26, 67, 79; reformers within, 2, 9, 11, 17n.4, 18n.9, 41, 43, 117; Shi'a, 5, 14, 17n.3, 19n.35, 21nn.72–73, 23, 36n.1, 105n.33, 111, 120n.6; Sufi, 41, 65, 66, 82n.3
Islamic Action Front (Jordan), 25, 118, 121n.31
Islamic Guards (Algeria), 73
Islamic Jama'a (Egypt), 16, 45, 46, 47, 48, 49, 51
Islamic law and jurisprudence, 4, 13, 46, 71, 72, 90, 91, 97, 100. *See also Shari'a*
Islamic Liberation Party (Technical Military Academy Group, Egypt), 16, 45, 48
Islamic Movement for Change (Saudi Arabia), 106n.44
Islamic Salvation Army (Algeria), 74
Islamic Salvation Front (Algeria). *See* FIS
Islamic state, 3–17 *passim*, 24, 45, 71–80 *passim*, 91, 93, 97, 113
Islamic Tendency Movement (Tunisia), 16, 28. *See also* al-Nahda Party

About the Author

MAHMUD A. FAKSH is associate professor of political science at the University of Southern Maine; he has also served as visiting professor of Political Science at Duke University. His articles have appeared in *Orbis*, *International Journal*, *Middle East Policy* and *Third World Quarterly* among others.

ISBN 0-275-95128-6

90000>

EAN

9 780275 951283

HARDCOVER BAR CODE